Olexander Hryb

Understanding Contemporary Russian Militarism
From Revolutionary to New Generation Warfare

With a foreword by Mark Laity

UKRAINIAN VOICES

Collected by Andreas Umland

58   Petro Rychlo
    „Zerrissne Saiten einer überlauten Harfe ..."
    Deutschjüdische Dichter der Bukowina
    ISBN 978-3-8382-1893-9

59   Volodymyr Paniotto
    Sociology in Jokes
    An Entertaining Introduction
    ISBN 978-3-8382-1857-1

60   Josef Wallmannsberger (ed.)
    Executing Renaissances
    The Poetological Nation of Ukraine
    ISBN 978-3-8382-1741-3

61   Pavlo Kazarin
    The Wild West of Eastern Europe
    A Ukrainian Guide on Breaking Free from Empire
    Translated from the Ukrainian by Dominique Hoffman
    ISBN 978-3-8382-1842-7

62   Ernest Gyidel
    Ukrainian Public Nationalism in the General Government
    The Case of Krakivski Visti, 1940–1944
    With a foreword by David R. Marples
    ISBN 978-3-8382-1865-6

The book series "Ukrainian Voices" publishes English- and German-language monographs, edited volumes, document collections, and anthologies of articles authored and composed by Ukrainian politicians, intellectuals, activists, officials, researchers, and diplomats. The series' aim is to introduce Western and other audiences to Ukrainian explorations, deliberations and interpretations of historic and current, domestic, and international affairs. The purpose of these books is to make non-Ukrainian readers familiar with how some prominent Ukrainians approach, view and assess their country's development and position in the world. The series was founded, and the volumes are collected by Andreas Umland, Dr. phil. (FU Berlin), Ph. D. (Cambridge), Associate Professor of Politics at the Kyiv-Mohyla Academy and an Analyst in the Stockholm Centre for Eastern European Studies at the Swedish Institute of International Affairs.

Olexander Hryb

UNDERSTANDING CONTEMPORARY RUSSIAN MILITARISM
From Revolutionary to New Generation Warfare

With a foreword by Mark Laity

Bibliografische Information der Deutschen Nationalbibliothek

Die Deutsche Nationalbibliothek verzeichnet diese Publikation in der Deutschen Nationalbibliografie; detaillierte bibliografische Daten sind im Internet über http://dnb.d-nb.de abrufbar.

Bibliographic information published by the Deutsche Nationalbibliothek
The Deutsche Nationalbibliothek lists this publication in the Deutsche Nationalbibliografie; detailed bibliographic data are available on the Internet at http://dnb.d-nb.de.

Cover by Hugh Beattie, inspired by AI

ISBN (Print): 978-3-8382-1927-1
ISBN (E-Book [PDF]): 978-3-8382-7927-5
© *ibidem*-Verlag, Hannover • Stuttgart 2025

Leuschnerstraße 40
30457 Hannover
Germany / Deutschland
info@ibidem.eu

Alle Rechte vorbehalten

Das Werk einschließlich aller seiner Teile ist urheberrechtlich geschützt. Jede Verwertung außerhalb der engen Grenzen des Urheberrechtsgesetzes ist ohne Zustimmung des Verlages unzulässig und strafbar. Dies gilt insbesondere für Vervielfältigungen, Übersetzungen, Mikroverfilmungen und elektronische Speicherformen sowie die Einspeicherung und Verarbeitung in elektronischen Systemen.

All rights reserved. No part of this publication may be reproduced, stored in or introduced into a retrieval system, or transmitted, in any form, or by any means (electronic, mechanical, photocopying, recording or otherwise) without the prior written permission of the publisher. Any person who commits any unauthorized act in relation to this publication may be liable to criminal prosecution and civil claims for damages.

Printed in the EU

'Nation Shall Speak Peace Unto Nation.'
BBC motto, 1927

Acknowledgements

This book started as a humble article in the *British Army Review* dedicated to understanding Russian information warfare (2019), so I would like to thank Dr Alex Finnen for co-ordinating the original peer-review and persevering with 18 months long publication process. Ever since a number of kind souls helped me to put together this monograph and some of them preferred not to be named. However, I am especially grateful for inspirational conversations with my senior military colleagues—Col Andrew Dennis, OBE and Col (Retd) Glen Grant who shared insights from their vast experience in military writing and provided feedback on my initial book drafts. Academic researchers and veteran Russia watchers such as Prof. Mark Galeotti, Dr Steven Main and James Sherr, OBE—all were inspiration for my work at some stage while writing this book. I am also grateful to a dedicated and hard-working librarian Rachel Daniels, who assisted with my research at the Russian Military Studies Archive (Barrington Library, Cranfield Defence and Security, Cranfield University). Prolific journalist and editor Thea Jourdan helped me improving my writing style in English, so I am enormously grateful for her time and dedication. Prof. Lubomyr Luciuk from the Royal Military College of Canada provided some useful comments on various sources that could illuminate historical chapters of this book better. I am especially indebted to the Ukrainian Voices' editor, Prof. Andreas Umland for including my second publication in this series and providing more Ukrainian authors with an academic platform lacking in the past. Last but not least, I am also grateful to all my military colleagues, with whom I had the honour to serve, for demonstrating great tolerance of my academic research activities. The views and opinions expressed are those of the author alone and should not be taken to represent those of His Majesty's Government, MOD, HM Armed Forces, any UK government agency or NATO.

Contents

Acknowledgements 5

Foreword by *Mark Laity* 9

Introduction 13

1. The Battle of Narratives 25
2. 'No Peace—No War' and the Origin of the Red Army *Modus Operandi* 47
3. The Great Patriotic War: Mythology and Conduct 65
4. The Cold War and Evolution of the Soviet Understanding of War 83
5. Cold War 2.0 and Russia's New Generation Warfare 93
6. "Information War is the main type of war" 111
7. Moscow's Black Magic or Reflexive Control in Russian Active Measures 131
8. The Full-Scale Invasion of Ukraine and Lessons Learned for NGW 151
9. Roadmap to Peace? 173

Conclusions 191

Bibliography 195

Foreword

This is a fascinating study of Russia and its relationship with the West from an informed perspective that we see too little of—a writer whose heritage and history means understanding the Russians is close, personal, and made all the more vital because it is linked to his nation's very survival. At the same time, it is deeply researched and thoughtful.

At its heart it highlights some consistent features of both Russia and its relationship with the West. In particular it how much of that relationship is based on misunderstandings of each other for a variety of reasons.

Firstly, the tendency to believe others basically think as we do and share similar outlooks and secondly the desire to believe what we want to believe rather than face up to reality. As the writer shows, Russia projects malign motivations on the West which align with their world view rather than ours. At a time when Western policymakers largely stopped seeing them as adversaries, Russian policymakers interpreted our actions very differently. At the same time, because many NATO nations wanted to believe in the end of history, they interpreted Russian activities far more benevolently than an objective judgement could justify. As the writer shows, first after Georgia, then following the first Ukraine aggression in 2014, too many Western leaders persisted in believing that somehow Russia could be appeased.

The writer's work shows though that Russian actions were consistent with their history and policies over decades and longer. His chapter on reflexive control highlights that Russia was well able to analyse and exploit the willingness of many actors in our nations to worry about allegedly escalatory actions on their part when it was Russia that was steadily turning the screw. In line with a phrase attributed to Donald Rumsfeld, 'Weakness is a form of provocation.'

Of course, some Soviet/Russian analysts were all too aware of the risks, but the tide was flowing against such views. The writer's analysis will still seem too hard-edged for some, and some of his interpretations can be debated, but the research and coherence of his writing cannot.

It is particularly useful that it is historically so well grounded. Putin's world view follows a line stretch back through previous leaders to Stalin and then the Czars. We should take seriously Putin channeling Peter the Great and Catherine the Great. Some may consider it delusional, but regardless it is driving him, and Russia's view of its own history is something we need to understand if we wish to understand manage Russia today.

Of most value though is the writer's close understanding and detailed analysis of Russian New Generation Warfare, especially in the context of Information Warfare. Arguably, and I would argue it, Russia's information warfare is a critical driver to much of what is happening in much of our societies.

Too much of the analysis of hybrid warfare and its information aspects falls quickly into tactical debates about disinformation which are essentially limited. Russian thinking about information warfare is far more sophisticated. Some, frankly, can seem a little odd, but the depth of the thinking cannot be challenged. What is clear is the centrality of information—Strategic Communication (StratCom)—to modern conflict.

In that context the writer comes up with some interesting thoughts on the role of StratCom to finding a way out of the current crises between Russia and ourselves. Certainly, properly understanding the drivers behind Russia's actions would have helped us in the past and must be vital for future policy. The same applies in reverse. How can we present ourselves in a way that both reassures Russia while not being seen as weak enough to be exploited. His own analysis of Russia's history and instincts demonstrates this is a big ask, but at the same time it is surely something that must be attempted.

Overall, the writer's analysis highlights that Russia's own prejudices led to some fatal misinterpretations of Ukraine, its people, capabilities and what they wanted. Arguably, they invaded Ukraine in February 2022 on a set of assumptions about the nature of Ukrainian society that proper analysis would have shown were wrong.

In the end, I suggest we are seeing a consequence of ignorance and lack of understanding about each other. We abandoned the classical precepts of deterrence that saw us through the Cold War in favour of appeasement, often labelled with euphemisms such as 'deescalating' or finding 'off-ramps'. Meanwhile the Russians persuaded themselves we were still a threat to them when we were not while at the same time believing they had a window of opportunity to exploit a current weakness.

It is surely a clear lesson that understanding your adversary is critical. It would not have made us friends but maybe we would not be where we are. This work is a valuable insight into Russia and how it sees us, as well as demonstrating the criticality of effective Strategic Communication to managing crisis and conflict in the modern information age.

Mark Laity, Senior Director, Stratcom Academy, UK
(former Director of the Communications Division at SHAPE, NATO)

'Putin relies on the ideology of patriotism and Eurasianism....
Putin sees his long presidency as a mission given by God.'
Gen. Dmitry Trenin, Member of the Council on Foreign and
Defence Policy (April 2018)

Introduction

In March 2015, the President of the Russian Federation, Vladimir Putin, commemorated the first anniversary of Crimean 'reunification' by delivering a speech in Simferopol. He addressed a carefully selected crowd of 'ordinary citizens' and spoke about Crimea as 'a Holy Land of the Rus', where Saint Volodymyr was baptised. Putin projected image of himself as a 'Gatherer of the Russian lands' — referencing the territorial gains of the Russian Tsars from 15th-16th centuries. In doing so, Putin was trying to achieve several objectives: legitimise his decision to go to war with Ukraine and justify what others call the illegal attempted annexation of Crimea, and create a new narrative linking the Kyivan Rus legacy to contemporary Russia, drawing parallels with himself personally through St Volodymyr.

Inadvertently, the Russian president admitted that he lied a year previously when he said that the invasion of Crimea was not planned as a military operation well in advance of the EuroMaidan uprising, known as Revolution of Dignity in Kyiv. He also exposed his personal belief in a mission given to him by God to reunite 'Holy Rus', which is how he sees Russia incorporating Ukraine et al. Russian historians had to scramble to rewrite historical conventions that until that very moment were not compelled to link Putin to St Volodymyr and Crimea, hence proving once again an adage that Russian history is less predictable than its future. It would be unnecessary to engage in factual dispelling of historical inaccuracies in these narratives as they are obvious to conscientious students of Russian history: 'Kyivan Rus' legacy belongs as much, if not more, to Ukraine and Belarus; there are no historical records confirming that Prince Volodymyr (Valdemar would be his Viking name) was baptised in Crimea, while linking St Volodymyr to the Putin aka 'KGB operative in the Kremlin' is anathema to millions of Orthodox Christians in Ukraine and worldwide. Yet, clearly Vladimir Putin felt that it was appropriate to push such narratives as the leader of the Russian Federation because in his eyes all his statements were true enough as dictated by political expedience and an act of faith on behalf of majority of Russians citizens. As Timothy Snyder explained: "Putin's aim was not to fool Ukrainians but to create a bond of willing ignorance with Russians, who were meant to understand that Putin was lying but to believe him anyway." (Snyder 2018. P1). Charles Clover explained this seeming contradiction in the following way: "Putin has correctly surmised that lies unite rather than divide Russia's political class. The greater and the more obvious the lie, the more his subjects demonstrate their loyalty by accepting it, and the more they participate in the great sacral mystery of Kremlin power." (Clover quoted in Snyder). In fact, as a commander-in-chief, Putin engaged also in military deception as part of the wider information war effort against the collective West. Military deception, according to Russian military doctrine, is a planned activity to manipulate the enemy's decision-making process and therefore is not simply a lie—it is a deliberate warfighting strategy. The term that is casually used for deception in the Russian armed forces is 'military cunning (*voyennaya hitrost'*). However, doctrinal terminology is much more elaborate as deception is conceptualised as *vvedeniye v zabluzhdeniye* (leading into a lie / trap), which is considered to be an organic element of the military art (*voyennoye iskusstvo*). In other words, Russians understand that President as their commander-in-chief is practising deception as part of masterful military art while tricking the enemies into a trap. But who is the enemy?

Considering that Putin consistently claimed that both Ukrainians and Russians are 'one people', he could not have meant to wage war on his own people in Crimea and wider Ukraine. Putin knew that most of the Ukrainians—just like most of the Russians—understood very well that he was engaging in deception for a higher purpose i.e. implying that he was telling a white lie. However, this was not the main reason. As Snyder explained in his article: "Russia wins the information war." Putin set up a successful trap of 'implausible deniability' and co-opted international press and international opinion influencers as partners in crime. He continued: "The narrative of the Russian invasion of Ukraine shifted in a subtle but profound way: it was not about what was happening to Ukrainians, but about what the Russian president chose to say about Ukraine. A real war became reality television, with Putin as the hero. Much of the press accepted its supporting role in the drama. Even as Western editors became more critical over time, their criticism was framed as their own doubts about Kremlin claims. When Putin later admitted that Russia had indeed invaded Ukraine, this only proved that the Western press had been a player in his show" (Snyder 2018, P.2). This technique, in fact, was known to President Putin since his old days as a KGB operative in East Germany when free press manipulation, using so called 'reflexive control' in 'active measures', was a dark and sophisticated art in which both KGB and the local Eastern German equivalent (Stasi) excelled. They later even invented the term 'peacewar' describing how human instinctive desire for peace and avoidance of war could be exploited and weaponised in order to exert influence over the enemy's public opinion and steer the target society to potentially a destructive course of action. However, if the Ukrainian people were not the target of Putin's military deception per se and therefore not the ultimate enemy (as 'one people' with Russia), then who was? The answer came a year later from Putin's spokesman Dmitriy Peskov, who admitted in TV interview that: "We are in a state of information war with the Anglo-Saxons" (Peskov 2018). The undeclared war in Ukraine, in other words, was a proxy war with the US and the rest of so-called Anglo-Saxons — the Five Eyes countries (the UK, Australia, Canada and the New Zeeland). Putin himself would state on various occasions that Russia is and always was under a war of sanction from the West (even before Crimean invasion in 2014) and therefore is in a state of 'undeclared war'. If this Hobbesian pessimistic world view of Russia being at war with the outside world were not bad enough, references to the Holy Rus'-Russia reflected another less familiar aspect of information war —

'theological warfare' (See: Moss 2019). As the quote from General Trenin, at the top of this introduction, suggests, President Putin believes in "his mission from God" and if we take it to be genuine in context of being at war with "Anglo-Saxons" then the confrontation might appear to be of apocalyptic proportions as it involves the two nuclear super-powers. As British naval analyst Edward Moss observed, the West needs a better understanding of the role of the Russian Orthodox Church to promote information warfare and identify subversion narratives in the media seeking to undermine Western values of plurality by promotion of so-called 'traditional values' that could be just as dangerous to the West as the promotion of extremism. "After all, the Russian state has more means at its disposal to attack the West than espionage and chemical weapons; it can just as easily attack the West with religious rhetoric as well with politically motivated misinformation. The Kremlin and the ROC truly believe that they are on the side of God; a nation that embraces that kind of theocracy makes the most dangerous kind of adversary" (Moss 2019, P.133).

The Kremlin's Holy War against the West is especially striking considering that merely 20 years previously, newly-elected President Putin suggested that Russia might actually join the US led North Atlantic Treaty Organization (NATO). So, what caused such a dramatic change of his worldview and what could be done to avoid staring into the nuclear abyss that both Moscow and Washington (with the rest of the world watching) are keen to avoid? Answer(s) to this question are especially important for the Anglo-Saxon community and wider NATO member countries considering that: a) not all of them *realise* that they are in a state of information war with Russia; b) there seems to be no clear end-state strategy towards Russia beyond so called 'smart-sanctions' that are misinterpreted by the Kremlin as part of 'perpetual' war on Russia; c) without a clear understanding of root causes of the conflict neither political nor military solutions could be easily found. While the declared Russian grievances against the West are well known from the narratives pushed by its media outlets such as Sputnik and RT (formerly Russia Today TV), there is a lot of confusion between what is a genuine grievance and what is deliberate deception. The eschatological aspect of the confrontation, so dear to the heart of *Russkiy Mir* (Russian World) warriors such as Aleksandr Dugin, are so esoteric that, with few exceptions in the Western academia, nobody takes it into account and hardly understands. And, yet, if the Third Rome (as Moscow proclaimed itself since 15h century) is waging a 'cathaphonic' (the End of the World) struggle on the Great Satan (the US), as Prof. Dugin and some of his fellow Eurasianists advocate, then the rest of the world should be paying attention. As one of the leading 'Anglo-Saxon' military anthropologists, David Kilcullen summarised in his book *The Dragons and the Snakes: How the Rest learned to fight the West,* top military strategists on both sides do not really understand what either party is doing: "Valeriy Gerasimov (Russian Chief of the Defence Staff) ... seems to have thought he was describing our way of war, not Russia's, and Russian planners tend to ascribe the same evil genius to us that some Westerners believe of them. In other words, it is entirely possible that none of us actually know what we are doing, that far from having cunningly executed master plans we are all reacting instinctively, often incompetently, in the moment — stumbling around in a fog, bumping into things without really understanding each other. This mutual incomprehension is a recipe for miscalculation, and nuclear miscalculation at that." (Kilcullen, 2020, P.224). Military anthropologists essentially are trying to answer the question why the enemy is enemy, and a friend is friend as well as "why we fight" (Martin 2019). This book is a result of a life-long quest for this answer by a researcher who spent half of his life behind the Iron Curtain being born and educated initially in Soviet Ukraine, then post-Communist Poland and the other half in the UK. The insights I picked up on this journey were informed by communist schooling, the Marxist-Leninist higher education, including Soviet military education, as well as Western liberal academia, my radio broadcasting for BBC World Service, and my work for the British Army as a cultural adviser on Eastern Europe. Having experience of being on both sides of the ideological conflict as a participant observer brings advantages of seeing the cognitive divide from various points of view. This book, therefore, is an attempt to look through the 'fog of war' and try to see it through the eyes of Russia looking at the West, the Russian immediate neighbours looking at Russia and the 'Anglo-Saxons' trying to understand Russia in the Eastern European context. Being fluent in English, Russian, Polish, and Ukrainian helped me to explore the original sources and try placing myself in 'everybody's shoes', so the method chosen for this study is one of comparative historical analysis as well as narratives assessment of written documents, radio and TV interviews by means of qualitative analysis of text, image and sound from open publicly available sources as well as personal interviews.

The first Chapter of the book looks at the essential definitions of what is culture as understood in military anthropology, visible and invisible (salient) elements of the 'cultural iceberg', cultural dimensions and their measurement, narrative assessment, and finally, inductive method of analysis whereas conclusions are based on the facts and patterns emerging from data. This chapter also sets out the contemporary cultural context of historical themes chosen by the current Russian leadership to create its narratives, either to explain or justify political and military decisions made and points of view taken. In other words, the subject of research is not only the historical events described in Russian political / military leadership statements but also the significance of context e.g., why some historical narratives were chosen, and others ignored. The idea is that by understanding the worldview of Putin the president we can gain insight into Putin a Russian patriot (nationalist), Putin a practising Christian believer and ultimately Putin the decision-maker and the Commander-in-Chief.

Chapter 2 will look at the origin of the Red Army culture, theory, and practice and how it informs the New Generation Warfare application a hundred years later. Bolsheviks waged a revolutionary class war based on their Marxist-Leninist dialectical view of uneven capitalist development that leads to spiralling inter-state contradictions in its imperialist form that inevitably leads to war. This pessimistic view of the inevitable armed conflict based on expanding markets and struggle for limited natural resources is still at the heart of contemporary Russian strategic thinking. Bolshevik strategy of 'No War—No Peace' invented by Leon Trotsky, when the Bolshevik government was threatened by the advancing German army in 1918, received its new re-incarnation in so-called 'Gerasimov Doctrine' when the Russian Chief of Staff quoted Red Army theorist thinker Isserson that war declaration is no longer required for the new type of warfare. (Gerasimov, 2013) That implies that the boundaries between a political war, operational deployment and combat resolution of the armed conflict are blurred in order to create a new faite-a-complete in the cognitive space and on the ground before the enemy can identify covert hostile course of action, decide on a political or military solution and react to the armed invasion which is already either in progress or accomplished. This chapter also considers the Bolshevik invention of the subversion war, or as Evgeniy Messner put it *miatezh-voina* (Мятеж-война), as a societal uprising which is an old time tried-and-tested military deception method that worked well for Stalin during the formative years of the USSR e.g. in Ukraine and Georgia; at the beginning of WW2 for invasions of the Baltic states, Romania and Finland; at the end of WW2 for subjugation of Central Europe and Eastern Germany; but also worked for Putin when he decided to pacify rebellious Republic of Ichkeriya (Chechnya) in 2000 or create his 'Peoples' Republics' in Georgia (2008) and Eastern Ukraine (2014).

Chapter 3 will examine the Great Patriotic War as a myth created by the Soviet leadership under Josef Stalin to explain its pact with Hitler at the start of WW2 and the subsequent Soviet-Nazi war that followed. On the one hand, the Soviet contribution to defeating Nazi Germany is often understated in Western literature and especially in popular memory. The sacrifice and monumental effort of the Soviet population mobilised for the war was truly epic. On the other hand, the Kremlin created a myth of the Great Patriotic war as a chosen Soviet glory precisely because the human and material losses were the direct result of Stalin's murderous pre-war policies, disastrous alliance with Hitler, and complete disregard for human life of its own and conquered population of Europe. An epic sacrifice was matched with an epic lie still exploited by the Kremlin militarist ideology under President Putin.

Chapter 4 will analyse how Soviet military art evolved during the Cold War and how the last Soviet war in Afghanistan spelled out the dissolution of the USSR. The Cold War experience fighting the West is essential to current understanding of political war that the Kremlin is engaged with the 'Anglo-Saxons' and wider NATO countries that has been already dubbed as Cold War 2.0. The Soviet experience in avoiding direct confrontation with the USA during the Cold War is still relevant as it informs attitudes of the current Russian political and military leadership. Once the Communist Party under Nikita Khrushchev figured out that a nuclear war cannot be won, the Soviet military had to develop an indirect form of confronting the imperialists without provoking an open war. Operational and tactical art of the Soviets therefore evolved in order to utilise proxy wars, the anti-guerrilla warfare and honing such skills as 'reflexive control' on a tactical and operational level.

Chapter 5 contains an analysis of the current Russian understanding of New Generation Warfare sometimes called 'hybrid' or 'liminal' warfare and is essentially a creative Russian interpretation of Western military art that envisages application of clandestine 'colour revolution' tactics to achieve military objectives by non-military means. The NGW concept informs us how Russian military strategists arrived at such conclusions, the lessons they draw and changes they implemented to counteract this hybrid form of new type of warfare that they imply the West is waging on the rest of the World. Ironically from the Western point of view, 'hybrid warfare' is how the 'Rest learned to Fight the West' (Kilcullen, 2020) and the chapter explores the source of clear mutual misunderstanding. On the one hand, Russian concerns regarding American ability to conduct non-contact warfare with high-precision weapons in both Iraq campaigns (1990 and 2001) were absolutely justified as they exposed potential vulnerability. This explains Moscow's substantial and relatively successful investment in new 'wonder-weapons' announced by President Putin in the 2018 re-election speech. On the other hand, the American-led NATO intervention in Serbia (1999), which from Western point of view was purely humanitarian, was perceived in Moscow as blatant American interventionism and application of a new type of aggression in a form of a 'colour revolution'. Moscow considered a humanitarian intervention as a new aggressive military tactic that led to a regime change in Serbia when NATO troops did not even need to arrive in Belgrade to achieve full military and political victory. This chapter argues that the Kosovo precedent, more than expansion of NATO in Central Europe, changed strategic calculations in Moscow that was still hoping at the time to build strategic partnership relations with Washington. However, a series of 'colour revolutions' that happened in Georgia (2003), Ukraine (2004) and the Arab Spring (2005) convinced the Kremlin that the US' objective is to change political regime in Russia as well. This led to changes in the Russian military and information security doctrines by 2011 and invasion of Ukraine in 2014. Russian ruling elites were already convinced that they are fighting a defensive war of a new type against the 'Anglo-Saxons' while the Western leadership was still hoping for a re-set with Russia in order to improve relations and Washington would not even contemplate fighting a 'hybrid war' as Moscow suspected it did. Chapter 5 therefore, looks at justified Russian concerns, perceived and real 'hybrid threats' and how they informed the decision-making process in Russia to launch military campaigns in Crimea, Syria and arrive at the conclusion that it is at war with the West.

Chapter 6 investigates evolution of Russian information warfare from its Soviet origins of military subversion and political war to the most current version adopted since 2011. The latter elevated information warfare to the dominant form of New Generation Warfare where the traditional kinetic element was reduced to 10-20% or might be not required at all. In other words, this chapter describes how Russian understanding of information war evolved from a supporting operation to deceive and distract the enemy, to a strategic weapon aiming to defeat through so called indigenous destructive ideas, while denying that war is being waged at all. Information war therefore became the main type of war while kinetic high-precision weapons are kept as a deterrent and as 'doomsday' insurance to be used only as the last resort.

Chapter 7 looks at the Russian Reflexive control theory and its application in the so called 'active' or 'supporting' measures that are the substance of the Information war. While neither theory nor 'active measures' methodology are new and show clear continuation from the Soviet military science, their application to the contemporary Russian 'hybrid manoeuvre' represents a new development. In fact, there is almost no academic research on the application of the Reflexive control theory in the contemporary Russian Information manoeuvre, so uncovering this Moscow's 'black magic' is important for understanding how to protect targeted societies.

Chapter 8 brings together all elements of the Russian New Generation Warfare to see how they were applied in Ukraine to estimate the measurement of success from the Russian methodology point of view. It shows that despite close historical ties with Ukraine, military strategists in Russia miscalculated Ukrainian resistance potential which ironically suggests lack of cultural understanding. The very fact that Russia needed kinetic military intervention in Eastern Ukraine and still could not win in this armed conflict after a decade illustrated the limitations of Russian 'hybrid warfare'. This also suggests that relative success of the takeover in Crimea is only possible if the targeted society is not prepared for a hybrid scenario and the decision-making time for politicians to react is disastrously slow, allowing the aggressor to accomplish the occupation almost without firing a shot. In other words, deception on such a scale was possible only by abusing the benefit of the doubt in international public opinion that is no longer extended to the Russian Federation leadership.

Final Chapter 9 looks at the real and perceived threats to Russia from both the Russian and Western point of view. It exposes contradictions in the Russian approach but also lack of attention on behalf of the 'Anglo-Saxons' that could at times perpetuate Russian fears. It suggests three likely scenarios of peaceful co-existence that are culturally acceptable to Russia, Russian neighbours and the collective West. The choice is ultimately in the hands of the Russian ruling elite that can eventually achieve a true 'European security zone from Lisbon to Vladivostok' but only on mutually acceptable terms. These terms could be based on common cultural understanding of 'just war theory' — essentially a Christian ethic concept accepted by Moscow and wider European Judeo-Christian civilization. Using eschatological verses, so dear to the heart of the '*Russkiy Mir*' proponents, the smog of the unholy information war could be dispelled indeed as we struggle not against the people but against a proverbial Kingdom of Darkness mentioned by St Paul in his letter to Ephesians: "Our struggle is not against flesh and blood but against the rulers, against the authorities, against the powers of this dark world and against the spiritual forces of evil in the heavenly realms." (Eph 6:12). In modern interpretation, as Dallas Willard suggests, these powers and forces are spiritual agencies that work with the idea-systems of evil that are "their main tool for dominating humanity. Christian spiritual reformation is a matter of recognizing in ourselves the idea-systems of evil." This understanding of war, as a set of essentially evil belief systems, has direct resemblance in the classic Russian literature which still forms the core of the modern Russian culture.

Russia's full-scale invasion of Ukraine, attempted on 24 February 2022, led to enormous human suffering of million Ukrainians when over 15 million citizens were displaced, over eight million became refugees and hundreds of thousands were killed and injured. The UN Tribunal eventually will investigate over 97,000 war crimes recorded by the Ukrainian Prosecutor General office by the summer of 2023, including rape, abduction and killing of children. (See: https://war.ukraine.ua/russia-war-crimes/) The scale of human suffering inflicted by the Russian state on the Ukrainian people has not been seen in Europe since WW2 and it will take years, if not decades, to achieve anything resembling a reconciliation between the two nations. However, it is in the Russian national interest to admit the responsibility for the heinous war crimes, repent and offer reconciliation with Ukraine and wider Europe. It is inevitable that the Russian people will have to go through the catharsis similar to that of Germany and Japan at the end of WW2. If successful, such catharsis will change Russia forever and the final chapter of this book will look at the potential options available to the ruling Russian elites as well as Europe. The eternal Russian questions: "Whose fault it is, what to do and how to build up (*obustroit*) Russia?" will undoubtedly cause heated debates both in Russia and the rest of the world but it is essential to begin this process as the only way to mutual reconciliation. As the Kremlin's spokesman Peskov said many times—"all wars end with peace negotiations." This book is a modest attempt to facilitate this intercultural dialogue.

1. The Battle of Narratives

The first Chapter of the book looks at definition of what culture is and how it is understood in military anthropology, including visible and invisible (salient) elements of the 'cultural iceberg', cultural dimensions and their measurement, narrative analysis, and assessment. This chapter also sets out the contemporary cultural context of historical themes chosen by the current Russian leadership to create its narratives either to explain / justify political and military decisions made and points of view taken. In other words, the subject of research is not only the historical events described in Russia political / military leadership statements but also the significance of context e.g. why some historical narratives were chosen, and others ignored. The idea is that by understanding the worldview of Putin the president, we can gain insight into Putin a Russian patriot (nationalist), Putin a practising Christian believer and ultimately Putin the decision-maker and Commander-in-Chief.

Wars of the 21st century are sometimes called 'people-centric', reflecting a consensus among the military that psychological victory over 'hearts and minds' is considered as essential as conventional victory on battlefields. Armed conflicts are always fought by humans among the humans and therefore understanding human nature and culture is essential. A traditional definition of culture usually found in Anthropology textbooks suggests that culture is "that complex whole which includes knowledge, belief, art, morals, law, customs, and any other capabilities and habit acquired by man as a member of society". (See Tylor, Edward B., Anthropology: An Introduction to the Study of Man and Civilization, London: Macmillan and Co., 1881 Google Scholar.)

Generals have been interested in the culture of their enemies since at least Sun Tzu wrote his famous study *The Art of War* 2500 years ago, suggesting that one should know his enemy and himself. Culture, as a combination of customs, ideas and social behaviours, is of interest to the modern-day military for the same reason — it can inform understanding of adversaries' likely reactions in case of armed conflict. While customs and material forms of culture, such as architecture, costumes and food, can be observed, they are often are portrayed as a visible part of a cultural iceberg. Most of the cultural iceberg is invisible as it consists of beliefs, ideas and behaviours that are essential for decision making but not necessarily written down, internalised, and self-consciously reproduced by individuals. Culture is often learned and forgotten and could be compared to invisible software that plays 'pre-recorded' themes of the human psyche. Understanding one's adversary is an ability to read that software just as well if not better than the person or a group of people who owns it. Military anthropology therefore studies human culture in context of armed conflict with a different intent to academic social anthropology. One of the latest examples from the US Army history is employment of social anthropologists in the so-called Human Terrain System project conducted in Afghanistan in 2000s. Anthropologists had been embedded with Army brigade combat teams to gather cultural intelligence, provide regional knowledge and orientation, and interpret the customs of indigenous peoples to military commanders in order to mitigate conflict and minimize the kinds of misunderstandings that can lead to ill-will, unwarranted violence, or inadvertent casualties. "The use of these HTS teams by the Army and Marine Corps are, in turn, only the most dramatic, publicly visible, and controversial facets of a much broader, evolving collaboration between scholars and soldiers, between social scientists and military, security, and intelligence forces (MIS). This emerging collaboration has come to be known as 'military anthropology.'" (See G Lucas on ethical issues discussion "Anthropologists in Arms" (usna.edu)). One of the reasons why understanding culture became so essential for the military strategists is their desire to avoid risky miscalculations among nuclear super-powers and avoid unintentional war with potentially cataclysmic consequences. Modern warfare is prohibitively expensive and often self-destructive, so understanding adversarial intent and calculations is a worthy endeavour, if only to avoid unintended / avoidable wars. Avoiding war with Russia due to miscalculation was stressed during public debates in the UK parliament by Stuart Anderson, MP. He said: "The former Chief of the Defence Staff, General Sir Nick Carter, has said that the biggest concern that kept him awake at night was miscalculation. I have recently read the book "Countdown to War" by Sean McMeekin, which describes the build-up to the First World War—35 days of probably the biggest miscalculation we have ever seen. That was the time it took from no war being expected to the start of a war, with catastrophic events. That happened very quickly. If we had had effective statecraft, it could have been avoided. Let us learn from history and understand the grand strategy of Russia, but it is vital at this time that the highest level of diplomacy is used to prevent another miscalculation". Russia's Grand Strategy—Hansard—UK Parliament

Considering that all cultures tend to be ethnocentric i.e., look on the outside world from its own point of view, it is not difficult to imagine how miscalculations can happen simply because conflicting parties perceive the same argument through opposing cultural lenses. Jonson argues that "a key insight from the field of strategic culture points out that communities with different cultures and values can look at the same thing but interpret it very differently". Likewise, "strategists and their institutions cannot be accultural and hence will continuously perceive and interpret the material realm culturally." (Poore 2003, 282). Culture should be seen as a context from which an understanding cannot be isolated. This has been particularly in the case of Russia as the Russian paradigm is "idiosyncratic, reflects a strong cultural imprint, and needs to be analysed in the context of its strategic culture" (Adamsky 2018, 35). (Quoted from Jonsson 2019).

Another dimension to military anthropology is no less important as cultural study helps to make a moral judgement on waging war as well:

> "This is not to suggest that we can do nothing more than describe judgements and justifications that people commonly put forward. We can analyse these moral claims, seek out their coherence, lay bare the principles that they exemplify. ...and then we can expose the hypocrisy of soldiers and statesmen who publicly acknowledge these commitments while seeking in fact only their own advantage. The exposure of hypocrisy is certainly the most ordinary, and it may also be the most important, form of moral criticism. We are rarely called upon to invent new ethical principles; if we did that, our criticism would not be comprehensible to the people whose behaviour we wanted to condemn. Rather, we hold such people to their own principles,

though we may draw these out and arrange them in ways they had not thought of before". (Walzer 2015, P. XXVII).

Russian foreign policy is often portrayed as unpredictable, and the West often seems to be surprised when Moscow 'suddenly' comes up with a list of grievances that were either not understood or simply ignored. Putin's December 2021 ultimatum to the US and NATO to withdraw its troops and infrastructure from Eastern Europe to pre-1997 levels or face 'military-technical' retribution, with potential escalation of armed conflict in Ukraine, posed a serious challenge to the West. "In a word, Russia is demanding that NATO commit suicide, and that the United States be reduced to the role of a regional power". (Thom, 2021)

Understanding the invisible cultural iceberg of Russian demands could help avoiding such surprises in relations with Moscow, acknowledging genuine concerns and exposing potential hypocrisy of declared grievances. Both concerns and grievances are often broadcasted by Moscow in a form of coherent themes or stories that are often called narratives. Often such narratives are deliberately manipulated in order to achieve undeclared effects, hence the need for a better narrative assessment and understanding.

This chapter compares Russian historical justifications in context of wider Kremlin's policy of historical memory that were used to present its case for waging wars in the 21st century. As was mentioned in introduction, such historical justifications reach as far as 9th century and refer to the history of Kyivan Rus and its baptism in order to justify Russian claims on Belarus and Ukraine. A good place to start is Kremlin's narrative on Crimea. "For, it was here, in the Crimea, in the ancient Chersonese, or Korsun, as it was called by Russian chroniclers, that Prince Vladimir received Holy Baptism and then christened the whole of Rus'. …And so it gives us every reason to state that for Russia the Crimea, ancient Korsun, the Chersonese, Sevastopol have an enormous civilizational and sacral meaning—in the same way as the Temple Mount in Jerusalem is meaningful for those who confess Islam or Judaism." (Quoted from Pravoslavie.ru https://orthochristian.com/75734.html)

Crimea

Neal Acherson's celebrated book *Black Sea* history suggests the following chronology of events related to Kyivan Rus and Crimea.

Eighth century Khazars establish empire in Black Sea steppe (including Crimea) and ally with Byzantine Empire.
862   Rurik from Scandinavia captures Novgorod (modern day Russia).
882   Capital of Rus-Viking state moved to Kyiv (modern day Ukraine).
991   Rurik's grandson Valdemar (Volodymyr in Ukrainian, Vladimir in Russian) allegedly baptised at Chersoneses, in Crimea, (a Greek colony at a time).
1204   Venetians establish colony at Soldaia (Sudak) in Crimea.
1223-41 Mongol-Tatar invasion of Kyiv Rus and east-central Europe.
1280   Foundation of Genoese colony at Kaffa, Crimea.
1423-40 Establishment of Crimean Tatar Khanate, independent of the Golden Horde, under the Giray dynasty.
1453   Ottoman Turks capture Constantinople.
1696   Peter the Great captures Azov from Turks and lays his eyes on the Azov and Black Sea.
1783   Empress Catherine II of Russia annexes Crimea; end of the independent Tatar Khanate.

The 991 reference to Valdemar's baptism in Crimea is alleged as there is no historical record that this was indeed the case. There are at least three medieval references to the baptism of Prince Volodymyr in Kyivan Rus chronicles. One suggesting that Prince was baptised in Pochayna river near Kyiv while another suggesting he was baptised in Vasylkiv—a small town 30 kms from the Ukrainian capital. The third reference, also known as the Korsun legend, indeed, suggests that Volodymyr was baptised in a coastal town of

Crimea Korsun (e.g. Chersoneses) because it was a Byzantine colony with a legitimate Greek Orthodox church, which was a precondition for Volodymyr's marriage with a Byzantine princess. This is the most elaborate legend that combines a few events that did happen, with some that did not, and wraps them up in a hagiographical story of a miracle when the prince went blind and then could see again once he accepted Christianity. The Korsun legend was little known in Moscow until it was mentioned by the Catherine II who conquered Crimea and then picked up by the Russian imperial navy command in 1825 precisely for the same reason as it was resurrected by President Putin in 2014 i.e. to legitimise Crimean conquest by Russia. https://incognita.day.kyiv.ua/u-%C2%ABstoron i-korsunskij%C2%BB...(2).html

In any case, how could a dynastic union between a Viking prince (whose mother was from Kyiv) with a Byzantine emperor's daughter in Constantinople who was baptised in a Greek Orthodox church circa 991, justify illegal occupation of Crimea in 2014 by Moscow? Chersoneses was a Greek (Byzantine) colony on the cost of Crimea that was under jurisdiction of the Khazar and Byzantium empires at the time with no recorded Slavic presence. Prince Volodymyr did invade Chersoneses briefly but never claimed its possession and, as per Korsun legend, was filled with Christian piety for peace and love towards the Greeks and especially the Byzantine princess.

In any rational way, therefore, these historical legendary events from the 9th century cannot justify decisions made in the 21st century that would suggest that Crimea was always Russian. In fact, Crimea was part of Khazar Empire from the 8th until the 13th century when it fell under the Golden Horde Mongol rule until the Crimean Tatar Khanate switched allegiance to the Ottoman Empire in the 15th century. The Golden Horde most likely gave Crimea its name Kerim (Krim) that meant 'fort' from their first capital Eski Kerim—'old fort.' (Ascherson, 2015. Location 572). In other words, Crimean history from the 8th century BC until the 15th century was a symbiotic relationship between coastal Greek and later Venetian colonies and the Eurasian inhabitants of the steppes starting with

Scythians, Sarmatians, Cimmerians, Goths, Huns, Khazars, Mongols and finally Crimean Tatars who ruled until 1783. So, how come Crimea was 'always Russian', or became so then? When General Suvorov's troops occupied Crimea, 90% of its population was Tatars with other ethnicities representing the remaining 10% and no recorded Muscovites. This is when the Crimea became a de-facto Russian possession but not because of gradual natural influx of Slavic population but mass expulsion of Tatars to the Ottoman Turkey who fled from persecution. General Suvorov prosecuted mass deportations of not only Crimean Tatars but also the Greek, German and other colonists who inhabited around 700 towns and villages on the Black Sea coast before the Russian invasion (Sereda, 2019). In other words, Crimea became Russian as a result of mass deportations and gradual colonisation throughout the 19th century. Economic development of Crimea by the Russian imperial governors was slow and mostly related to militarization of the peninsula, construction of both the new Black Sea navy and its naval base in Sevastopol on the ruins of Greek Chersoneses as well as destroyed Tatar settlements. Crimea was not 'reunited' in any sense of the word, but conquered and colonised by the new imperial master. Even the name Sevastopol was given to the city of 'Russian glory' by mistake as it was meant to be Kherson — to resemble ancient Chersoneses. However, inept couriers from Catherine II mixed up the postal bags and delivered the decree with a name 'Kherson' to another city being constructed in Southern Ukraine at the time. Neal Acherson compares claims on Crimea as anybody's exclusive right or possession to a joke:

> "Crimea, whose beauty provokes almost sexual yearnings of possessions in all its visitors, has demonstrated this joke in every century of its history. It has no natives, no aboriginals. …Voyaging communities settled in Crimea (the Scythians lived here for nearly a thousand years) but in the end they dispersed or moved on. …Only in recent times has the Crimean truth — that it belongs to everybody and to nobody — been violated. Three of these violations, which would be merely absurd if they did not imply so much blood and suffering, are the declarations of three autocrats. In 1783, Catherine II ("the Great") proclaimed that the Crimean peninsula was henceforth and for all time to become Russian. In 1954, Nikita Khruschev, seeking to divert his own people from their own miseries, announced that he was transferring Crimea from Russia to become for all time Ukrainian. And in 2014, Vladimir

Putin told the world that Crimea was to be torn out of Ukraine and to become, again, for all time Russian". (Acherson, 2015, Location 659).

Yet, the Ukrainian Constitution adopted in 1996, did recognise the Crimean Tatars and a tiny minority of Crimean Karaims as the *indigenous* population of the Crimean Autonomous Republic. In fact, independent Ukraine became the only nation-state in Europe that allowed resettlement of an entire people on its sovereign territory from another part of the world in the 20th century. Deported by Stalin in 1944, Crimean Tatars were allowed to come back to their ancestral lands from Central Asia only after 1991. Crimean Tatars, unlike ethnic Russians in Crimea, have no other homeland, and their entire history since 1783 was one of marginalisation and persecution by successive Russian governments. By the time of the Crimean War (1853-56), Tatar populations on the peninsula was reduced from absolute majority to 60%. The first Bolshevik massacres in 1920 killed an estimated 150,000 Crimeans including thousands of Tatars. The following terror-famine killed half of the population in Tatar's capital Bakhchisarai, so by 1923, Tatars constituted only a quarter of the Crimean population:

> "The historian Alan Fisher, in his book the Crimean Tatars, calculates that 150,000 Tatars, half the Tatar population in 1917, had been killed, deported or forced into exile outside of the Soviet Union by 1933. A renewed slaughter of educated Tatars, including the Moslem clergy, took place during the Great Purges of 1937-8" (Acherson, 2015, Location 737).

The next bloody purge of the Crimean native population was conducted during WW2 by SS Einsatzgruppe D, led by Otto Ohlendorf, that "executed an estimated 130,000 Crimeans, including the entire gypsy population of Crimea, the remaining Jews and …most of the Karaims. Tens of thousands of Tatars were among Ohlendorf's victims". (Acherson, 2015 Location 763). When the Soviets came back, they delivered the ultimate blow and the entire Crimean Tatar people were deported to Central Asia with thousands dying en route. This is really when Crimea, for the first time, became Russian indeed. With the indigenous population killed or deported, entire collective farms from the Russian Federation were resettled in Crimea and took over empty properties and land of evicted owners.

However, once, Russian *kolkhozniks* failed to master the essential skills of farming difficult steppe soils requiring irrigation (i.e. 80% of Crimean agricultural land), the Soviet Government made a pragmatic decision to hand over Crimea to the Ukrainian SSR with its massive human and water resources. What was essentially an economic decision to change the internal Soviet administrative borders was presented by CPSU Chairman Khruschev — native of Ukrainian Donetsk — as a gift to the Ukrainian people in order to celebrate the 1654 'reunification' with Russia. This opened a new Ukrainian page in the history of Crimea but did not end the suffering of the previously evicted inhabitants. Although, rehabilitated by Khruschev, Crimean Tatars were allowed to return only by the governments of independent Ukraine after 1991. Despite all the difficulties of resettlement, reintegration and often local communal hostilities, Crimean Tatars became staunch supporters of Ukrainian independence and, by the time of the Russian invasion in 2014, constituted one third of Crimean population. According to the UN reports, Crimean Tatars face once again human rights abuses, extrajudicial killings, forced emigration and systematic persecution under the Russian rule (UN Ukraine reports, 2021). For them there is little doubt that the empire is back, and their homeland has been once again proclaimed to be 'eternally Russian". As Conservative British MP Alec Shelbrooke informed the British parliament on 6th January 2022, there is strong evidence of ethnic cleansing taking place: "It is also worth putting on the record in the House that there are many reports of the ethnic cleansing of Tatars in Crimea. There are reports that 25,000 people have disappeared. There is a complete lockdown on the verification by outside international media of what is taking place in Crimea". (UK Parliament, 2022).

Likewise, Ukrainians who refused to take Russian passports were forced to emigrate or face political persecution, loss of property and intimidation. The only school in Crimea that taught pupils in Ukrainian language was forced to switch to Russian language of instruction. New Russian authorities were committed to eradicate also Ukrainian churches and made the Crimean political organization *Mejlis* an illegal entity. At the same time, Russian language publications such as Novoross.info published numerous accusations of Ukrainians being fascists and Crimean Tatars being Islamic radicals. Ukrainian media were banned since 2014 and the assets of most Ukrainian commercial or state enterprises were nationalised. Even UkrNaftogaz' new Oil&Gas offshore platforms in the Black Sea were captured, including one that is in closer proximity to Odessa than Crimea. This was followed by rapid militarization of Crimea. Both Ukrainian and Tatar residents, that amounted to almost half of the pre-2014 population, were forced to serve in the RF army violating international legislations that does not allow youth on occupied territories to be drafted in the armed forces of an occupying power. As of 2022, the citizens of occupied Crimea have been also mobilised into the RF Armed Forces and sent to fight fellow Ukrainians, the subject of future investigation into war crimes committed as a result of the Russian aggression against Ukraine. In addition, more than two hundred thousand of RF citizens were resettled in Crimea to change the population ratio in favour of ethnic Russians:

> "Russia has been actively trying to increase the size of its "loyal" population by promoting and encouraging the in-migration of its citizens to Crimea. According to the Office of the Federal State Statistics Service in Crimea and Sevastopol, since 2014, 205,559 Russians moved to Crimea, of whom 88,445 settled in Sevastopol (Crimeahrg.org, January 6). As of January 2021, the population of Sevastopol was 513,149 (Goroda Rossii, accessed March 14). Ukrainian authorities from the Ministry of Reintegration of Temporarily Occupied Territories and representatives of the Crimean Human Rights Group believe the real figures of such new settlers are much greater (Informator.ua, January 6)". (Jamestown Foundation, 2021)

Yet, few countries in the world recognised that Crimea is 'forever Russian'. Instead, Crimea has turned into a militarised 'fort' once again and any criticism of Kremlin's action only produces more statements from Moscow about Russia as a 'besieged fortress' surrounded by enemies.

Ukraine and Donbas

Russian 'reunification' of Crimea has opened a further set of revanchist historical claims: initially with regards to so called Novorosiya and then eventually, the whole of Ukraine as 'eternally Russian'. President Putin tried to 'educate' President George Bush back in 2008 that Ukraine is a historical aberration—a collection of lands given to Ukrainians by generous Russians: "You have to understand, George, that Ukraine is not even a country. What is Ukraine? Part of its territories is Eastern Europe, but the greater part is a gift from us". (The Huffington Post, 16 March 2014).

The claim harked back again to the historical legacy of Kyivan Rus and was elaborated by President Putin in 2021. (Article by Vladimir Putin "On the Historical Unity of Russians and Ukrainians" • President of Russia (kremlin.ru)).

The article, aimed at international audiences, postulated territorial claims justified by common territory, history, language and culture of Malorussians (Little Russians) as part of 'one people' with 'Great Russians'. History is only a backdrop to support narratives that Ukraine is merely a borderland of Russia, According to these, the Ukrainian language was the same as Russian until it was distorted by 'Polonisation'; Ukrainians are 'Little Russians'; Ukrainian nation-state aspirations were artificially inspired by Polish and Austrian 19-20 century politicians to divide the Russians; the Ukrainian Soviet Socialist Republic was an aberration created by Lenin; independent Ukraine has no legal rights for territory received from the USSR after 1922; contemporary Ukraine is turning into the project 'anti-Russia' by misguided by Western powers; ethnic Russians are persecuted and the identity of millions can disappear if not protected by the Kremlin; attacks on the Russian identity in Ukraine are equal to the use of weapons of mass destruction; Ukrainian government introduced 'anti-Russian' discriminatory law on indigenous ethnic minorities under the protection of large-scale NATO exercises.

In reality, all these accusations amounted to the information warfare preparation of the battlespace setting out Russian 'legitimate rights' and grievances, Ukrainian and NATO misdeeds as well as justification of Russian 'counter-attack' against externally-managed Ukrainian authorities using 'weapons of mass destruction' on ethnic Russians—a Casus Belli par excellence. So, is there a grain of truth in any of the suggested 'historical' statements and political allegations in President Putin's article?

Narrative 1: Kyivan Rus as the Russian medieval state

"Russians, Ukrainians, and Belarusians are all descendants of Ancient Rus, which was the largest state in Europe. Slavic and other tribes across the vast territory—from Ladoga, Novgorod, and Pskov to Kiev and Chernigov—were bound together by one language (which we now refer to as Old Russian), economic ties, the rule of the princes of the Rurik dynasty, and—after the baptism of Rus—the Orthodox faith. The spiritual choice made by St. Vladimir, who was both Prince of Novgorod and Grand Prince of Kiev, still largely determines our affinity today. The throne of Kiev held a dominant position in Ancient Rus. This had been the custom since the late 9th century. The Tale of Bygone Years captured for posterity the words of Oleg the Prophet about Kiev, 'Let it be the mother of all Russian cities.'"

Facts: Eastern Slavs used so called Old-Church Slavonic language as the official language of Kyivan Rus and not 'Old-Russian'. The Old-Church Slavonic was introduced by the Greek clergy using medieval Bulgarian language as a Slavic lingua-franca for the church writings and was not used by local population colloquially. Eastern Slavic tribes spoke a variety of lingos with regional variations but still mutually understood. The name Rus and ethnic name *Russkiy* translated in the Kremlin's article as 'Russian' requires additional explanation in terms of transliteration as well. Below is the list of meanings referencing ethnic name "Russkiy" in various contemporary languages:

- *Russky* (русский) — ethnic Russian (Russisch in German) vs *rossiisky* (Российский), Russlaendisch,
- *Russkiye* (русские in Russian) vs *Rossiyane* (Россияне) — ethnic Russian vs citizens of Russia
- *Rus'kyi* (Руський in Ukrainian), old Ukrainian referring to either Kyivan Rus or later periods of Ukrainian history (as late as 1915 depending on regions). E.g. вул. Руська (Rus'ka street) in Western Ukrainian Lviv refers to a street where Ukrainians lived in the 17th century as oppose to a Polish majority of the city.
- *Rus'ki* (Руські in Ukrainian) refers to people of Kievan Rus i.e. one of historical ethnic name for Ukrainians e.g. русичі, русини. The Ukrainian word for Russians is *rosiyany* (росіяни), *moskali* (москалі). The later word refered initially to Russian soldiers and then became pejorative to describe all Russians.
- *Ruski* (in Polish) — pejorative for a Russian, although might sometimes include also Ukrainians and Byelorussians (or anyone to the East of Poland i.e. ze Wschodu). *Rosjanie* is Polish for Russians.

In other words, "Rus'ki" in Ukrainian language not only does not mean Russian but also does not recognise the right of contemporary Russians to use it as an ethnic self-name. Regional authorities in Lviv and Rivne even demanded in 2021 that the Ukrainian Government stops referring to 'Russian' Federation and start using the old name 'Muscovite'. A relevant petition collected over 25,000 signatures by February 2023 and should have been discussed by the Ukrainian government (Ukrinform 2023).

If we look at 17th century Dutch map of Ukraine we can see why:

As we can see above, the Latin inscription *Russia Pars* (in Western Ukraine) refers to the land of the Western Rus' incorporated into the Polish Kingdom since 1340, while the Moscow Grand Dutchy is portrayed as a separate entity different from Ukraine. The Moscow Grand Dutchy was not officially called 'Russia' until Peter 1 proclaimed so by a decree in 1721. From the Ukrainian language point of view 'Ukraina' is not a 'borderland' but literally 'in-land'. Inland might simply refer to the heartland of the Kyivan Rus land delineated by the Carpathian mountains in the West, Prypiat river marches in the North, Dnieper river in the East and hostile nomadic steppe in the south. Peter I claimed all this territory by choosing the name Russia which is not unusual misappropriation of other peoples' names by a bigger neighbour. German settlers on the Eastern shores of the Baltic similarly 'borrowed' the name of indigenous Baltic tribes known as 'Prussy' hence the name 'Prussians' adopted by Germans as of the 17th century. Original Prussian language, likely similar to modern Lithuanian, did not survive in written form to tell the story of non-Germanic Prussians who were fully assimilated. However, the Ukrainian language clearly does not recognise the misappropriation of the name 'Rus'kyi' by the contemporary Russian politicians. So, how about the claim that Ukrainian and Russian languages were the same?

Narrative 2: Russian and Ukrainian languages were the same

"The incorporation of the western Russian lands into the single state was not merely the result of political and diplomatic decisions. It was underlain by the common faith, shared cultural traditions, and — I would like to emphasize it once again — language similarity. Thus, as early as the beginning of the 17th century, one of the hierarchs of the Uniate Church, Joseph Rutsky, communicated to Rome that people in Moscovia called Russians from the Polish-Lithuanian Commonwealth their brothers, that their written language was absolutely identical, and differences in the vernacular were insignificant. He drew an analogy with the residents of Rome and Bergamo".

Facts: Rutsky referred to the Ukrainians as 'Rus'ky' not Russian to reflect their common name as descendants of Kyivan Rus. People in Moscovia did not use the name 'Russi'a until 1721. hence misplacing the names is a deliberate confusion to create an effect that 'Russian's of the Polish-Lithuanian Commonwealth were the same as 'people of Moscovia'. It is true that both used Old Church Slavonic in canonical texts, and it was similar if not identical, but it was clearly not the Russian language of Aleksandr Pushkin. With regards of vernacular used by locals we can judge from the fact that Hetman Bohdan Kmelnytsky, praised by Putin for 'reunification' of Cossack Ukraine with Moscow Kingdom, used interpreters to discuss a political-military alliance in 1654. The original text of the treaty has never been released by Moscow, if it ever existed in writing, so we do not know what language was used by both parties at the time. However, *Kievskaya starina* published, in 1883, a colloquial Ukrainian text from 1619, showed a clear continuity with contemporary Ukrainian language that Russians struggle to understand when spoken (Mova kozakiv, 2016).

Curiously contemporary Russian language has more in common with Bulgarian, rather than Ukrainian or Belarussian, even though Bulgaria does not share a land border with RF. That suggests that the Old Church Slavonic based on old Bulgarian was used as a foundation for the Russian language refined by Pushkin and Gogol. Contemporary Ukrainian language has more in common with Polish than Russian. For instance, the Ukrainian language has 30% different vocabulary with Polish making it like the difference between French and Italian. At the same time, the Ukrainian language is 38% different from Russian language making it as different as contemporary English and Dutch. (The difference between Russian and Bulgarian is only 27%) (Radchuk, 2000).

So, what about Ukrainian territory within 1922 border as suggested in the article?

Narrative 3. Ukraine was created by Lenin

"You want to establish a state of your own: you are welcome! But what are the terms? I will recall the assessment given by one of the most prominent political figures of new Russia, first mayor of Saint Petersburg, Anatoly Sobchak. As a legal expert who believed that every decision must be legitimate, in 1992, he shared the following opinion: the republics that were founders of the Union, having denounced the 1922 Union Treaty, must return to the boundaries they had had before joining the Soviet Union. All other territorial acquisitions are subject to discussion, negotiations, given that the ground has been revoked. In other words, when you leave, take what you brought with you".

The map below shows the border changes between Ukraine and Russian Federation in 1918-1928.

The key highlighted differences, related to the border between Ukraine and Russian Federation, are related to Crimea and Donbas (Vortman, 2014). However, the deep green area of Donbas, that was transferred to Ukrainian SSR in April 1920, had been 'returned' to the RF in October 1925. Bolsheviks took into the account ethnographic and cultural mix of the population and generally accepted the borders of Ukraine established by the Ukrainian Peoples Republic (UNR) in 1918 (Yefymenko, 2014).

The key cities such as Mariupol, Yuzivka (Donetsk) and Luhansk are firmly within Ukrainian borders. So, does it mean that Donbas is not subject for renegotiations with Moscow at the start of 2022 invasion? Even more embarrassingly for the authors of Putin's article — undisputed Ukrainian territory in 1922 included what is now known as the Transnistrian Peoples' Republic, a Moldovan break-away territory under effective control of RF at present. Territories where Ukrainian SSR expanded since 1922 included parts of modern Poland, Romania and Hungary (due to the USSR Westward expansion) but certainly not Russian Federation.

As Andrew Wilson pointed out this narrative simply does not make sense: "From 1939 to 1954, the Bolsheviks added territory to Ukraine from inter-war Poland, Czechoslovakia and Romania, together with Crimea in 1954. Putin proposes the nonsensical idea that 'when you leave [the dissolution of the USSR in 1991], take what you brought with you'—referring to the territory that the Ukrainian SSR had when the USSR was created in 1922. But, apart from Crimea, all of Putin's Novorossiya—eastern and Black Sea Ukraine—was then part of Ukraine". (Wilson, 2021 Russia and Ukraine: 'One People' as Putin Claims? | Royal United Services Institute (rusi.org)) So, what is Kremlin's justification for the change of borders in Donbas? Apparently, Ukraine does not need Donbas anymore, says Mr Putin:

> "I am becoming more and more convinced of this: Kiev simply does not need Donbas. Why? Because, firstly, the inhabitants of these regions will never accept the order that they have tried and are trying to impose by force, blockade and threats. And secondly, the outcome of both Minsk 1 and Minsk 2 which give a real chance to peacefully restore the territorial integrity of Ukraine by coming to an agreement directly with the DPR and LPR with Russia, Germany and France as mediators, contradicts the entire logic of the anti-Russia project. And it can only be sustained by the constant cultivation of the image of an internal and external enemy. And I would add—under the protection and control of the Western powers" (Ibid.).

The justification for border change seems to be Ukrainian attempts to use Donbas, under control of Western powers, to perpetuate project 'anti-Russia' using Donbas 'resistance' as an image of an enemy. This amounts to attempts of ethnic cleansing, perhaps even genocide, and forced identity change that amounts to the use of weapons of mass destruction against the ethnic Russians. The Kremlin is careful not to blame such policy on the Ukrainian people, as they are allegedly innocent victims of the Ukrainian government dominated by corrupt oligarchs who keep their stolen money in the West and serve Western geopolitical interests. After all the Ukrainians are 'one people' with the Russians, so it is all about Western machinations that started with the Poles in 19th century and continued by the Austrian security services fostering a separate Ukrainian identity during WW1 and Nazi Germany in WW2 (Putin 2020) (Об Украине (интервью ТАСС) • Президент России (kremlin.ru)). From the Kremlin's point of view, 21st Century Ukraine is, in fact, project 'anti-Russia' which is directly orchestrated by Washington and Brussels: "We are witnessing not just complete dependence but direct external control, including the supervision of the Ukrainian authorities, security services and armed forces by foreign advisers, military 'development' of the territory of Ukraine and deployment of NATO infrastructure". The article ends with a statement of belief supporting the grand narrative of a 'greater Russian nation' incorporating Ukraine: "I am confident that true sovereignty of Ukraine is possible only in partnership with Russia. ...For we are one people".

Putin's article presents a wealth of narratives that tells us more about the Kremlin and 'collective' Putin than the actual history of Eastern Europe. It is not surprising that the UK Secretary of State for Defence, Ben Wallace, urged everyone to read Putin's essay in order to understand the Kremlin's intent:

> "We should all worry because what flows from the pen of President Putin himself is a seven-thousand-word essay that puts ethnonationalism at the heart of his ambitions. Not the narrative now being peddled. Not the straw man of NATO encroachment. It provides the skewed and selective reasoning to justify, at best, the subjugation of Ukraine and at worse the forced unification of that sovereign country. President Putin's article completely ignores the wishes of the citizens of Ukraine, while evoking that same type of ethnonationalism which played out across Europe for centuries and still has the potential to awaken the same destructive forces of ancient hatred". (Wallace 2022, gov.uk "An Article by the Defence Secretary on the situation in Ukraine".)

Some of the narratives in the 'collective Putin's' article reflects authoritarian personality of its authors, while others are shared by wider Russian society and reflect Russian cultural beliefs and attitudes. Considering that a lot of narratives are used to justify a military-political decision to threaten invasion of Ukraine and challenging NATO in Eastern Europe, it is worth considering these narratives in terms of Russian militarism i.e. the belief that geopolitical challenges could be resolved through a military campaign or an open armed conflict. As Anne Applebaum observed Putin's line on Ukraine is more emotional and ideological than rational:

> "He then sent that essay to every soldier in the Russian army. Putin's interest in invading, occupying, dividing, or otherwise destroying Ukraine—a country that has no nuclear weapons and could not invade Russia—is not strategic. It is emotional. The collapse of the Soviet Union was, in his words, "the

greatest geopolitical catastrophe of the 20th century." An expanded Russian occupation of Ukrainian territory might, in his view, help right that wrong". No One in Kyiv Knows Whether Russia Is Bluffing – The Atlantic

It was long known that the way in which a military decision-maker as an individual perceives and acts towards his environment is partly determined by the quality and strength of his motives, needs, attitudes, and emotions: "Prejudice, ignorance, fear of failure, over-conformity and sheer stupidity may disrupt leadership-decisions as surely as they interfere with planning or technical decisions. All are products of the same brain". (Dixon 1976, P. 20). Dixon's classical study, *On the psychology of Military Incompetence*, was largely based on British and American military history but considered Russian case studies as well and equally applies across military cultures. As a former bomb disposal officer himself, Dixon could not agree that military incompetence, leading to bloody disasters, are results of just "ignorance and ordinary stupidity". As a psychologist, he arrived at a conclusion that that there is a weak dividing-line between militarism and obsessional neurosis: "The syndrome that includes such attitudes as religious dogmatism, ethnocentrism, intolerance of minority groups, punitiveness, anti-hedonism, conformity, conventionality, superstition, resistance to scientific progress, and a liking for militarism. In other words, the syndrome is scarcely distinguishable from the Berkeley concept of authoritarianism" (Dixon, 1976, P. 447). In his view, this combination of attitudes functions as an ego-defence of a decision making general against feelings of inferiority and insecurity. Hence, the proposal to remove such military decision makers from enacting wars: "The world cannot afford the excitement of entrusting its hydrogen bombs to impulsive, maverick individuals. For this job we still require the naturally inhibited, totally obedient, 'bullshit'-ridden bureaucrat". (Ibid, P.449). Could Putin's personal decision to invade Ukraine in February 2022 be a result of such obsessional neurosis or rather a wider reflection of culture of militarism inherited by the KGB officers from the Soviet society?

Historically, the CPSU (civilian) control of the military made the USSR less prone to miscalculations as the Soviet generals alone could not decide whether to launch a war. Contemporary RF government is fully controlled by the ex-KGB senior officers and there is no civilian oversight comparable to CPSU. Having the military in charge of the decision to go to war allows for more unpredictability in their decision-making process. As Keir Giles put it in his *Moscow Rules,* never assume that you can choose when or whether to be at war with Russia: "(Rule) 10. Don't think that you can choose whether to be at war with Russia or not. Sometimes de-escalation, taken to its logical conclusion, equates to surrender. At the same time, Russia will never be 'at peace' with you. Normal relations with Russia include fending off a wide range of hostile actions from Moscow; this is the default state throughout history, and Western nations should by now be realising this is the norm" (Giles, 2019).

Situation when Russia is in a state of 'No Peace—No War' harks back to the very foundation days of the Red Army and the Treaty of Brest-Litovsk in 1918. Hence understanding evolution of the 20th century Soviet military doctrine and practice will help to understand the resurgence of Russian militarism in the 21st century.

2. 'No Peace — No War' and the Origin of the Red Army *Modus Operandi*

When the Russian Empire started to disintegrate at the end of WW1, it was still largely an agrarian society and a very unlikely place where a proletarian revolution could occur. Karl Marx considered Russia a backward country with an Asian mode of production that would take a long time to catch up with industrialised Europe. However, the German General Staff took a different, more optimistic view, while facing inevitable defeat against Entante Powers on both fronts in 1917. On 9th April 1917, 32 Russian Bolsheviks boarded the train in Zurich and started their journey to St Peterburg to launch an uprising. The future self-declared leader of the 'world's proletariat', Vladimir Lenin, was on the train, sponsored by Kaiser Wilhelm II who invested in subversion of the interim Russian government led by Aleksandr Kerensky: "On November 7, 1917, a coup d'état went down in history as the October Revolution. The interim government was toppled, the Soviets seized power, and Russia later terminated the Triple Entente military alliance with France and Britain. For Russia, it was effectively the end of the war. Kaiser Wilhelm II had spent around half a billion euros ($582 million) in today's money to weaken his wartime enemy" (Wagener, 2017) https://www.dw.com/en/how-germany-got-the-russian-revolution-off-the-ground/a-41195312

The German Chief of Staff, General Erich von Ludendorff, wrote unequivocally in his memoires: "In sending Lenin to Russia, our government took upon itself a special responsibility. His journey through Germany was justified from the military point of view; Russia had to made to fall"[1]. This quote was re-discovered by Soviet general / turned historian Dmitriy Volkogonov who also established that funding was transferred via Alexander Helphand known as Parvus. The later acted as intermediary between the German High Command and the Bolsheviks: "The fact is that Lenin's most trusted agents, Ganetsky and Kozlovsky, received large sums

---

1 Ludendorff, E. Moi vospominaniya o voine 1914-1918, Moscow, 1924. P.89.

of money from Parvus. The Bolshevik denial of this fact was as vigorous as it was unconvincing: the fact alone that they could maintain seventeen daily newspapers with circulation of more than 300,000 while complaining of empty Party coffers was proof enough that funds were coming from somewhere, and that it was a source they preferred to keep secret. ...Former Tsarist police general A.I.Spiridovich, using documents from the St.Petersburg prosecutor's office established that the Bolshevik Central Committee received money from abroad via Parvus, Ganetsky, Kozlovksy and Sumenson" (Volkogonov, 1996. Loc 4355).

Lenin's return to his home country was followed with great attention in Berlin. "Lenin's entry into Russia was a success. He is working according to your wishes," was the message Germany's top army command sent to its Foreign Office. Lenin seemed to enjoy the best of two worlds for a revolutionary at the time: lavish sponsorship from the 'hated' capitalist Germany and success of his communist project in Russia. However, he and his People's Commissar of War, Leon Trotsky, could not explain to ordinary Russians why they had to surrender territories to the enemy that was clearly losing the war. Hence, both came up with a formula 'No Peace—No War' that allowed demobilisation of millions of peasants and workers who hated the life in the trenches and were eager to return home to their families. Volkogonov's publication of Lenin's collaboration with the German Military Command was a profound shock to Post-Soviet Russia that uncovered that Soviet mythology of Lenin as an independent revolutionary actor was not only false but also that Bolshevik success was to a large extent a result of a successful Western (German) conspiracy and a strategic military deception operation (Byl li Lenin... diletant.media 2017; Byl li Lenin... ria.ru 2020,).

Hence the modern Russian elite's obsession with Western anti-Russian conspiracies could be partially understood by formative experience of the Bolshevik founders of the USSR. The other formative experience was reliance on brutal violence of the Red Army command towards its own soldiers and anti-Bolshevik opposition that survived to the present day in blurring the lines between military operations against external enemies and suppression of internal opposition. In a similar fashion the distinction between peace and war became theoretical as war rhetoric and vocabulary was used routinely. The Civil war front became the 'labour front' when soldiers were not immediately demobilised but simply re-allocated to unpaid labour front duties.

Bolsheviks waged a revolutionary class war based on their Marxist-Leninist dialectical view of uneven capitalist development that leads to spiralling inter-state contradictions in its imperialist form that inevitably leads to war. This pessimistic view of the inevitable armed conflict based on expanding markets and struggle for limited natural resources is still at the heart of contemporary Russian strategic thinking. Bolshevik strategy of 'No Peace – No War' invented by Leon Trotsky, when the Bolshevik government was threatened by the advancing German army in 1918, received its new re-incarnation in so-called 'Gerasimov Doctrine' when the Russian Chief of Staff quoted Red Army theorist thinker Isserson that war declaration is no longer required in the new type of warfare (Gerasimov, 2013). Isserson captured the spirit of the future Blitzkrieg ahead of his time: "War is not declared at all. It simply begins with a pre-deployed military force. Mobilization and concentration do not refer to the period after the onset of the state of war, as it was in 1914, but are imperceptibly, gradually carried out long before that. Of course, it is impossible to completely hide this. In one size or another, concentration becomes known. However, there is always one step from the threat of war to entry into war. It raises doubts as to whether a valid military action is being prepared or whether it is only a threat. And while one side remains in this group, the other, determined to act, continues to concentrate until, finally, a huge armed force is deployed on the border. After that, it remains only to give a signal, and the war immediately erupts on its full scale." (Isserson, 1940) Quoted from ВОЕННАЯ ЛИТЕРАТУРА – [Военная мысль] – Иссерсон Г.С. Новые формы борьбы (lib.ru)

That implies that the boundaries between a political war, operational deployment and combat resolution of the armed conflict are blurred on purpose in order to create a new faite-a-complete in the cognitive space and on the ground before the enemy can identify covert hostile course of action, decide on political or military solutions and react to armed invasion which is already either in progress or accomplished. So, where did this Soviet and modern Russian pessimistic view of mankind as warring parties come from?

A look at Bolshevik understanding of causes of war is very illuminating, argues Oscar Jonsson: "In Marxist thought, the root cause of war was the existence of class societies. The exploiting ruling class would continually use war to further its economic interests, and in this light the cause of war was economic (Light 1988, 212). The chief of the Red Army, Ioakim Vatsetis (1923, 33), opined, emblematic of the view that persisted throughout the Soviet Union, that "a future war will in a sense be a class war, evoked by rivalry on purely economic grounds". In Lenin's view, war was necessary in the condition of transforming the world and reaching the ultimate good. For Soviet leaders, "the socialistic transformation of society without an armed struggle was unconceivable" (Lider 1977, P.232). This struggle was not limited to an interstate level; rather, it was militarizing the whole of social life (Lenin 1916, P.3). Frunze agreed, arguing that "absolutely all aspects of social life are absorbed by war and subordinated to them" (Frunze 1921, P.28)" (Jonsson, 2019, P.44).

Jonsson suggests that there was a paradox at the core of the Marxist view of war (when perceived as something evil stemming from Western imperialism) but also positive (facilitating revolutionary change). For Lenin, "war is a reflection of the internal policy conducted by given country before the war" (Lenin 1919, P.152). For Trotsky: "war is a hostile encounter between human groups equipped with instruments for killing and destroying, with the direct aim of winning physical dominance over the enemy." (Trotsky 1922) Trotsky thus emphasized the physically violent aspect of war and, like Clausewitz, supported the notion that war's nature remains the same while the ways of fighting change (due to human technology development — OH). Trotsky saw "the task of war to destroy the enemy's manpower. This can be achieved by means of a blow." (Jonsson, 2019, P.49).

Volkogonov noted that Lenin postulated the need for a swift revolutionary violence but it was Trotsky who implemented theory in practice that led to a disastrous spiral of violence in the Russian Civil War: "When in March 1922 Lenin wrote, in his secret letter to the Politburo, "If it is necessary to achieve a particular political goal by means of a number of cruel measures, then they should be carried out in the most energetic way and in the shortest possible time," Trotsky was in complete agreement with him. This was the deeply ingrained flaw in Russian Jacobinism, of which Trotsky was one of the most eloquent exponents. (Volkogonov, 1996. Loc 519). Vladimir Lenin instructed his security forces (*chekisty*) on 9 August 1918 "to use all powers... implement mass terror immediately, execute <the enemies>. No time should be wasted. Conduct mass searches. Shoot for possession of arms. Deport all unreliable ones and *mensheviks*. We must conduct merciless terror against the *kullaks*, priests and white guards. All unreliable ones have to be locked up in the concentration camps out of city" (Napriach vse sily...Novaya Gazeta 2021).

While initially Trotsky, as People's Commissar for war, planned to abolish the regular army in favour of irregular revolutionary guerrilla warfighting tactics the reality of large-scale military operations during the Civil War changed his mind quickly. His five-volume collection *How Revolution was armed* (1923-24) therefore indicated evolution of the Red Army from partisan warfare, both voluntary and regular (conscripted) service, and underlined the decisive role of the commissars in orchestrating strategy and inducing discipline. Speaking on 7 December 1919 at the 7th Congress of Soviets, he declared: "I must say that in the form of our commissars and leading Communists we have a new order of Samurai, who without caste privileges will know how to die and will teach others to die for the cause of the working class". (Trotskii, Sochineniya, vol.17. pt 2, P.326 Quoted from Volkogonov, 1996. Loc 10004). Commissars quickly turned into executioners where revolutionary justice was delivered on the spot with a shot to the head of hesitating soldiers. Trotsky's lieutenants, clad in black leather armed with revolvers, looked almost glamorous as they travelled with him on an armoured train from one front to another delivering execution orders. "It is impossible to maintain discipline without a revolver," claimed their boss demanding more revolutionary executions. In reality, however, the commissars were not so much the gentrified Samurai bound with a code of honour, but a Bolshevik reincarnation of *oprichniki* — the brutal executioners of the 17th century Tzar, Ivan the Terrible, ironically, with anti-Tsarist revolutionary rhetoric. (It is very telling that the date when Ivan the Terrible established *oprichnina* was chosen as the Day of the Land Forces in Putin's Russia). Trotsky was open that brutal repression of conscripts must follow immediately upon a breach of discipline as required to achieve military aims. Russian peasants and workers demobilised from the German front were soon mobilised for the Civil War efforts and treated as openly inhumanely as requested by the 'Eternal Revolutionary' Commissar of War who created rear-guard units shooting in the back of retreating soldiers: "An army cannot be built without [repression]. Masses of men cannot be led to death unless the army command has the death penalty in its arsenal. So long as those malicious tailless apes that are so proud of their technical achievements — the animals that we call men — will build armies and wage wars, the command will always be obliged to place the soldiers between the possible death at the front and the inevitable one in the rear." (Trotsky, My Life, op.cit. P.411 Quoted from Volkogonov, 1996. Loc 3943). Dmitriy Volkogonov researched how families of mobilised former Tsarist officers who deserted were held hostages and shot; colleagues of deserted officers would be taken hostages in concentration camps; families aiding Wrangel's White Army were deported to Siberia etc. Quite quickly, brutality became part of formative years of the Red Army: "The threat of punishment gradually entered the structure and functioning of the army, and also entered people's minds as a moral norm, "revolver law", the revolutionary imperative, proletarian necessity" (Volkogonov, 1996 Loc 3954).

According to Volkogonov, blocking units appeared for the first time in August 1918 on the Eastern front in the 1st Army under the command of Tuchachevsky who was the first to issue orders to shoot, and would be shot himself at the order of Stalin years later.

Tukhachevsky implemented, however, an explicit directive from the Commissar of War himself: "In fact the role of the blocking units during an attack must be more active. They must be deployed closely behind our lines and when necessary, give a shove to stragglers and the hesitant. As far as possible, blocking units must have either a truck with a machine-gun or a light vehicle with a machine-gun" (Ibid., d.87, L.459). Trotsky's intent was clear—to threat the retreating conscript army with machine-gun fire and execute "stragglers" if required. Volkogonov concludes that Stalin simply adopted the same policy in 1941-42 when he created SMERSH units that executed retreating Red Army soldiers "merely applying the experience of the Civil War under new conditions" (Volkogonov, 1996, Loc 4032). Symbolically, Vladimir's Putin father served in similar special 'annihilation (*isstrebitelnyi*) battalion' of NKVD during WW2 (Ne bylo nenavisti… 2015 https://m.lenta.ru/articles/20 15/04/30/putin_family/) while his proud son recreated the institution of commissars as political officers in the Russian army in 2021.

WW2 annihilation battalions were also Stalin's adaptation of formative Red Army experience of exterminating internal 'enemies of the people', starting with anti-Bolshevik clergy, town bourgeoise and wealthier farmers branded as 'kulaks'. The Red Terror, according to Lenin, meant to bring justice to the working people, of course: "I come to the inescapable conclusion that we must now launch the most decisive and merciless battle against the Black Hundreds clergy and crush their resistance with such ferocity that they will not forget it for several decades… Confiscating of valuables, especially of the richest monasteries and churches, must be carried out with the most merciless determination, stopping at nothing and in the shortest possible time. The bigger the number of reactionary clergy and reactionary bourgeois we manage to shoot in the process the better". (TsPA IML, f2. Op1, d.22947, LL1-6. Quoted from Volkogonov, 1996, Loc.4793). Annihilating class enemies both internally and across Russian frontiers hence was the main effort of annihilation detachments from the start of the Bolshevik revolution and reached its peak at the end of the Civil War. Mass execution of class enemy, e.g. anyone educated and better off than the poorest of workers, became the norm on territory taken over from the retreating White armies. Gen Mungo Melvin researched the annihilation of the educated population of Crimea in 1920 when retreating Wrangel army left the peninsula in the hands of the Red Terror squads: "Taking the whole of Russia into consideration, it is estimated that the largest concentration of killings in the Reds' reign of terror overall occurred in Crimea, where at least 15,000 and perhaps, up to 100,000, people perished. While the numbers involved remain hotly disputed, the balance of historical analysis suggests at least 50,000 were killed. The Chekist methods of execution varied according to proclivities of their local leaders and activists — numbers of whom had marked psychopathic tendencies. In Yalta, many of the Whites, their families and suspected sympathisers had heavy stones attached to their bound feet and were subsequently shot in the back of the neck. Their bodies were then dumped unceremoniously into the sea. In Simferopol, over 20,000 were executed; their bodies were piled on top of each other in the wooded ravines of the Maryno district, now covered by a reservoir. The German mass murders of Jews in Kiev and Simferopol during the Second World War would follow a similar pattern. Whether the executions took place in 1920-21 or in 1941-42, and whatever the nationality or motives of the executors, the killings were none the less heinous crimes against humanity". (Melvin, 2017, P.427-428). Annihilation of former Tsarist state employees and military officers with their families continued until the spring 1921 when notorious Troika tribunals were dissolved. Sevastopol, the 'glory of Russian arms' lost around 30,000 inhabitants with White officers being hanged in the streets.

Militarization of an entire society reached its logical peak in the policy of 'war communism' introduced between June 1919 until March 2021. This was nothing short of reintroduction of militarised forced labour when workers had no rights and peasants were obliged to give up their produce to the military authorities. Bolsheviks came to power promising all land to peasants, factories to workers and peace to all, but turned everyone into dispossessed slave labour to the Bolshevik state that nationalised and owned everything. (Peasants used to own small plots of land, agricultural tools, and cattle before the Bolshevik revolution). Conscripted peasants and workers were marched to fight on the fronts of the Civil War and those who survived were marched to labour camps subsequently. Volkogonov noted that Trotsky oversaw the conversion of at least seven full armies into labour camps with the first GULAG being established in Ukraine. (GULAG stands for the main directorate for labour camps management). Commissar for War stated his position of forced labour clearly: "[We] must make it clear to ourselves once and for all that the very principle of free labour as radically and irreversibly as socialization of the means of production, has replaced capitalist ownership" Quoted from Volkogonov, 1996, Loc 4752). As Simon Pirani observed in his book, *The Russian Revolution in Retreat,* the Bolsheviks replaced the capitalist exploitation of labour with state exploitation that nearly ruined Russia: "The economy collapsed, peasants resisted grain requisitioning, famine and disease spread unhindered and the population suffered unprecedented hardship. Society was close to breaking down. In industry, most of which was nationalised within weeks of Bolsheviks taking power, attributed of alienated labour—labour discipline and top-down management—were imposed, as the Bolshevik government struggled to revive the broken economy. Indeed, under these conditions of desperate shortage, labour could *only* be alienated labour, and on that basis social relationships were formed that could only be exploitative". (Pirani, 2008, P.18). War communism eventually had to be abandoned after mass resistance and bloody repressions but the Civil War costs Russia between 7 and 12 million lives, most of them civilian. The rain of Red Terror, however, was suspended only temporarily with introduction of so called New Economic Policy in 1921. Farmers were allowed to revive agriculture and feed starving workers by selling their produce until the end of 1920s. Mass collectivization started in earnest from 1929 but met fierce resistance of peasants who did not want to give up their land, cattle, and modest tools of production in return for unpaid labour on collective farms. Lenin's successor Josef Stalin crashed peasants' revolts by surrounding villages with troops and starving entire communities in Kuban, Ukraine and Don Cossack region to death over 1932-33. Genocide by starvation in Ukraine alone killed between 4 and 7 millions, mostly ethnic Ukrainians. (Conquest, 1986; Luciuk, 2008; Applebaum 2017). Similar militarist response to a socio-economic challenges in Kazakhstan where pastoral population resisted forced collective farming caused another 1.5 million lives. (Volkava, 2012).

While Lenin conceded eventually that Communism would be built initially in Russia alone, Trotsky dreamed of Worldwide Communist revolution and, therefore, demanded to extend annihilation of class enemies abroad using subversion and exported revolution. Soviet ideology throughout its existence held that all wars stemmed from class struggle and that the only wars that could be just were those working toward its abolition, which the Soviet wars in whatever form did by virtue of their socio-political character (Miller 1964, P. 268 – quoted from Jonsson). Thus, Jonsson concludes, Soviet wars were legitimate because of what the Soviet Union was, not what it did: The moral thinking was based on a systematic character rather than particular actions. This view is notable since it made concepts such as justness in the means of fighting (*just in bello*) aggression and self-defence less relevant (key concepts in Western just war theory) (Jonsson, 2019. P.57). Volkogonov's research shows that Trotsky's theory of permanent worldwide revolution had practical implications as well. On 29 July 1924, at a meeting of the board of the Military Science Society, Trotsky "stressed the need to compose a Manual of Civil War", which leaders of socialist revolutions could use as a handbook, pointing out that if the leaders were not prepared, any uprising was doomed to failure. ...A manual of Civil War, he was convinced, "would become necessary element in higher-level military-revolutionary training" (Trotskii, Sochineniya, Vol.12, P.395 Quoted from Volkogonov, 1996, Loc. 4617). Such an export version of class struggle and annihilation of class enemies was well understood by White Army emigree officer Evgeniy Messner who considered such subversion war or *Мятеж-война* as the Modus operandi of the Red Army (Messner, 2005). Messner explained how subversion war in various forms of a societal uprising worked well for Stalin during the formative years of the USSR e.g. in Ukraine and Georgia; at the beginning of WW2 for invasions of the Baltic states, Romania and Finland and at the end of WW2 for subjugation of Central Europe and Eastern Germany.

Evgeniy Messner (1891-1974) served as an artillery officer in the Tsarist Army during the First World War, acted as a Chief of Staff in Kornilov's division of the 'White' Wrangel Army during the Russian Civil War and a head of propaganda in the 'Russland' Division of Wehrmacht during WW2. Messner later emigrated to Argentina where he worked as an academic / military writer and created his concept of *Miatezh-voina* – Mutiny / rebellion / subversion war. The Mutiny War theory went largely unnoticed in the West but was studied by the KGB and Soviet / Russian military strategists ever since, predating the concept of the New Generation Warfare. (Messner is understood as a moderniser in the current Russian military thinking as opposed to a restorationist, who argues in favour of conventional warfare methods in order to restore the 'Russian military glory').

Messner's theory was informed by his conventional military experience against German and Austrian armies during WW1 as well as unconventional warfare experience fighting the Bolsheviks' revolutionary army (1918-20) and Yugoslav partisans during WW2. While observing proxy conflicts during the Cold War confrontation between the Soviet / Chinese Communists and the West he arrived at visionary conclusions about the changing character of warfare. His foundational works, *The Face of Modern War* (Лик современной войны, 1959), *Mutiny – the Name of the Third World War* (Мятеж – имя третьей всемирной, 1960), *Mutiny-war* (Мятежевойна, 1971) were re-published by the Moscow Military University and became available for a wider Russian public only in 2005. Messner sometimes referred to Miatezh-voina as a 'Subversive war' but conceptually his theory is closer to what RAND describes as Political warfare overlapping with other forms of power (See: Figure 1). (Robinson 2019)

Figure 1. Where Political Warfare Fits Within the Implements of Power

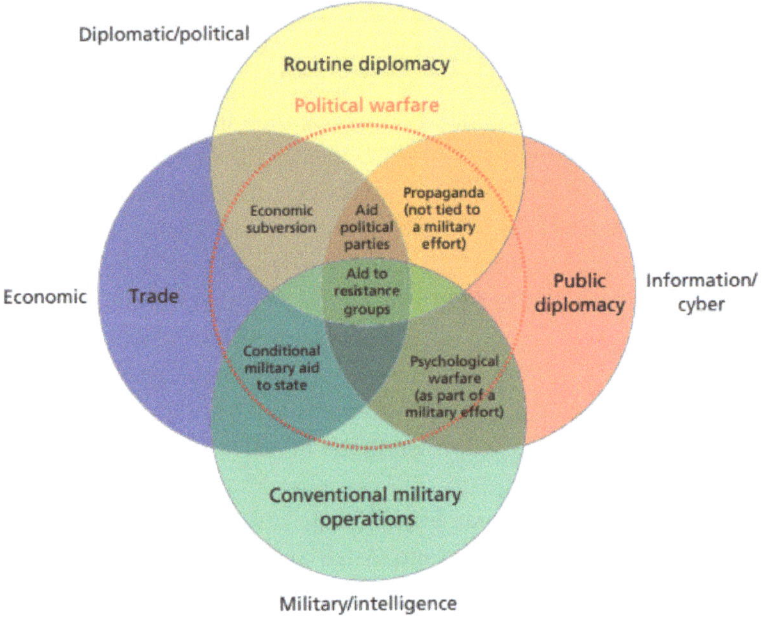

Diplomatic/political
- Routine diplomacy
- Political warfare
  - Economic subversion
  - Aid political parties
  - Propaganda (not tied to a military effort)
  - Aid to resistance groups
  - Conditional military aid to state
  - Psychological warfare (as part of a military effort)

Economic — Trade

Public diplomacy — Information/cyber

Conventional military operations

Military/intelligence

NOTE: All activities are illustrative, rather than an exhaustive list of possible actions.

Soviet political warfare was ideological as it was based on a dogmatic belief that the USSR is on a mission to create an ideal classless society free of exploitation of workers by the owners of production means. Hence subversion of class enemies abroad was a foundation of warfare where conventional military operations would follow up on the clandestine work. Jonsson suggests that seeing war as inevitable and peace as a mere pause between wars has implications for how war is viewed ethically, which is another aspect of the Soviet understanding of war: "War was viewed positively in the Soviet Union in the sense that it could speed up the transformation of the world into communism. This built on an idea from Marx, who stated that war was 'the midwife helping the birth of a new society from the loins of the old order' (Fedotov-White 1936, P.326). Soviet wars were just, and imperialist wars were not. ...Just wars were those in defense of the motherland and socialist countries, revolutionary wars of the working classes, wars of national liberation, and wars in defense of imperialist aggression. Unjust wars were imperialist aggression directed at socialist states, wars between the exploiting classes and the working class, colonial wars, and aggressive imperialist wars within the capitalist system (Scott and Scott 1988, 34)" (Jonsson, 2019, P. 57).

Once Bolsheviks figured out that their 'ethical' ends justified the use of any means—deception, sometimes known as *voyennaya hitrost'* or *maskirovka*, was integrated into the doctrine and practice. As Thomas Rid describes in his *Secret History of Disinformation and Political Warfare*, military deception was not limited to passive defence but quickly evolved in a proactive art of so called 'active measures': "On January 11, 1923, a remarkable institutional innovation saw the light of day. Artuzov created an office of *dezinformatsiya*, or disinformation. The GPU reportedly coordinated with the Revolutionary Military Council, Russia's highest military authority, to set up a special bureau to "prepare disinformation for Western military intelligence services." The goal, according to a GPU participant, was to deter military intervention by the Western powers. The GPU *deza* office would produce fake Politburo minutes, memoranda, and misleading military reports to exaggerate Soviet strength. The new office was authorized by the party's Central Committee and initially "placed forged stories in the official Soviet press" (Rid, 2020, P.25). The new proactive strategy quickly brought a spectacular success in a form of operation *Trust* when a fake White Russian counterrevolutionary organization managed to lure and capture not only various Russian monarchists but also a legendary British SIS agent known as the "ace of spies" — Sidney Reilly (https://www.theguardian.com/uk/2002/sep/07/russia.artsandhumanities). "(Trust) would serve, throughout the entire Cold War, as a towering example of an intelligence tactic with a bright future: a way to subvert, support and exploit political activists, 'like a sticky fly strip attracting insects'", as the official SVR history put it. (Rid, 2020, P. 32). OGPU not only created a successful international monarchist conspiracy to annihilate internal and external opposition but also to create an effective influence operation abroad. For instance, fake monarchists invited an influential White émigré and Eurasianist ideologue, Vasiliy Shulgin, to visit them in Moscow under cover and took him "for a ride" throughout Soviet Russia. Unsuspecting Shulgin was impressed with improved living conditions of ordinary Russians that he was allowed to observe under OGPU covert supervision and then wrote a relatively positive book on his travels when he returned to the West. Shulgin therefore was initially used to spread positive spin among Russian emigration circles where he was trusted. However, once Op Trust was exposed as a trap, OGPU effectively not only discredited Shulgin but also his entire Eurasianist movement that started to decline from the late 1920's. Destroying Shulgin's reputation once, however, was not enough for zealous Bolshevik chekists. They tracked him down in Soviet occupied Central Europe after WW2, brought him back to the USSR and locked up in captivity, so he could continue to write positive Soviet 'memoirs' and discredit the White émigré movement. OGPU-NKVD-KGB therefore continuously engaged in operational games with Russian dissidents abroad throughout the USSR existence. Ironically, Eurasianist ideology would be resurrected by KGB-FSB as a controlled form of Russian nationalism and adopted as a semi-official ideology in Putin's Russia (See Hryb, 2020). More importantly, late KGB elites running modern Russia inevitably ended up viewing the world as a combination of conspiracies that are to be engaged with and used to their own advantage.

Soviet military thought therefore combined Leninist-Trotskist interpretation of Marxist ideology with operational art based on mass brutality, annihilation of internal and external class enemies, proactive military deception and externally oriented *Miatezh voina* (subversion war) aiming at fermenting civil wars abroad and therefore expanding Bolshevik revolution worldwide. While 'eternal revolutionary' Leon Trotsky was expelled from the USSR and later killed on personal orders from Stalin, his theory and methodology was widely applied and tested in successful subversion of neighbouring Georgia, Ukraine and the Central Asian countries that would go through the 'exported civil wars' stage before being taken over by 'national communist' governments and incorporated in the USSR in early 1920s. Similar tactics were used for the Baltic States and Moldova at the start of WW2. This new successful experience was used to further develop the 'scientific dialectics' of revolutionary war theory undertaken further by Josef Stalin, who coined five permanently operating factors that would ensure victory in war.

One of the key components of what in Stalin's view, made Soviet military science scientific, argues Jonsson, was its focus on history. "Historical analysis was a constituent part of Marxist-Leninist dialectical materialism and seen as critical in the development of Soviet, and later Russian, Military theory." As the seminal theorist Svechin put it, "All of strategy is basically a contemplation of military history," and "the study of strategy is of little use without military historical knowledge" (Svechin 1927, 77. Quoted from Jonson, 2020, P.55). Stalin's contribution to the Soviet military thought was relatively modest despite his rank of Generalissimos. He accepted Lenin's adaptation of Clausewitz in the relation of politics and war, and war as a continuation of politics by class violence — already present in Marxist theory (Stalin 1946). This was Stalin's typical positioning as the guardian of Leninism, including in the military theory: Lenin "not as a military expert, but as a politician . . . used the works of Clausewitz" to gain support for the view of the role of war and politics (Stalin 1946). In Jonson's view, "therefore, Stalin did not go against Lenin's reliance on Clausewitz; rather he accepted it and justified it as if they were already a part of Marxist theory from the start". (Jonsson, P 50, Loc 701). Even official Stalinist publications struggled to pinpoint Stalin's substantive contributions beyond his total glorification. For instance, one of the regime's apologists, Nikolai Bulganin, wrote an article *Stalin and the Soviet Armed Forces* where he defined Stalin's most important insight into the military logistics:

> "Comrade Stalin has also thoroughly worked out problems of the art of war as a constituent part of the military science. He has created the theory of the art of operations and modern tactics and strategy. ...A most important feature of the art of war created by Comrade Stalin is thorough preparation and all-round supply for an operation. Comrade Stalin has always pointed out that the working out of a good plan of operations is not by itself preparation

for the operation. The plan of operations is only the beginning. Of decisive importance are preparations to execute the plan, all-round supplies of men, materiel, reserves, etc". (Bulganin, 1950 Quoted from https://www.marxists.org/archive/bulganin/1949/12/21.htm)

Stalin's real influence on the Red Army development before WW2, however, was paradoxically negative as he presided over annihilation of the entire military command in 1937-38, including its most talented marshal Tukhachevsky, who was wrongly accused of conspiratorial cooperation with Wehrmacht. This preceded with *'zachistka'* (clearance) of all military academies where leading theorists were accused of mythical crimes and shot. Neither Stalin nor his Red army leader, Kliment Voroshilov, seemed to care: "The beating of Soviet military scientists was carried out with the knowledge and approval of Stalin and Voroshilov. According to military commanders who had been in close contact with Stalin for a long time (G.K. Zhukov, A.M. Vasilevsky, N.G. Kuznetsov), the General Secretary of the Party, who soon after the total defeat of the Red Army cadres was to take on the duties of the Supreme Commander-in-Chief, knew little military theory. The chief "military adviser" of the leader, Klim Voroshilov, who headed the Red Army for fifteen pre-war years, also did not particularly favour it, as well as military theorists. Although by duty he was obliged to know their true value" (Cherushev, 2018).

Russian scholar Yulia Kantor described in her book, *Cursed friendship: the secret history of Soviet-German cooperation in 1920-30s*, that Stalin beheaded the entire military command following his conspiratorial paranoia:

> "If in 1937 the repressions affected mainly the highest command staff, then in 1938 Stalin's terror affected about 40 thousand servicemen of various military ranks in all military districts. The army was not just beheaded but demoralized. A monstrous psychological climate developed in the military environment: in the second quarter of 1937, the number of suicides increased sharply (in the LVO — by 27 percent, in the BVI — by 40 percent, in the CEP — by 50 percent, in the Black Sea Fleet — by 200 percent). The military has ceased to understand who you can now trust if your immediate commander and military superior can easily turn out to be an enemy and a spy. Here is what the impartial statistics say: during 1937-1938, all (except Budenny) district commanders were replaced, as well as all their deputies and district chiefs of staff, 88 percent of corps commanders, 98 percent of division and

brigade commanders, 79 percent of regimental commanders, 87 percent of battalion and division commanders, 100 percent of the composition of regional military commissariats". (Kantor, 2016 Quoted from https://lenta.ru/articles/2016/03/19/redarmy/).

Massive losses of educated and talented commanders explained, to a large extent, the poor performance and mass casualties of the Red Army at the beginning of WW2.

Yet, there is one personal accomplishment of historical proportions that Stalin must be credited for — a secretive Molotov-Ribbentrop Pact that split Eastern Europe between the two totalitarian states. The secret protocols remained unpublished by Moscow until 1993 and confirmed continuing controversy over this fateful decision that saw Wehrmacht and the Red Army invading Poland in September 1939. Despite obvious ideological differences, the Soviet leadership entered into a conspiratorial arrangement that reflected the peculiarities of both German and Russian culture which scored high on uncertainty avoidance. The secret plan looked like a masterstroke as the USSR acquired Bessarabia, Western Ukraine and Belarus as well as the Baltic States, declaring their 'liberation'. However, moving Soviet frontiers West meant abandoning established border fortifications and exposing the Red Army on the new hasty defences — unprepared for the Blitzkrieg that followed in June 1941. The price of miscalculating Hitler's intent was horrendous, with 26 million Soviet citizens dead by 1945. We can conclude, however, that Soviet formative experience was based not only on being a subject of international conspiracy that brought Lenin to power but also the USSR as an active participant in such conspiracies, e.g. a successful conspiracy between Hitler and Stalin that lasted from August 1939 until June 1941. A conspiratorial mindset became deeply ingrained in the Soviet and Russian political culture and played a crucial role throughout the Cold War until the dissolution of the USSR which was itself triggered by a failed conspiracy of GKChP.

3. The Great Patriotic War
Mythology and Conduct

Chapter 3 will examine the Great Patriotic War as a myth created by the Soviet leadership under Josef Stalin to explain its alliance with Hitler at the start of WW2 and the subsequent Soviet-German war that followed. On the one hand, the Soviet contribution to defeating Nazi Germany is often understated in Western literature and prevalent public memory. The sacrifice and monumental effort of the Soviet population mobilised for the war was truly epic. On the other hand, the Kremlin created a myth of the Great Patriotic War as a chosen Soviet glory precisely because there could not be any rational justifications for the human and material losses suffered by the Soviet people because of Stalin's murderous pre-war policies, disastrous alliance with Hitler, and complete disregard for human life of its own and conquered population of Europe. On the other hand, an epic sacrifice was matched with an epic lie of the Soviet dictator, resurrected and exploited by the Kremlin militarist ideology under President Putin.

Soviet contribution to the defeat of Nazi Germany was, indeed, decisive in terms of the actual fighting and pushing the enemy from the whole of Eastern Europe to Berlin. The Russian Ministry of Defence provides plausible figures showing the correlation between German forces fighting on its Eastern (Soviet) front and those fighting against the rest of the allies:

> "The victory in World War II was achieved through the joint efforts of the countries participating in the Anti-Hitler Coalition. The contribution of the Western allies, who defeated and captured 176 divisions, was significant. But it was the Soviet people who bore the brunt of the struggle. For almost four years, the Soviet-German front riveted to itself the bulk of the forces and means of fascist Germany. From 190 to 270 of the most combat-ready divisions of the fascist bloc, i.e., more than 3/4 of their total number, simultaneously acted against the Soviet troops. On the Soviet-German front, 607 enemy divisions were defeated and captured. The total human losses of the German armed forces in World War II reached 13.4 million people, on the Soviet-German front—10 million people. The irretrievable losses of Germany and its allies on the Soviet-German front amounted to 8,649.5 thousand people. During the war, Soviet troops destroyed and captured more

than 75% of all weapons and military equipment of the enemy." (Russian Ministry of Defence, https://mil.ru/winner_may/lessons/win_fash.htm) (Entsyklopedia... 2010) «Энциклопедия Победы. Справочник для обучающихся государственных образовательных учреждений по истории Великой Отечественной войны 1941-1945 гг.» – М.: Издательство «Армпресс», 2010.

These figures are broadly accepted by Western historians who are specialists in WW2, even though they are largely absent from the public memory in the West. British historian Max Hastings indicated in his book, *Inferno: World at War, 1939-1945*, that not only the Nazi Germany lost three quarters of its army on the Eastern front, but also the USSR paid 95% of the blood price:

> "It was the Western Allies' extreme good fortune that the Russians, and not themselves, paid almost the entire 'butcher's bill' for [defeating Nazi Germany], accepting 95 per cent of the military casualties of the three major powers of the Grand Alliance". (Washington Post, 2015).

The Washington Post also acknowledged that American society is largely ignorant about these facts, which the nationalist rhetoric of President Putin could exploit: "It is essential for Americans to acknowledge and respect these realities. Russians are acutely aware that the magnitude of their sacrifice is not understood in the United States. Indeed Vladimir Putin's regime has won popular support in part by exploiting Russians' sense that their country is not respected in the world and their history is not understood" (Washington Post 2018).

The official figure from the same Russian military sources breaks down the Soviet losses providing the context of statistical figures:

> "The total human losses of the USSR during the war amounted to 26.6 million people. Among them are soldiers and partisans who were killed in battle and died of wounds, who died of starvation and disease, who died from bombing and shelling, peaceful Soviet citizens, who were shot by punishers and prisoners of war tortured to death in concentration camps, as well as party, Komsomol and Soviet activists. The irretrievable demographic losses of the Soviet Armed Forces during the Great Patriotic War of 1941-1945 and the Soviet-Japanese War of 1945 amounted to 8 million 668.4 thousand military personnel. At the same time, the Red Army and Navy lost 8 million 509.3 thousand, internal troops – 97.7 thousand, and border troops – 61.4

THE GREAT PATRIOTIC WAR 67

thousand people. According to military reports, sanitary losses amounted to 18 million 344.1 thousand people. (Including the wounded, shell-shocked — 15 million 205.6 thousand, sick — 3 million 47.8 thousand, frostbite — 90.9 thousand)." (Ibid, 2010)

What neither Soviet (Russian) nor Western public cares to remember is the conduct of war that led to such losses and the extent to which ethnic republics of the USSR absorbed most of such terrible blood price. As George Orwell mentioned back in 1947, there was an unspoken taboo in the West to discuss Soviet conduct in WW2. (Ironically, Orwell introduced the 'Cold War' term as "peace that is no peace" See: Grant & Zieman 2018) https://manchesteruniversitypress.co.uk/wp-content/uploads/2018/07/Sample-978178 499440.pdf).

Orwell's understanding of Communist myth-making came from his experience in the Spanish Civil War, where he came across the Soviet ideological mind games, so well reflected in his books, *Animal Farm and Homage to Catalonia*. Indeed, the Soviet-German war (1941-45) became a spectacular exercise in Soviet myth-making from day one.

The myth

The main drivers of such myth-making reflected necessity to obscure: Soviet-German imperialist division of Eastern Europe between August 1939 and June 1941; Stalin's irrational refusal to act on the military intelligence warnings about Op Barbarossa; 93% losses of the Red Army stationed on Western Soviet borders in the opening weeks of German invasion as well as the need to find a scapegoat for the spectacular initial German success.

Great Patriotic War literally means in Russian, Great Fatherland War. There was only one Fatherland war previously in Russian history — the Napoleonic invasion in 1812. By linking the two events, Stalin wanted to mobilise a population disenfranchised by mass repressions, for the defence of the USSR, because he understood the magnitude of the German threat. So, strictly speaking, the Great Patriotic War is a Soviet-German war that started on 22 June 1941 and ended on 9 May 1945. In Western historiography, this war is mostly known as the WW2 Eastern Front and, therefore, simply another WW2 war theatre. WW2, however, started with a joint invasion of Poland by Hitler and Stalin in September 1939 as per the Molotov-Ribbentrop agreement. Therefore, the USSR started WW2 on the offensive by invading Eastern Poland, Finland, Estonia, Latvia, Lithuania, and Romania. The USSR annexed the conquered territories as per the agreement with Hitler. These facts became inconvenient once Nazi Germany invaded the USSR in 1941 and hence violated the original Non-aggression Pact and its unofficial protocols. The initial Soviet narrative about the 'liberation' of territories annexed between 1939 and 1941 had to change to their 'defence'. Hence, the Red Army liberation saga had to be changed from conquest-liberation to the 'defensive' (Great) Fatherland War. Soviet textbooks emphasised the GPW to the extent that an average citizen could not tell the difference between the GWP and WW2. GPW became WW2's main event and therefore acquired the 'sacred' mythical value of the sacrificial victory over evil, whereby the USSR liberated the whole world from the Nazi horrors. This narrative was magnified by Leonid Brezhnev in 1965 and it changed little until the end of the USSR in 1991. Putin took the myth to a new level of perfection when he accused Poland of starting WW2 in his 2019 comments on the Molotov-Ribbentrop Pact anniversary. The Polish Institute of National Remembrance (IPN), a state body responsible for researching Nazi and communist crimes against the Polish nation, issued a lengthy statement disputing Putin's attempts to "undermine fundamental facts about the role of the Soviet Union in unleashing the slaughter of World War Two" (NFP Putin… 2019). Putin's development of the GPW narrative makes perfect sense, however, if understood as weaponization of historical trauma to mobilise the population for renewed 'liberation' of neighbours from imagined 'fascists'. Positioning of new conquest as anti-fascist resistance also conveniently presents the future victim as a 'fascist' opponent at the expense of factual truth.

Truth is said to be the first victim of any war, and WW2 was no exception. Just like Hitler claimed that Germany wanted peace but was forced to fight Poland on 1 September 1939, Stalin claimed that the USSR was forced to invade Poland on 17th September to protect the Ukrainian and Belorussian minorities. The 'liberated' citizens of Eastern Poland witnessed how the Polish army was attacked by both German and Soviet troops, taken prisoners, and often immediately executed. Some witness reports suggested that the Red Army used artillery to kill POWs more efficiently. The invasion was well planned as the Soviet military intelligence had names of Polish veterans from 1920 Polish-Russian war who were blacklisted for immediate extra-judicial executions on the occupied territories of Western Ukraine and Western Belarus. The so-called *osadniki*, or military colonists, were rewarded by the Polish government with land and seeding capital for settling in the regions bordering the USSR between the two world wars. Twenty years later, they were hunted down and killed by the vengeful Soviet death squads alongside other Polish officials. (The Russian security services used a similar tactic in 2022 when Ukrainian ATO veterans and territorial defence volunteers were hunted down in the occupied territories of Ukraine, showing continuity of institutional memory). The mass execution of Polish officers did not stop after the end of border clashes. Stalin would personally sign the death warrant that would lead to the execution of 22,000 officers and government officials in Katyn forest (Smolensk) in April-May 1940.

During the first weeks of WW2 German troops often overrun the Molotov-Ribbentrop demarcation lines in pursuit of the retreating Polish army as it happened, for instance, in Lwow (Lviv). The Red Army officers had to liaise and re-negotiate the disengagement areas as partners in the crime of dismembering independent Poland. It was a matter of symbolic pride for the Red Army to hold a victorious parade alongside the German troops in Brest on 22 September 1939 – two decades after the Bolshevik government had to sign a humiliating Brest-Litovsk treaty. The parade was received by General Heinz Guderian, who would lead German tank formations back into the Soviet hinterland two years later. The Soviet propaganda, however, did a good job erasing both Brest Nazi-Soviet parade and Katyn massacre from the memory of the occupied population and Soviet history in general. Instead, the Soviet history books would commemorate the Brest fortress' border guards who resisted the German invasion on 22 June 1941. Soviet governments also blamed the Germans for the Katyn massacre even though the mass graves were discovered by Wehrmacht in 1943 and reported to the International Red Cross. To muddy the waters, the Soviets drummed up a story of a previously little-known Khatyn village in Belarus burned down by the German troops in one of the anti-partisan reprisals. Khatyn was a German massacre of 149 villagers, but by amplifying it, the Soviets tried to cover up their war crime of much bigger significance in Katyn. Facts and fiction were intertwined from the beginning to the end in Soviet history books, and many narratives were transferred into Western literature without due critical scrutiny. A celebrated British historian Anthony Bever illustrated his narrative on the Eastern front developments in *World War 2* book using predominantly writings of Vasiliy Grossman—a celebrated Red Army war propagandist who worked for the official Red Army publication, the *Red Star*. The uncritical transfer of Soviet narratives into Western history books created a sense of false understanding of Soviet (Russian) history that is reflected in the German term "Russlandversteher"—someone who thinks he understands Russia.

Practically all Soviet and many Western historians took Soviet official hagiography of GPW for granted. Many referred to the 1943 Kursk battle as the biggest tank formation encounter in history, with over 500 German and 1500 tanks destroyed in Soviet counteroffensive. However, German Lutsk-Dubno-Brody offensive in late June 1941 involved around 3140 Soviet and just over 600 German tanks in a battle that ended in spectacular Soviet defeat by 4 July 1941. Despite the superior armour of T-34 and KV-1 tanks, the Soviet logistic lines were quickly overwhelmed. Only 671 Soviet tanks escaped the 'Bloody Triangle' to be finished off in the Kyiv encirclement that followed in September 1941 (Kamenir 2023). Some Western historians, of course, did take a critical view of the Soviet conduct of war, of course. Norman Davies' "Europe at War 1939-45. No simple victory" admitted that mainstream Western historiography was misled by a false sense of solidarity with a former WW2 ally (the USSR) and has not changed its narrative on Soviet conduct of war well into 21 century (Davies, 2007).

As we can see, inconvenient truths about massive Soviet losses at the beginning of the Soviet-German war were conveniently erased from public memory and glossed over by a myth of the victorious Great Patriotic War that united wise Communist leaders with their heroic Soviet people. So, what can we learn from the actual military history of the Soviet-German armed conflict that can illuminate patterns of Russian military behaviour relevant today?

The conduct of the war by the Red Army

In March 2023 a Russian military analyst Roman Skomorokhov called on the readers of the *Military Review* (TopWar.ru) to "stop referring to the image of the Great Patriotic War" previously widely abused in the press under the slogan: "*Mozhem povtorit!*" (We can repeat it!). He argued that the RF was not the USSR in terms of population, politics and military technology. His analysis suggested, however, that many mistakes committed by the Red Army at the beginning of the GPW were still familiar to the Russian troops fighting in Ukraine in 2023:

> "Why today they (mistakes) have been openly forgotten and only frontal strikes remain from the entire military doctrine of the Great Patriotic War, many today do not understand. And it is painfully insulting to observe a picture similar to 1941: the masses of infantry and equipment are going to storm the settlement without reconnaissance, without air support, they just go in. Everything is in the best traditions of June-July 1941. It is useless to ask questions, there will be no answers. What our generals are learning today is difficult to say. But so far, and this is clear from the reports of the Ministry of Defence, our army can execute a frontal attack on a settlement occupied by the enemy with masses of infantry, supported by tanks and infantry fighting vehicles. This is the level of (sophistication) from the First World War. Especially given the complete lack of interaction between units and subunits in terms of communications." (Skomorokhov, 2023)

Indeed, the German and Finish recollections from the Eastern front are full of disbelief at how mercilessly Soviet generals were 'burning through' entire divisions in multiple waves of senseless frontal attacks. Generaloberst Erhard Rauss, Commander of 4th and 3rd Panzer Armies was debriefed by the US intelligence after WW2 on the Russian Combat methods:

"In the attack the Russian fought unto death. Despite most thorough German defensive measures he would continue to forward, completely disregarding losses. ...another determining factor has been introduced into the Red Army by the political commissar—unqualified obedience. Carried out to utter finality. It has made a raw mass of men a first-rate fighting machine. <...> In this connection, it must be remembered that Russia is an autocratically ruled state—an absolute dictatorship demanding and compelling the complete subordination of the individual. That blind obedience of the masses, the mainspring of the Red Army, is the triumph of communism and the explanation of its military success." (Rauss, Russian Combat Methods in WW2. P. 23.)

Unqualified obedience of the Soviet soldiers might have seemed like a triumph of Communism from a totalitarian Nazi cultural point of view. However, a Russian witness of the GPW Nikolay Nikulin explained such obedience by a sheer terror experienced by the frontline troops who feared death from their own death squads more than the enemy:

"The troops went on the attack, driven by horror. The meeting with the Germans was terrible, with their machine guns and tanks, the fiery meat grinder of bombing and artillery shelling. No less terrifying was the implacable threat of execution. To keep the amorphous mass of poorly trained soldiers in check, executions were carried out before the battle. They grabbed some frail stragglers, or those who blurted something out, or random deserters, of which there were always enough. They lined up the division with the letter "П" and finished off the unfortunate without deliberation. This preventive political work resulted in a greater fear of the NKVD and the commissars than of the Germans. And in the offensive, if you turn back, you will receive a bullet from the rear-guard detachment. Fear forced the soldiers to go to their deaths. This is what our wise party, the leader and organizer of our victories, counted on. ...Hence the combat readiness of our valiant troops." (Nikulin, 2007, P.101)

Nikulin's *War Memoirs* was drafted in 1970s but published only in 2007. As a young student Nikolai volunteered to defend his native Leningrad in June 1941 and was lucky to survive the entire war as an artillery soldier. He avoided talking about war all his life while working as an art historian in the State Hermitage Museum, looking after collections of Western art. His recollections meant to be a reconciliation from what could be described today as severe PTSD. As a historian, he was aware of his own bias and self-censorship, admitting that he omitted the worst atrocities from his recollections. That makes his work even more powerful when drawing explanation of 'survival of the fittest' in that war:

> "A hundred (Russian) Ivans would get up and wander through the deep snow under the crosshairs of the German machine guns. And the Germans in warm bunkers, well-fed and drunk, impudent, predicted it all; everything was calculated, approaches were zeroed in, and advancing troops were hit, like in a shooting range. The (Russian) Colonel knows that the attack is useless, that there will only be more corpses. There were cases when a division, starting the battle, had 6-7 thousand bayonets, and at the end of the operation, its losses were 10-12 thousand — due to constant replenishment! ...But the Colonel carries out the order and drives people into the attack. If his soul hurts and he has a conscience, he runs into the battle and dies. There is a kind of natural selection. The faint of heart and the sensitive do not survive. There remain only cruel, strong personalities capable of fighting under the prevailing conditions. They know only one method of war — to crush the mass of bodies. Someone will eventually kill the German." (Ibid. P.23).

German soldiers that previously conquered most of Europe quickly realised that they were up against a different enemy, not only in terms of mindset but also military culture. The US Army Lt Col Tsouras, who edited the recollections of Wehrmacht officers, observed: "The German soldier needed little imagination to think he was fighting in hell. Here was no etiquette of war. One German who had fought as a panzergrenadier on both fronts commented that in the West (1944-45), war was still fought as an honourable game where no one went out his way to be vicious and where fighting tended to taper off after five in the afternoon — but in the East, "The Russians were trying to kill you — all the time!". (Rauss, 1995, Russian Combat Methods in WW2. P.14).

Out of the two totalitarian systems, the Soviet one turned out to be more ruthless as it did not spare neither enemy combatants nor its own soldiers. Nor did Moscow spare the civilian population of the occupied and then retaken areas of Western Soviet republics. Massive losses of frontline units were replenished by pressing all men of fighting age, often teenagers, into combat, sometimes without training or even uniforms or rifles. Hundreds of thousands of 'liberated' Ukrainians, Belarussians or Moldovans were pushed into the meatgrinder just to uncover the German defensive positions for a follow-up human waves attack. General Rauss was impressed by the Soviet 'efficiency' in rounding up civilians for combat:

> "For example, the inhabitants of a threatened city, or perhaps, the entire male population of areas which the Germans had recently evacuated, were gathered up quickly by means of excellent organization. Regardless of age, nationality, deferred status, or fitness, they were thrown into battle. They were supposed to learn in combat all that was necessary, and to acquire weapons from their dead comrades. The Russians themselves were aware of the fact that these men were no soldiers, but they filled the gaps and supplemented the sinking numbers of the human mass. During the fighting in a bridgehead southeast of Kremenchuk in September 1943, the Russians at night-time used to drive ahead of their armed soldiers large numbers of civilians whom they had gathered up, so that the German infantry might expand its scant supply of ammunition. The Russians repeated the same tactics again and again." (Ibid. P. 42)

The plight of civilians under brutal German occupation was exacerbated by the scorched earth policy conducted by the Soviet partisans behind the enemy lines. Although Stalin coined the term the 'partisan movement,' latest research by a Russian historian Alexander Gogun reveals that 'partisans' was a cover name for Stalin's commandos: organised, directed, supplied and fully funded by the Soviet special forces organised under the umbrella of Central Staff of the Partisan movement (TsShPD) or local staffs such as the Ukrainian Staff of Partisan Movement (UShPD). The 'partisans' carried out acts of terror and sabotage as directly instructed in Stalin's order No.00189 on 5 September 1942: "The resolution of these main tasks requires the broad launch of partisan combat operations by all partisan detachments, as well as of sabotage, terrorist, and intelligence work in the enemy rear." (Quoted from Gogun, 2016, P.126). Soviet internal documents referred to acts of terrorism as "T assignments" or "extermination actions". Therefore, Gogun argues: "The red partisans were not insurgents (rebels) but commandos (saboteurs, scouts, and terrorists)" (Ibidem, P.255). The principal objective of partisan commandos was to destroy and burn down all populated points (locations) and civilian infrastructure up to 60 km behind the German-Soviet frontline and up to 30 km left and right of every road potentially used by German army logistic units on the occupied territories. It meant, in practice burning collective farms, grain barns representing people's livelihoods, schools and clubs, so the German military could not use them. According to partisan UShPD official reports "Ukrainian partisans destroyed 402 industrial enterprises, 59 electric power stations, 42 pumping stations, 1,117 separator (milk) stations, 915 storehouses, 1,444 tractors, 2,231 other farming machines, 5,422 wagons, 153 engines, and 5,280 horses". (Ibid, P.82). According to the records of the Intelligence Directorate of UShPD, partisan counterintelligence exposed 9,883 people as spies, traitors, and other accomplices of the German aggressors ...and shot 2,927 of them" (Ibid, P.125). Two thirds of the Soviet partisan victims were civilians and even Soviet NKVD leader, Lavrentiy Beria, recognised that many partisan detachments were engaged in banditry, looting, and raping innocent civilian populations. As a result of destitution inflicted by both the Nazi regime and Soviet 'liberators', Ukraine suffered a severe famine immediately after the war that cost the lives of up to 800,000 citizens. This is on top of millions of refugees, forced labourers and 8 million who died during WW2: "According to the estimates of the Ukrainian Institute of Demography, approximately 5.2 million civilians died on the territory of Ukraine, and over 3.5 million were relocated into the deep hinterland together with the factories where they worked. Over 2.8 million Ukrainians died while fighting in the ranks of the Red Army" (Prymachenko, 2017). Only Belarussian SSR suffered a higher proportion of population losses during WW2: "On the territory of today's Belarus, about two million people were killed during the Second World War. More than a million more people fled the Germans, and another two million were deported or displaced. Beginning in 1944, the Soviets deported another quarter million people to Poland, and thousands more to the Gulag. By war's end, something like half the population of Belarus had either been killed or moved." (Snyder, 2022). According to Snyder, no other country suffered more than Belarus in WW2 because of both German and Soviet conduct of war (even though numerically, Ukrainian losses were higher).

Rape was initially used by the Soviet partisans as an intimidation and terror tool and then continued by the advancing Soviet army units once they reached Eastern '*kresy*' (territories) of pre-war Poland that were incorporated in the USSR and especially Eastern Prussia. The 'russification' of Kenigsberg, soon to be Kaliningrad, started with ethnic cleansing: "Soviet soldier", a propaganda poster pointed out, "You are now on German soil. The hour of revenge has struck". Terrible atrocities were committed, villages burned, and refugees slaughtered, but what amounted to a programme of mass rape left the most indelible mark on the German population. "It was inspired less by sexual frenzy than by a burning lust for vengeance and an overwhelming desire to degrade and humiliate the German nation" (Kerrigan, 2018, P. 173).

There is plenty of evidence suggesting that mass rape was encouraged by the Soviet Army chain of command. WW2 veteran Nikulin recalled that his sexual abstinence was considered as deviant behaviour by soldiers in his unit who did not miss an opportunity to engage in sex with women in 'liberated' territories. On one occasion, Nikulin described how soldiers on both sides of frontline were showered with leaflets written in Russian and German language just before assault on the city of Danzig (Gdansk):

> "They said something like this: 'I, Marshal Rokossovsky, order the Danzig garrison to lay down their arms within twenty-four hours. Otherwise, the city will be stormed, and all responsibility for civilian casualties and destruction will fall on the heads of the German command ... 'The text of the leaflets was in Russian and German languages. It was clearly intended for both warring parties. Rokossovsky acted in the best Suvorov traditions: 'Boys, here is the fortress! There are wine and women! Take it—enjoy for three days! And let's blame everything on the Turks!'. Then business as usual: a drunken frenzy, hellish shelling and bombing. With obscene abuse soldiers went forward and only one out of ten made it. Then the fun began. Fluff flew from featherbeds, songs, dances, plenty of grub, you can roam around the shops, and apartments. Houses are burning, and women are screaming. Everyone had so much fun!" (Nikulin, 2007, P.101).

Weaponization of rape was sanctioned at the highest level of the Soviet government and became almost official policy once the Soviet Army entered Germany. Soldiers engaged in gang rape of entire families with three generations of women often being abused simultaneously. Teenage girls often had broken spines, and many committed suicides. Some German women engaged in 'survival prostitution' to get food from the invaders and feed their children. (Soviet army song suggested at the time "Love today, Frau and food tomorrow"). Others would choose to house one Soviet soldier as an official 'boyfriend' who would protect them from potential gang rape by others. As Michael Kerrigan observed, the collective punishment of German women with 'strategic rape; was sanctioned from top to bottom of the Soviet military-political apparatus: "Stalin took an indulgent view of the Red Army's sexual depredations on its way through Germany and Berlin itself (where 100,000 women and girls are believed to be raped). Given what he had been through, it was understandable if a victorious Soviet soldier felt inclined to have a bit of "fun with a woman" or to "take some trifle", the dictator said. His political officers went further, urging men on in hideous attack that mirrored that of the Germans on Soviet women four years before". (Kerrigan, 2018, P. 173).

In a sense, the mass terror against the civilian population and 'strategic rape' were psychological operations that would inflict paralysis and instil fear into the German populations preventing them from resisting. Terror against civilians was much more effective in comparison with atrocities inflicted on the German POWs and frontline troops. Generaloberst Rauss was rather dismissive of the Soviet Army tactical PsyOps against Wehrmacht as crude and naïve for the most part because, it did not correspond to the psychology and mentality of the German soldier in any way and therefore it was ineffective. This is despite the fact that Soviet propaganda distributed 668 millions leaflets targeting German soldiers in 1941 alone. Rauss observed that the Red Army tactics included demonstrative acts of mutilation of POWs in order to intimidate the enemy:

> "During the first years of the war the Russians apparently had sought to impress the German troops and lower their morale by committing numerous atrocities against them. The great number of such crimes, committed on all sectors of the front especially in 1941-42, but also during later German counteroffensives, tends to support that presumption. <...> During the battle of Zhizdra, in early March 1943, a battalion of the German 590th Grenadier

Regiment was assigned the mission of mopping up a sector of overgrown with brush. The attack failed. When, on 19 March 1943, the sector again passed into German hands after a counterattack by the corps, 40 corpses of soldiers from the battalion were found with their eyes gouged out, or their ears, noses, and genitals cut off. Corpses found in another sector of the battlefield bore signs of similar mutilations" (Ibid., P.105).

Soviet propaganda encouraged Soviet soldiers and partisans to kill German soldiers by all means possible. The Red Star (Krasnaya Zvezda) newspaper published poetry of a Soviet celebrity Konstantin Simonov titled: "Kill him". The last lines included a call to action: "Kill at least one! Kill as soon as you can! Kill at first sight! Kill once again!". Another prolific Soviet propagandist, Illia Ehrenburg, published over 1500 articles that dehumanised Germans and called for revenge. Ehrenburg stated: "We understood that Germans are not humans. From now on, the word "German" is the worst curse for us. From now on, if you hear the word "German", press the shotgun trigger. Do not talk. Do not grumble. Just kill. If you have not killed at least one German per day, the day is wasted. ...Kill the German. Don't miss. Don't blink. Just kill". Many Soviet newspapers had regular columns titled: "Have you killed a German today?" (TopWar.ru; 2 January 2023). Hate speech produced by the Soviet press on mass-scale created psychological conditioning for acts of violence not only against German combatants but against all Germans, explaining mass war crimes against civilians later in the war.

Killing Germans by all means possible even included attempts of using bacteriological weapons. Alexander Gogun discovered Soviet archive materials suggesting that a network of Red Army saboteur doctors deliberately infected German guards and officers in Slavuta POW camp established for Red Army troops in 1942. Dr Mikhailov distributed glass tubes with typhus-carrying lice, and as a result, 28 German guards were infected with spotted typhus and 8 died. "This is the only known case of the operational use of a weapon of mass destruction (WMD) in World War II in the European theatre of war. Its modest scale should not be underestimated, for typhus is a bacteriological weapon and therefore an example of a WMD, especially if one considers its capacity and even tendency toward self-propagation" (Gogun, P.145). Soviet archives did not mention that once the wave of typhus struck Slavuta camp with Soviet POWs, German military authorities designated it as *Gross Lazaret 301* where POWs were dumped to die. Approximately 150,000 people died during the epidemics and from starvation. Gogun suggests that if the Soviet agents indeed infected guards and POWs as per their reports, then Dr Mikhailov's men were as responsible for their deaths as German authorities.

The Soviet government never admitted its responsibility for the ethnic cleansing of entire German populations on those territories that were captured in 1944-45 and repopulated. German Red Cross figures suggest that up to two and half million German refugees were killed while trying to relocate from territories under Soviet control in Central and Eastern Europe to the future Federal Republic of Germany territories. However, it does not mean that such crimes were not known in the West. A distinguished US General George Patton, co-operated with the Soviet Army while defeating Wehrmacht, but was left with no illusions with regards to the conduct of the war by the Soviet ally:

> "The Russians are Mongols. They are Slavs and a lot of them used to be ruled by Ancient Byzantium. From Genghiz Kahn to Stalin, they have not changed. They never will... The difficulty in understanding the Russian is that we do not take cognizance of the fact that he is not European, but an Asiatic, and therefore thinks deviously. We can no more understand a Russian than a Chinese or a Japanese, and from what I have seen of them, I have no particular desire to understand the except to ascertain how much lead or iron it takes to kill them. In addition to his other amiable characteristics, the Russian has no regard for human life, and they are all out sons-of-bitches, barbarians, and chronic drunks." (http://www.freerepublic.com/focus/f-news/1775305/posts General George Patton).

The fact that the USSR never had to face the reckoning for such crimes against humanity created a belief in Moscow that this was something the Kremlin could get away with in future. A million civilian Afghans lost their life as a result of Soviet invasion in 1979-89 in addition to 90,000 mujaheddins and 18,000 Afghan soldiers (Taylor, 2014). Over 100,000 Chechens died in two Russian campaigns that rehearsed the invasion of Ukraine in 2014 with its 'filtration' camps, indiscriminate shelling of residential areas, gang rape, and executions (Mirovalev, 2023). The term 'Ruscism' (or Rushism) was first used in reference to Russian atrocities in Chechnya by its first President Dzhokhar Dudayev in 1995. Ruscism was defined by Dudayev as a Russian version of super-violent fascism. Ukrainian parliament recognised in May 2023 ruscism as a Russian state militarist ideology: "Ruscism is militarism, cult of the leader's personality and sacralisation of state institutions, self-glorification of the Russian Federation through violent oppression and / or denial of the existence of other ethnicities, the imposition of the Russian language and culture on other peoples, propaganda of the 'Russian world doctrine', systemic violation of norms and principles of the international law, sovereign rights of other countries, their territorial integrity, and internationally recognised borders" (Novaya Gazeta 2 May 2023). The term was also used by the NATO Parliamentary Assembly denouncing "Russia's employment of hunger as a weapon as part of its ideology and practices of ruscism" (NATO 2023).

Unsurprisingly, the 'we can repeat it' mantra of Russian propagandists in February 2022 had the same menacing promise of brutal conduct of war by exploiting the repurposed myth of GPW. The descendants of NKVD and Smersh executioners who monopolised the victory from the peoples of the USSR in the aftermath of WW2 tried to manipulate historical memory in Putin's Russia to justify new imperial conquest.

This was predicted by the Russian WW2 veteran and art historian Nikulin, who almost word by word repeated similar predictions by a former artillery officer Leo Tolstoy a hundred years before him: "Stupid senseless murder of our own soldiers took place. One must think that this selection of the Russian people is a time bomb: it will explode in several generations, in XXI or XXII century, when the mass of scum selected and cherished by the Bolsheviks will give rise to new generations of their kind" (Nikulin, 2007, P.23).

Tolstoy's predictions were published in 1895 but equally could apply to Russia in the 20th and 21st centuries showing the enduring nature of Russian militarism and the Russian way of conducting war:

"The bells will ring, and the Russian people will dress in golden robes and begin to pray for the murders. And the old, long-known terrible thing will begin. People will fuss under the guise of patriotism, all sorts of officials will fuss, anticipating the opportunity to steal more money, the military will fuss receiving double pay for killing people. They will receive ribbons, galloon crosses and stars. They will drown their souls with songs, debauchery, vulgarity and vodka. They will disengage from peaceful labour, from their wives, mothers and children. They will suffer cold, starve, get sick, die of diseases on the battlefields, while killing people whom they have never seen and did not know, who have done nothing wrong to them. And when there are thousands of Russian sick, wounded and killed, there will be no one to pick them up from the fields. And when the air is already infected with the pus of cannon fodder, they will somehow dump the wounded in heaps. The dead will be buried at random, while their bodies sprinkled with lime. And again they will lead the crowd of savages further and become furious and completely brutalised. Love will disappear among the barbarians for decades and ages. And again, they will say that the war was necessary, and they will accustom the future generation to this idea, thereby corrupting their souls and hearts." (Tolstoy, 1895, Christianity and Patriotism. Tolstoy.ru).

This enduring nature of Russian militarism was not lost on the WW2 generation of war leaders such as General Patton and lead to the Cold War confrontation: "Russia KNOWS what she wants. WORLD DOMINATION. And she is laying her plans accordingly. We, on the other hand, and England and France to a lesser extent, don't know what we want. We get less than nothing as a result. If we have to fight them, now is the time" (The Patton, 2007).

4. The Cold War and Evolution of the Soviet Understanding of War

The USSR emerged victorious from the ashes of WW2 and transformed from a pariah state to a rising superpower and a co-founder of the United Nations with a veto power. Despite colossal losses in blood and treasure, which massively overmatched Germany's, Soviet leadership gradually turned this pyrrhic victory into a regime foundation myth titled "the Great Patriotic War 1941-45". Ordinary Soviet citizens were educated to believe that the GPW was a triumph of Soviet arms over Nazi ideology deliberately omitting inconvenient truths such as collaboration with Hitler (September 1939 – June 1941) and wars of conquest waged by the USSR against its neighbours throughout WW2.

The USSR acquired new union members such as the three Baltic states and Moldova under the pretext of sham referenda organised after a military invasion of those countries. In addition, the Russian Federation expanded at the expense of Germany (East Prussia), Finland (Karelia) and Japan (the Northern Territories) while Ukrainian and Belarussian Republics acquired substantial territories belonging to Poland prior to WW2. The USSR also created an entire 'socialist camp' in Central Europe that included all territories which Soviet army liberated from German occupation, including East Germany. What Trotsky failed in terms of expanding 'world revolution' in 1920 Stalin achieved in 1945 with substantial help from the USA's land-lease—a massive supply of armaments and war materiel offered in return for defeating Hitler. (The role of land-lease was hardly mentioned in Soviet history books even though Russia settled the debt only in 2006). The Yalta peace conference (4-11 February 1945) cemented the Soviet leadership's conspiratorial belief that the West recognised the Soviet sphere of influence in the countries overrun by the Soviet army and agreed to the new Iron curtain over Central Europe effectively lasting until the end of the USSR. Hence, the Kremlin's conviction that great power status could only be achieved and maintained by military means became the foundation of Soviet militarism based on WW2 experience. As Dmitry Volkogonov observed, despite some tactical differences among the Bolshevik leaders, Lenin, Trotsky and Stalin were united in their believe that only social violence can bring about required change both nationally and internationally: "Despite some major differences, what all three men shared was reliance on social violence, a belief in the absolute certainty of only one ideology, and the conviction that they had the right to dispose of the destinies of nations. <…> here lay the paradox of Bolshevism: having proclaimed freedom as the aim of their revolution, they did not see that they were taking it away not only from the 'ex-people', but also from those they had promised to make 'everything', the people who trusted them. It was the party-cum-state they invested with freedom, then the bureaucratic machine, and finally the dictator." (Volkogonov, 1996).

In fact, Soviet military success was the only success that a ruined country could be proud of after WW2, so Stalin doubled down on further militarisation at the expense of starving post-war population. Up to a million Soviet civilians died from starvation in 1947 while the USSR allocated grain in support of communist regimes established in Central Europe. Aggressive military stance of the Soviet army and political leadership soon led to confrontation with former anti-Hitler coalition allies. The so-called Berlin blockade (24 June 1948 – 12 May 1949) became one of the first manifestations of what would become known as the Cold War. (The USSR tried to block all supplies to Western Berlin controlled by the Allies). Stalin's belief in inevitability of conflict between socialist and capitalist states became a self-fulfilling prophecy and defined his rule until his death on 5 March 1950. Soviet pessimistic outlook was further aggravated by acquisition of the atomic weapons and realisation of potential consequences of armed conflict with a nuclear armed United States. Should the Stalinist successors retain the power the confrontation could have turned tragically for all parties. However, a palace coup led by Nikita Khruschev in 1953 ousted key Stalin's hardliners, including the notorious head of NKVD Lavrentiy Beria, who was executed. Khruschev was a skilled party apparatchik, but his coup would not have been possible without the help of the still popular among rank-and-file war hero Marshal Zhukov. They both were abused by Stalin and feared persecution from Lavrentiy Beria, hence the Communist Party leadership effectively conspired with the Army leadership against the security apparatus and the Stalinists. Khruschev released millions of GULAG prisoners and condemned Stalin's purges in his speech at the 20th Party Congress in 1956. The Khruschev's Thaw lasted until another palace coup in October 1964 removed him from the office. However, his main contribution in the Soviet understanding of war was profound and became known as the 'peaceful co-existence theory'.

According to Jonsson, the Leninist understanding of war as an inevitable consequence of capitalist development was maintained from the formation of the Soviet Union until Nikita Khrushchev amended it after the Soviet Union's first successful test of an explosive nuclear device: "There is, of course, a Marxist-Leninist precept that wars are inevitable as long as imperialism exists… but war is not fatalistically inevitable. Today, there are mighty social and political forces possessing formidable means to prevent the imperialists from unleashing war." (Khruschev, cited in Booth 1981, 84-85). The "formidable means" that Khruschev referred to was the ultimate weapon of mass destruction and he maintained the view that imperialist systems were still the ultimate cause of war.

Daunted with the inevitability of war, Khruschev launched the idea of peaceful coexistence. He wrote an article in Foreign Affairs in 1959 introducing the concept to the American audiences. Khruschev argued that there were two ways to deal with a neighbour one dislikes: war (which in the age of atomic and hydrogen weapons of mass distraction would be dire for all) or peaceful coexistence. Khruschev saw that "the new alignment of international forces …offers ground for the assertion that a new world war is no longer a fatal inevitability, that it can be averted." (Khruschev, 1959)

Despite Khruschev's attempt to achieve mutual understanding between the USSR and the USA, the logic of an arms race led both countries to the Cuban missile crisis (October 1962) that nearly ended in a nuclear exchange. Met with a tough response from President Kennedy, the Kremlin backed down and withdraw its missiles from Cuba in exchange for a similar step by the US in Italy and Turkey. However, the most important lesson for both parties was implemented in the creation of a nuclear hotline that could avert unintended escalation between the nuclear superpowers. Nuclear de-escalation was further enhanced during President Lyndon Johnson's meeting with Head of the Soviet Government Andrey Kosygin in Glassboro (23-25 June 1967) when both leaders discussed for the first-time the possibility of limiting the nuclear arsenal. According to a leading Russian expert on the US-Soviet relations Viktor Kremenyuk, this meeting laid foundations of the 'strategic theory'. Namely, when nuclear forces capability is similar for both the US and the USSR "the most logical behaviour model is based on a certain form of trust or understanding of mutual logic and behavioural motivation with relevant consultation mechanism and information exchange". In other words, both parties found themselves in a situation of Mutually Assured Destruction (MAD) and it was in their precious interest to make sure that "the adversary not merely guessed on possible retaliation but firmly knew what steps will be taken in case of an attack." (Kremenyuk, 2022, P.168).

Leonid Brezhnev, who replaced Khruschev in 1964, maintained the concept of peaceful coexistence based on the strategic theory of Mutually Assured Destruction (MAD), even though he seemed less optimistic. For him, peaceful coexistence did not diminish the conflict; rather, "we must be prepared for this struggle to become more intense and an even sharper form of confrontation between the two social systems." (quoted in Lider 1977, P.265). While maintaining Khruschev's notion of war as avoidable, the Soviet Military Encyclopaedia noted that it did not "signify the complete elimination of the possibility of war in the modern age. The nature of imperialism has not changed." Wars in capitalist society are fought to acquire labour and access markets and imperialist war "exacerbates all of the contradictions of capitalism to extremes and to an enormous degree intensifies the scale, the intensity, and the sphere of spread of wars." (Grechko and Ogarkov 1993, P.365-66). As we can see there is a consistent continuity of this Marxist-Leninist premise from Lenin to Stalin, Khruschev and Brezhnev, so it should not have been a surprise that such formulation survived in post-Soviet Russia where Putin's confrontation with the West is fundamentally perceived as fighting back against Western imperialist struggle to control world's natural resources.

Kremenyuk argues that both Moscow and Washington went through a period of "a mutual learning curve" that helped to create the "culture of containment" leading to several agreements and Strategic Arms Reductions Talks (START). However, President Reagan's administration returned to escalation of the Cold War from Moscow's point of view: "With the arrival of a right-wing Republican administration led by Ronald Reagan, the new spiral of the Cold War started and continued until mid-1980's. Reagan revived the ultimate objective for containment strategy from early Cold War, namely, destruction of Soviet system by exhausting it through arms race, trade sanctions and the 'Reagan doctrine'. The latter counted that the USSR would bleed out in the third world armed conflicts." (Kremenyuk, 2022).

Soviet occupation in Afghanistan indeed became one of the last straws that broke the Soviet camel's back. However, Brezhnev's decision to invade was caused by his own belief in the "international duty" that justified Soviet military intervention if the "socialist camp" was under threat. This is sometimes called the Brezhnev doctrine, but the term has never been used in the USSR. Soviet invasion of Afghanistan was framed internally as the "internationalist duty" to aid the Afghan people who aspired to build socialism. However, nobody really consulted the Afghan people in 1979 and the invasion followed the logic of the Soviet conquest in Central Asia throughout 1920s (subversion, palace coup, establishment of the people's republic regime etc). Moscow's move reflected Russian cultural *stremlenie na Vostok* (longing for the East) since at least 19th century coupled with Marxist-Leninist ideology of 'liberation' from the Capitalist yoke as merely justification of Soviet militarist practice where invading its neighbours became the norm. Soviet leadership and the military command believed that the Soviet Army had never been defeated on the battlefield and therefore Afghanistan was meant to be another "small victorious war". After all, the Soviet Army successfully invaded Hungary (1956), Czechoslovakia

(1968) and plans were in the making to instigate a military crackdown in Poland (1981-83). This time the initiative to invade came not from the Communist Party but from the Soviet Army command and the KGB. Brezhnev hesitated but agreed to go along with what meant to be a relatively quick and painless operation against an adversary with practically no conventional modern army. The Soviet war in Afghanistan proved, however, to be one of the decisive factors in triggering a spell of reforms known as Perestroika and eventually the demise of the USSR.

Although the Soviet Army technically was not defeated by the Western- backed Mujaheddin insurgency, the Soviet economy suffered from over commitment to military expenditures worldwide and fell into "*zastoy*" (stagnation), prompting a major change of policy aiming at saving the USSR. Once CPSU First Secretary Mikhail Gorbachev figured out that proxy wars in the developing world could not be won by the Soviet Union, he responded to Reagan's challenge by initiating '*razriadka*' (de-escalation) that eventually led to the end of Cold war proclaimed at the Malta summit in December 1989. According to Kremenyuk, "The new leadership of the USSR led by Mikhail Gorbachev responded asymmetrically to combative American strategy by de-facto unilaterally winding down confrontation with the USA. It became evident that reducing armed forces and military expenditures, de-escalation with the USA, Western Europe and China, renewed disarmament negotiations with limitations of both conventional and nuclear weapons, gradual withdrawal of Soviet troops from Afghanistan and de-escalation of regional conflicts were in the national interests of the USSR and lightened the burden of 'imperial overload." (Kremenyuk, 2022).

Gorbachev's new thinking, however, was not only determined by social-economic and military factors but also by ideological crises that led to the demise of the USSR. The Soviet ruling elite no longer believed in Khruschev's premise that "our generation will live under communism" and was not satisfied with Brezhnev's premise of life under "the really existing socialism". Perestroika meant to introduce political pluralism (a multi-party system) and economic liberalisation (market economy for small enterprises) aiming at ending CPSU's monopoly on power and improving the competitiveness of the Soviet economy. However, once Gorbachev was elected as the first president of the USSR in March 1990 it became clear that the power shifted away from the Communist party, the military apparatus, and the KGB to the presidential administration and to some extent regional republican governments supporting Gorbachev's Perestroika. The first and the last Soviet president tried to balance between the Soviet old guard and increasingly more assertive regional elites by proposing the new union of 'free' republics united by a popular idea of rising living standards associated by then with "Swedish socialism" rather than planned Soviet economy. President Gorbachev campaigned for the new Union Treaty and received 80% support at a referendum held in the nine largest republics on 17 March 1991, which upheld the idea of preserving the USSR. However, the KGB, the Soviet Army and Communist party hardliners staged a failed coup against the president on 19 August 1991 that led to the 'sovereignty parades' of the key Soviet republics catalysing the formal dissolution of the Soviet Union on 26 December 1991.

Militarism as a statecraft, therefore, was a consistent feature throughout the existence of the Soviet state up to its final days when a failed military-led palace coup finished off the Union of Soviet Socialist Republics. KGB Chairman Vladimir Kryuchkov and Marshal Dmitriy Yazov managed to trigger destruction of the USSR as a state that has never been defeated militarily by its adversaries. In reality, the Soviet Union was brought down by the lack of faith of the Russian and regional ethnic elites that no longer believed in unachievable Communism and 'really-existing' Soviet socialism. The key role was played not by the 'separatist' republics, most of which voted to preserve the USSR that year, but by the leader of the Russian Federation, Boris Yeltsin, for whom dissolution of the USSR was the only chance to wrestle power from the Soviet President.

For the moment it seemed that the Russian elites were content to dispose of the 'imperial' mentality and desire to control militarily the Warsaw Pact countries or even former republics of the USSR. The later were allowed to keep practically all Soviet army assets they wanted with exception of nuclear weapons. Yeltsin's family and a group of well-connected individuals (soon to be known as the oligarchs) were busy plundering assets of the Soviet economy making themselves super-rich. At the same time, much of the general population were sliding into poverty caused by unprecedented transition from socialist state-run economy to unregulated capitalism that was dubbed as the 'shock therapy'. Soviet militarism was defeated by sheer greed of the Soviet ruling elites that did not stop stripping state assets until everyone in Russia, except the oligarchs, found themselves in much reduced circumstances of the so called evil *"likhiye* 1990's" or a modern version of Russian *"smuta"* (the Time of Troubles). The defeat of the Russian armed forces by the Chechen rebels led by ex-Soviet air-force General Dzhokhar Dudayev in the first Chechen War (1994-96) became a rude awakening and a major blow to the Russian military prestige. The Kremlin could not understand how the Chechen irregulars could have defeated their combined arms divisions that once commanded fear of the entire NATO block. It also prompted the military and political elite to re-think its understanding of war and peace. Moscow responded initially with a knee-jerk reaction of mass repressions against civilian Chechen population, filtration (concentration) camps, intimidation and collective punishment. This is when the Russian army learned that systematic war crimes against its own population is a tolerated practice not used in the Soviet army for generations practically since Stalin's times. (Young Russian officers for whom both Chechen campaigns became their formative military experience would lead the RF divisions into Ukraine repeating the same patterns of behaviour but on a bigger scale). However, mounting human costs to the conscript Russian army taking massive casualties caused an outcry among Russian voters and Yeltsin accepted a negotiated solution. The humiliating defeat in the First Chechen war was blamed on the Chechen victory in information confrontation when Russian public simply lost support for the war efforts.

President Yeltsin initially fully supported Russian integration with the Western liberal system as the main goal was to develop the Russian Federation as a modern capitalist state with social welfare provisions. However, his declared intent coupled with reality of epic embezzlement of previously state-owned assets contrasted with the experience of the overwhelming majority of the Russian population.

As David Kilcullen (2020) observed, the consequences of the Russian transformation to a market economy in the 1990's were widespread and dire: "In the 1990s, life expectancy fell eight years for Russian men and two for Russian women, productive capacity dropped 8 percent per year from 1989 to 2001, capital flight averaged $1.5 billion a month, and the number of people living in poverty across the former Soviet Union rose from 14 million in 1989 to 147 million in 1998. Mafia murders skyrocketed, with hundreds killed as rival gangs and competing oligarchs fought for control of lucrative, newly privatized industries and booming illicit businesses. It was a social, humanitarian, and economic catastrophe unprecedented in peacetime" (Kilcullen, 2020. P.129).

Russian intellectuals could not fail to notice that the consequences of Yeltsin's transformation felt like a defeat in war, considering demographic losses. "...The toll from murder, suicide, heart attacks, and accidents gave Russia the death rate of a country at war" (Satter, 2007). It did not take a long time to trigger reflections among the intelligentsia that the Cold War defeat and the collapse of the USSR was a result of a clandestine Anglo-Saxon subversion war waged on the Russian Federation. In other words, a substantial part of the Russian establishment started to believe that the real cause of economic, social, and military decline of the Russian Federation was not rooted in corruption of the rulers but in secret information war conducted by external enemies.

President of the Russian Academy of Military Science Makhmut Garyev wrote a major work in 1998 — *If War comes tomorrow? The contours of Future Armed Conflict* where he agreed with some late Soviet theorists suggesting reconsidering the nature of war solely as an armed struggle and stressed the role of psychological warfare. He argued that armed struggle is "a part of war — war being a complex social and political phenomenon embracing all spheres of life in the nations engaged, with diverse ways of fighting the enemy including industrial, political and psychological means, with armed struggle being paramount among them." (Gareyev 1998, P.viii). Another area of continuity with Soviet understanding in Gareyev's thinking is the causes of war, which he saw as economic, even if they were "disguised as religious, ideological, and other motives." (Gareyev 1998, P.19). Gareyev's argument was that regardless of the benefits that military technology can bring, psychological factors such as strength of will and morale will be decisive for winning the information dominance in future wars: "The main efforts in the struggle with the enemy will be directed not towards the physical destruction of each unit of weaponry, but towards the destruction of their common information space, sources of intelligence, channels of navigation, and control systems of communication and targeting in general." (Gareyev 1998, P.49).

The Russian information warfare theorist Igor Panarin, a former KGB general and a member of the Academy of Military science, argued in his 2010 book, *Pervaya mirovaya informatsionnaya voina: Razval SSSR*, that the first information world war started with an assault against Russia in 1943. Russian theorists therefore started to re-evaluate their experience during the Cold War in much more conspiratorial terms. According to Panarin, the information war was launched by Winston Churchill, who was later developed by George Kennan, and went on until the engineered election of Mikhail Gorbachev, whom Panarin saw as responsible for the dissolution of the USSR (Panarin 2010). In a follow up article titled *Vtoraya mirovaya informatsionnaya voina: Voina protiv Rossii*, he launched the idea that a second information world war was ongoing. The war's main purpose was seen to be the West's goal of eliminating an alternative world model that rivalled liberal colonialism (Panarin 2012. Quoted from Jonsson. 2019). Initially such conspiratorial belief was a minority's faith among the old Soviet Guards like Gareyev — a legendary WW2 veteran. However, when President Yeltsin handed over his powers to ex-KGB officer Vladimir Putin in December 1999, the premise that Russia is in a state of information war with the Anglo-Saxons and NATO started to evolve into a dominant thinking among the RF military command, security services and the Kremlin.

5. Cold War 2.0 and Russia's New Generation Warfare

Chapter 5 analyses the current Russian understanding of New Generation Warfare sometimes called 'hybrid' or 'liminal' warfare and is essentially a Russian interpretation of a Western military art that envisages application of clandestine 'colour revolution' tactics to achieve military objectives by non-military means. The New Generation Warfare (NGW) concept informs us how Russian military strategists arrived at such conclusions, the lessons they draw and changes they implemented to counteract this hybrid form of new type of warfare that they imply the West is waging on the rest of the World. Ironically from the Western point of view, 'hybrid warfare' is how the "Rest learned to Fight the West" (Kilcullen, 2020) and this chapter explores the source of clear mutual misunderstanding. On the one hand, Russian concerns regarding American ability to conduct non-contact warfare with high-precision weapons in both Iraq campaigns (1990 and 2001) were absolutely justified as they exposed potential vulnerability. This explains Moscow substantial and relatively successful investment in new 'wonder-weapons' announced by President Putin in the 2018 re-election speech. On the other hand, American-led NATO intervention in Serbia (1999), which from Western point of view was rather reluctant and purely humanitarian, was perceived in Moscow as blatant American expansionism. From Moscow's point of view, this was the first clear application of a new type of aggression in a form of a 'colour revolution' that led to a regime change in Serbia, so that NATO troops did not even need to arrive in Belgrade to achieve a full military and political victory. This chapter argues that the Kosovo precedent, more than expansion of NATO in Central Europe, changed strategic calculations in Moscow that was still hoping at the time to build strategic partnership relations with Washington. However, a series of 'colour revolutions' that happened in Georgia (2003), Ukraine (2004) and the Arab Spring (2005) convinced the Kremlin that the US' objective is changing regime in Russia as well.

This led to changes in the Russian military and information security doctrines by 2011 and invasion of Ukraine in 2013. Russian ruling elites were already convinced that they were fighting a defensive war of a new type against the 'Anglo-Saxons' while the West was still hoping for a re-set with Russia in order to improve relations. Washington and London would not even dream about fighting a 'hybrid war' as Moscow suspected it did. Chapter 4 therefore, looks at justified Russian concerns, perceived and real 'hybrid threats' and how they informed the decision- making process in Russia to launch military campaigns in Crimea, Syria and how Russia arrived at the conclusion that it is in a state of information war with the Anglo-Saxons.

Information war accounts up to 70-80% of New Generation Warfare tactics as understood by the Russian CDS General Gerasimov. Although there are clear signs that Russia is reconstructing a previously existing Soviet model of mass mobilisation for a large-scale conventional army-on-army conflict, it does not necessarily mean that the Kremlin is planning to launch a conventional war against the West.

On the contrary, there are suggestions that by 2019 the ruling elite believed that Russia has already won the conventional arms race with the West and therefore was relatively secure within its borders. Having secured its homeland, the Kremlin felt confident to conduct aggressive information war on the territory of its adversaries. As influential Russian security official Sergey Karaganov triumphally declared:

> "By carrying out a successful military reform, by rearming and reforming general-purpose forces, and by starting to deploy the latest generation of high-tech strategic weapons, Russia has pre-emptively ruined the United States' hopes to regain military superiority, and has so far won the arms race without getting involved in it. It seems that by crushing those hopes, Russia, not even fully realizing it yet, has finally knocked down the foundation out of the West's five-hundred-years dominance in world politics, economy and culture. That foundation was ensured by the West's military supremacy. Dozens of countries and previously suppressed civilizations now have much greater opportunities for free and sovereign development". (Rossiyskaya Gazeta, 26 December 2019).

Once, Russia has deployed its first hypersonic nuclear-capable missiles in December 2019, Vladimir Putin boasted that it put the RF in a class of its own and compared the Avangard hypersonic glide vehicle to the 1957 Soviet launch of the first satellite. It looked like the Kremlin was engaging into a deterrence rhetoric, but against whom?

Russian political and military elites expect a global military confrontation within next 15 years:

> "If you look at Russian military reviews and programmatic foreign policy articles, it's easy to see that the thinking in Putin's environment of *siloviks* is dominated by the following frame: The world is moving towards a global war in the 2035 horizon, and if there will be no war, there will be a large-scale clash between the US and China and a new 'redistribution of the world'. Russia is in a weak position compared with the capabilities of the United States, NATO, the EU as a whole and China. The political class in Russia believes that Putin is leading Russia to a strategically advantageous position on the eve of a global 'redistribution of the world'. And since Russia is weaker, they are convinced that it must follow guerrilla tactics" (A.Morozov; 20 Jan 2020, BBC Monitoring).

This strategy of 'guerrilla warfare' was best described by Russian white emigre strategist Evgeniy Messner in his book *Miatezh Voina* or *Subversion War* (Russkiy Voyennyi Sbornik, 2005) and approximates what RAND describes as a political war.

The latter aims at disrupting targeted societies rather than attacking adversarial armed forces in the nuclear age. Expecting a worldwide armed conflict caused by violent struggle for redistribution of world's markets and natural resources is consistent with Soviet, essentially Marxist-Leninist interpretation of history in general. This is how both Marxist-Leninist and current Russian historiography explained causes of WW1 and WW2. Prediction of causes for a potential WW3 is similar as well as consistent with the fatalistic outlook of Russian culture and psyche. Putin's Russia perceives the capitalist world in terms of perpetual struggle for new markets / bigger profits and the Kremlin positions itself as defending its economic interests militarily. Russian interpretation of the New Generation Warfare suggests however, that future worldwide war will be fought mostly unconventionally in the information /

cognitive space and the Grey Zone, with conventional warfare being only a supporting act if required at all. The key element of the New Generation Warfare is the Information War. The latter could manifest itself in undermining other societies on two levels: cognitive and cyber-physical. Cognitive level is covered by influence operations, psy-ops and 'active measures' while cyber-physical by hacking into National critical infrastructure, tearing underwater cables, sowing chaos by disrupting economic value chains and military networks subversion.

This is consistent with the US DoD expectation that Russia will develop capabilities to operate below the threshold of conflict to take control of strategic objectives before an opponent can respond. Considering global climate change and the opening of the Arctic resources for human exploitation, it is inevitable that Russia sees the Arctic and the North Sea Route opening for trans-Atlantic trade as the key potential conflict zone in the medium-to-longer term timescale. Military leadership of both the USSR and the RF always considered the Arctic seas as the most likely vector of attack from the Atlantic maritime powers e.g. the US and Great Britain. From a political, economic and military point of view, this region became critical to Russian geopolitical calculations or, as Aleksandr Dugin put it, became the "Russian destiny".

Deconstructing Russia's grievances: What are the most dangerous conflicting objectives?

Fear and greed over the Arctic. In October 2020, the Russian Government published its assessment suggesting that Global climate change opened up new economic opportunities in the Arctic Ocean. However, Western activities, in what used to be from Moscow's point of view their deep hinterland, started to threaten Russian national security.

The Arctic Council of the Russian Parliament published an extensive assessment of Russian national interests in the region (2019) and explicitly underlined the importance of the Arctic for national defence: "The Arctic was and is the key region in preserving the balance of strategic deterrence. The shortest routes to attack Russia via air and space runs through the near Arctic territory. Massive attacks on Russia by nuclear and non-nuclear cruise missiles could be launched from the surface (or air) of the Arctic seas" (P.12). This document specifies the Russian view that conflict of political, military and economic interests could lead to an international armed conflict:

"The following adversary's capabilities in the Arctic should be considered as potential threats to the military security of the Russian Federation in the Arctic:

- Ability to use high precision weapons (submarine or aircraft based) on the Northern strategic air & space vector;
- Expansion of strategic air-defence with new mobile elements located on surface ships in the Norwegian and Greenland Seas; dual purpose radar infrastructure used for military purposes on Svalbard and in Northern Norway.
- Ability to deploy strategic non-nuclear high-precision weapons (cruise missiles) based on surface ships or nuclear-powered submarines in the Greenland, Norwegian, Barents and Western Kara Seas;
- Ability to deploy anti-submarine warfare units and effectively counter our submarines." (P.314).

Russia considers modernised NATO installations as far as RAF Saxa Vord or Thule airbase in Greenland as examples of 'intensified military competition' aiming at the Arctic direction (P.316).

Russian narratives assume that 'some countries' (the Anglo-Americans) plot to take control over the Northern Sea Route and that Russia must do everything in order to protect it as part of its sovereign maritime space and the sea shelf (Polonskiy 2019).

In response, the RF's state armament programme envisaged to deploy a new group of armed forces in the 'strategic arctic area' (*napravleniye*) by 2025. This new force will fall under the jurisdiction of the Northern fleet, being responsible not only for the RF continental shelf, the Northern Sea Route but also all areas up to the North Pole (P.323). Such narratives are spread via international media using third party's channels to portray any anticipated Russian actions as defensive. Some Russian experts, however, qualify potential military threat from the North Atlantic vector as not immediate:

> "We cannot exclude possibilities when aggressive intentions of NATO countries would transform into military incursions against Russia in a long-term or even in a medium-term timeframe. Preparations for such actions intensified recently and the hybrid war against our country and our allies becomes more entrenched" (Belobrov, 2019. P.74).

Crossing the threashold: Russian revisionism in the Arctic and how might it turn into a confrontation & conflict?

Despite a tense standoff between Russia and the Euro Atlantic security community in Central and Eastern Europe, this was not the direction of threat Russian military strategists considered of critical importance despite Cold War rhetoric. As General Slipchenko of the Russian Military Academy succinctly concluded: "Nobody is going to invade us by land anymore". The expected vector of high-precision weapons since the Cold War was from the High North as it was the shortest route to fly missiles from the US toward the Russian strategic targets. The shrinking Arctic ice cap also can expose the hiding Russian strategic submarines in the region to add insult to the injury, hence Moscow strategists need a new approach or a new type of deterrence.

Western fears that that Russia might physically seize key terrain around the North pole and present it as a *fait accompli* finds direct supporting evidence in the Arctic. The Russian Arctic bid to the UN, submitted in 2015, extends as far as the North Pole, despite ratification of the UN Convention on the Law of the Sea that limited its territorial waters to 12 miles and exclusive economic zone to 200 miles. Therefore, Russia is currently a revisionist power claiming up to 1.7 million square kilometres of Arctic Sea shelf extending more than 350 nautical miles from the shore. This could lead to either conventional armed confrontation if not carefully managed or, most likely, a covert and asymmetric (hybrid) competition over the disputed sea shelf. Militarisation of the Russian Arctic therefore indicates Moscow's future intent to seize the underwater shelf and de-facto annexing this vast territory if the legal claim would be rejected by the UN. Joanna Hosa from the European Council on Foreign Relations legitimately asked back in 2018 — "Has Russia already won the scramble for the Arctic"?

> "Other countries should prepare for Russia continuing to want more than it receives under UNCLOS. Given its strong interest in the Lomonosov ridge, the military changes it is making in the Arctic, and its wider drive to influence the shape of the world order, it is not unimaginable that Russia may simply move in to begin exploiting the Lomonosov ridge, creating a fait accompli that only other major powers could undo. At the moment, it is not clear who would wish to confront Russia in this way, or even whether they have the full complement of strategy, skills, and technology to do so". (Hosa, 2018)

This assumption is consistent with the US DoD assessment of Russia's violation of international law when it comes to navigating the Northern Sea Route by third parties:

> "Russia regulates maritime operations in the NSR, contrary to international law, and has reportedly threatened to use force against vessels that fail to abide by Russian regulations. Russia could choose to unilaterally establish those limits if the procedures prove unfavourable and could utilize its military capabilities in an effort to deny access to disputed Arctic waters or resources." (DOD Arctic Strategy 2019 P. 6)

Conventional confrontation scenario

Izvestia newspaper reported (Dec 2019) that the Russian Army would deploy "Arctic Helicopter Carriers" or mobile airfields already tested by the Baltic Navy. The new technologies would allegedly permit military personnel to deploy an airfield network beyond the Arctic Circle in a matter of hours and provide capability to reinforce, resupply and defend captured territory. Russia is the only country that has experience of establishing stations on drifting ice, so this new mobile airfield capability would give another technological edge to Russian de-facto 'ice grab'. Despite COVID-19 epidemics, Russian VDV troops successfully tested its new capability to parachute in the Arctic from 10,000 meters and conduct search and destroy operations against foreign 'subversion groups' on Russian most northern territory—France Josef Land. The previous summer, Russia also successfully tested its first seaborne nuclear power plant that could sail across the Arctic and provide energy to support long-term operations in a required area. In other words, there is a physical infrastructure in place to support any Arctic 'land/ice-grab' and make it sustainable long-term.

At the same time, the West's ice-breakers fleet is very limited in the Arctic and challenging any Russian territorial takeover might be impossible without investment in such capability. The US is the only country that declared its intent to enforce international law in the Arctic when it comes to preserving freedoms of the sea:

> "Maintaining freedoms of navigation and overflight are critical to ensuring that the Arctic remains a free and open domain and that U.S. forces retain the global mobility guaranteed under international law. DoD will continue to fly, sail, and operate wherever international law allows. When necessary and appropriate, the United States will challenge excessive maritime claims in the Arctic to preserve the rules-based international order and the rights and freedoms of the international community in navigation and overflight, as well as for other, related high seas uses". (DOD Arctic Strategy 2019, P.13)

Russian military planners are fully aware of American intent in the Arctic and keep themselves busy strengthening defences in the High North. Russian Minister of Defence Sergey Shoigu stated explicitly back in February 2015 that Russia is prepared to fight in the Arctic in order to defend its national interests: "Permanent military presence in the Arctic and possibility to defend state interests by means of warfare is considered to be essential part of general policy to defend national security" (Shoigu, 2015).

Despite the official line that Russian defences are impenetrable from the High North "vector" the unofficial online Russian Military review (TopWar.ru) published detailed analysis that with current state of affairs, the Northern Navy and the naval nuclear strategic forces did not stand a chance in conventional confrontation with the US and other NATO allies (Klimov 2019).

The TopWar.ru war gaming scenario suggested the following results of an American led NATO strike:

1. Russian strategic nuclear submarines deployed at sea would be destroyed by NATO aviation before the actual armed conflict starts in a pre-emptive strike.
2. Strategic nuclear submarines would be destroyed also in its bases, blocked from escaping by deployed-from-air sea mines or torpedoed by NATO submarines.
3. Russian submarines would be targeted in the Barents Sea by NATO surface ships armed with missiles and located outside of the Russian coastal based anti-missile defence range e.g. "Bastions".
4. All Northern Fleet naval bases close to NATO borders would be destroyed with all ammunition and materiel stored there.
5. The defeated remains for the Northern Navy would attempt to retreat toward the Southeast of the Barents Sea but would be destroyed in the process.
6. Anti-missile defences based on various Arctic islands would be supressed with key bases captured after helicopters paratrooper forces positioned for future strikes and advances into the Siberian hinterland.

With no options other than nuclear, such confrontation scenario would lead to the use of land-based ICBMs and consequently a Mutually Assured Destruction. Although the Military Review offered a mitigating course of actions to avoid the conventional armed forces defeat in the Arctic (see the chart below) it stated that the current military leadership prefers to ignore necessary investments due to lack of funding to match Soviet level of military build-up in the High North. Or does Russian Defence Staff rely on the alternative asymmetrical means?

Hybrid conflict scenario

Our assumption that future warfare will be less confined to the battlespace and more focused on disrupting societies could also be relevant to the HN with Russian influence operations being likely conducted against the UK, Norway, Denmark/Greenland, Canada and the US. As described by Conservative MP Bob Seely, who researched Russian hybrid warfare tactics: "This conflict is not primarily military and uses violence and force economically. It also uses psychologically-based information operations as both a prelude to war, an alternative to war, and a handmaiden in war." Therefore, we can expect Russia to engage in further horizontal escalation through multiple points of low-level conflict in order to control, absorb and exhaust allied forces. As described by Tunku Varadarajan in the Wall Street Journal, Russia is "economically modest and technologically mediocre, so they look for ways to compensate, and subversion of competitors is an obvious, low-cost strategy". Interviewed on CNN in 2007, Retired KGB General Oleg Kalugin described "active measures" as "the heart and soul of Soviet intelligence":

> "Not intelligence collection, but subversion: active measures to weaken the West, to drive wedges in the Western community alliances of all sorts, particularly NATO, to sow discord among allies, to weaken the United States in the eyes of the people of Europe, Asia, Africa, Latin America, and thus to prepare ground in case the war really occurs."

CIA veteran John Sipher concludes that in this sense, "active measures have long been part and parcel of Russia's larger use of irregular/asymmetric warfare and intelligence operations meant to influence their adversaries and prepare the ground in case a real war occurs." (Sipher, 2018).

Kremlin's preference for non-kinetic competition with the Anglo-Saxons is supported by the latest academic research as well. Fridman's book on Russian 'Hybrid Warfare' arrives at the conclusion that "the current threat that Russia poses to the West is of non-military nature. This does not mean that the military has no role to play... Instead, it simply means that the Russian leadership prefers to operate in the non-military spectrum of confrontations, rather than a direct open military conflict" (Fridman, 2018. P.169). There is indirect confirmation that such approach is becoming a mainstream in the Russian military thinking. A PhD thesis presented at the Military University (affiliated to the Russian MoD) in 2019 begins with an assumption that "current military affairs transition from classic understanding of war to non-classic where war utilises non-physical application of violence" e.g. psychological, information, consciousness-centric (*konscientalnaya*) and hybrid concepts of war (Kaftan, 2019. P.15).

We can expect Russia, therefore, to rely on the mix of information warfare, legal ambiguity of the Arctic (lawfare) and the threat of conventional armed forces retaliation to prevent international military intervention in the HN. Russia has been successful previously in using economic leverage inviting Western Oil & Gas majors to set up joint ventures in the disputed areas (e.g. Nord Stream 2) and encouraging the Western Oil & Gas lobby to oppose sanctions on deep sea technology required for the Arctic upstream development. Concurrently, Russia could involve China in exploration and development of claimed / disputed Arctic shelf, rising international stakes in the confrontation with the USA and the wider West. The China Petroleum Corporation has already replaced Western companies as the key investor in Yamal gas field developments while the Northern Sea Route has been designated by China as the 'Arctic Silk Road' since 2017. Hybrid / asymmetric confrontation would be therefore most likely preferred Russian option. As a Chatham House report (2019) suggested, "Russia's military leadership rules out starting a conflict in the Arctic, and would push any Arctic- based conflict towards sea lines of communication between the North Atlantic and the Baltic Sea" (Boulegue, 2019). However, a conventional armed conflict following an 'Arctic grab' should not be ruled out if the hybrid approach would not bring satisfactory results. Considering Russian conventional vulnerability from the Arctic vector, the West should expect what General Gerasimov called an "active defence", suggests Michael Kofman:

> "This is a set of pre-emptive non-military and military measures, deterrence and escalation management approaches based on cost imposition. The Russian armed forces are geared towards being able to pre-emptively neutralize an emerging threat or deter by showing the ability and willingness to inflict unacceptable consequences on the potential adversary. As Gerasimov said, 'acting quickly we must pre-empt our adversary with preventive measures, identify his vulnerabilities in a timely manner, and create the threat that unacceptable damage will be inflicted.' (Kofman, 2020)"

So, what "pre-emptive non-military and military measures" Russia did, and still could, apply in the region? According to EUvsDisinfo — the European External Action Service's East StratCom Task Force for combating Russian disinformation, Russia conducted 818 disinformation activities against the UK, Baltic and Nordic states in five years since 2015 when documentation began (EUvsDisInfo.eu)[2]. These information attacks represent only a tip of the iceberg and prove wider systematic efforts to wage and win an information war with the West, essentially with the US and the UK with Nordic and Baltic countries targeted as proxies. One of the key tactics in such information war is to identify, exploit and weaponize indigenous self-destructing cultural ideas (e.g. hard Brexit) in order to undermine targeted societies in view of destroying their social fabric and will to fight using 'reflexive control' (See Chapter 6). A number of UK parliamentary reports indicated substantial subversive Russian influence in Britain (See: *Moscow's Gold: Russian Corruption in the UK,* House of Commons Foreign Affairs Committee, 8th Report, 2018) and ongoing disinformation and cyber threats. Cyber-attacks against national critical infrastructure become a new normal in global conflict, however, conceptually in Russian military thinking, it is part of Information Warfare on a cyber-physical level. In other words, it is part of Russian asymmetric response that potentially can provide a physically distractive edge to information war in future. (Similarly, as air-power was considered initially at its infancy as a reconnaissance tool but evolved into a destructive new war domain with invention of heavy bombers, missiles etc).

However, what could be overall Russian strategic objectives in targeting the UK establishment, critical national infrastructure, and wider society? Moscow did not see post-Brexit Britain as a resurging global military power but rather a hesitant American ally. Hence, Russian influence efforts were likely to ensure that London

---

2 Last searched on 1 May 2020 https://euvsdisinfo.eu/disinformation-cases/?text=&date=&disinfo_countries%5B%5D=77548&disinfo_countries%5B%5D=77621&disinfo_countries%5B%5D=77560&disinfo_countries%5B%5D=77575&disinfo_countries%5B%5D=77561&disinfo_countries%5B%5D=77574

did not commit to the US efforts more than a bare minimum of military support. Evgeniy Savchenko explained in the Russian General Staff's official publication *Military Thought*:

> London remains one of the key close allies of Washington and despite substantial change of foreign policy, continues to demonstrate allegiance to the 'special relationship' with the US. However, in reality, such allegiance is merely symbolic. For instance, British government announced that Britain would send 75 instructors to train Ukrainian Armed Forces. . ... At the same time, since the 2016 Brexit referendum, it is unlikely that Britain will increase defence spending and increase the scale of its military engagement to support the US. In other words, such support will remain at the minimal acceptable to London level... (Savchenko, 2017).

Hence, Russian overall strategy could be better understood through the lens of Moscow's confrontation with Washington. It is Russian-American *détente* that informs best the ultimate Russian information war objective, with Russian ambitions not being limited to the Arctic but acquiring a truly global character. As one of the Russian information warfare experts Vladimir Lepskiy explains, Moscow should opt out for the 'controlled chaos' weapon against the West as a Russian asymmetrical response to the US dominated unipolar world.

One of the key Russian 'controlled chaos' concepts is deconstructing subjects of development into objects of exploitation. It is assumed that humankind is ready for a 'meta-system civilization shift' and, therefore, Russia should propose an "asymmetrical response to 21 century's information wars and facilitate re-assembly of subjects of international development". Considering that Western technology-based civilization exhausted its development, Russia can lead to a new world order based on a 'socio-humanitarian civilization' where humankind will become a subject of its own destiny: "The suggested approach represents Russia's asymmetrical response to the information wars of the 21st century. It will ensure Russian leadership of planetary social change enabling it to re-assemble subjects of international development and create conditions of the dynamic and secure development of Russia as well as the international community" (Lepskiy 2019. P.7). In other words, Russian ruling elites want no less than a new multipolar world order where the role of the US and the UK (the Anglo-Saxons) would be downgraded in principle and the unipolar world of Western domination destroyed through a complex web of 'reflexive control' active measures (Analysed in Chapters 5-6).

Implications for the Anglo-Saxons

The military thinkers in the UK have been long calling on the UK government to address the new Russian threat. Former CGS General Mark Carleton-Smith pointed out in 2018 that Britain should not underestimate the 'hybrid threat' to the world order: "Mistaking hybrid warfare as an ancillary branch of twentieth century conflict misses the scale of the challenge. Beginning with the click of a mouse, from cyber-attacks to disinformation campaigns, the adversary is manoeuvring across multiple domains uncontested. Failing to recognise and respond to these realities not only risks strategic defeat before the first shots are fired, it has the potential to upend the international order" (Carleton-Smith, 2018). Similarly, Sir Nicholas Carter said that "First of all, I think we should recognize that Russia respects strength and people who stand up to them" (Carter, 2019).

Since 1991 the UK government policy towards Russia was mostly one of opportunistic emerging market penetration for economic gain. Thanks to BP's risky involvement with Rosneft, the UK became one of the top leaders in Foreign Direct Investment in Russia, despite the fact that Rosneft, where BP held a 20% stake, was under the US sanction, something that has been re-valuated only in 2022 (Millard, 2020). Until then, selling 20% Rosneft to BP could have been Kremlin's strategic act of reflexive control over Britain in the first place that explains why extracting from this deal was so difficult. Firstly, Moscow used BP investment to legitimise Rosneft's status as an international Oil&Gas major while litigation with former Yukos owners was still in progress over looted assets. Secondly, BP investments became a major leverage over politics in Britain considering the power of O&G lobby as well as banks, pension funds etc. that invested into BP shares. Could that explain why release of the report on Russian interference in the UK elections prepared by the parliamentary intelligence committee in 2019 became such a controversy? (Over 56 thousand UK citizens signed a petition to release the report by April 2020).

So, what should the UK be doing differently? Again the military answer is probably easier to formulate than a political one:

> "We should identify Russian weaknesses and then manoeuvre asymmetrically against them. First and foremost, perhaps we should be in the business of building real institutional capacity in neighbouring states so that they have the strength and confidence to stand up to Russia and the internal resilience to withstand pressures designed to bring them down from within. We should be making more progress on reducing energy dependency on Russia. We should be telling the Russian population what's really going on. We should be protecting our critical capabilities; hence the importance of cyber. And we should be looking to identify our own vulnerabilities to Russian malign influence and disinformation, and act to reduce them. Next, I think, we need to demonstrate our preparedness to commit. 'Boots on ground' is not a positive term at the moment, but our allies on NATO's eastern flank absolutely appreciate that a platoon of infantry is worth a squadron of F-16s when it comes to commitment". General Sir Nicholas Carter, Chief of the General Staff (Carter 2019).

Conclusions: Russian strategic goals in the HN and NA derive from its overall strategy to unhinge the unipolar world dominated by the 'Anglo-Saxons' and establish a multipolar one with Russia among others like China, at the top table. Russia competes with the US and the UK over access to the Arctic natural resources, ownership of the sea shelf (up to the North Pole) and control of the Northern Sea Route. Moscow actively rebuilds its defences in the HN and projects its military power in the NA trying to prevent and delay hypothetical attack on its coastal bases and bastions. Considering its relative economic weakness against the combined EU and NATO security community, the Russian ruling elite relies on conventional forces deterrence for defence and information war for fighting the battle in the cognitive space against its adversaries. The very fact that Russian leadership is taking offensive actions against a superior US-led NATO forces suggests their confidence in reliable conventional defence of its homeland. Even if President Putin's announcements regarding the new 'wonder-weapons' are part of 'perception management' nobody seems to be challenging Russian credibility to deliver MAD in case of conventional confrontation with the West. This allowed some Russian experts to believe that Moscow has already won the new arms race and is free to act on an international scale to advance its strategic goals at the expense of the West (i.e. the Anglo-Saxons) with a sense of impunity. Russian strategists like Aleksandr Dugin, have commented extensively that Brexit not only aborted Britain as a great power but also manifested the end of the Western domination: "Brexit is the collapse of the West and it is a victory for humanity, which is opposed to the West and seeks to go its own way. ...Britain is not just leaving the EU — it is disappearing from history" (Dugin, 2017). Considering that Dugin advocated Russian policy to isolate Britain from the EU since 1997 he belongs to the school of thought among Russian strategists that can even claim 'victory' of active measures and reflexive control that facilitated Britain's "disappearance from history". This interpretation of geopolitics emboldens Kremlin's attempts to place "Eurasian (Russian) civilization" at the heart of the new multi-polar world and out-compete the Anglo-Saxons using asymmetric information warfare.

Ironically, Russian strategists claim that the most effective information war techniques such as exploitation of 'controlled chaos' or 'self-destructive cultural ideas' are of Western origin, so the West should be superior in this asymmetric competition. Indeed, the remedies are known, and, for instance, the US Army War College published a number of detailed recommendations on *Deterring Russia in the Grey Zone*: "U.S. policymakers must carefully construct overt and covert measures while committing ample resources to regain information dominance over Russia. The key to policy development is viewing the information environment through both an overseas and domestic lens and includes:

Overseas:

- Fully funding the Department of State's Global Engagement Center (GEC);
- Supporting NATO information operations; and
- Employing covert actions.

Domestic:

- Creating an Office of Foreign Influence (OFI);
- Drafting of key legislation by Congress; and
- Presidential support and leadership". (McCarthy, 2019. P.48)

Under President Trump administration, American efforts were hindered by lack of adequate support and questionable leadership on behalf of President Donald Trump who "consistently broke from political orthodoxy in his effusive praise of Russian President Vladimir Putin" (Kaczynski, 2017). This was a serious hindrance in the Grey Zone deterrence as counteractions to Russian misinformation campaign recommended for the U.S. policymakers included considering "a more robust covert action campaign that:

- Undercuts Russia's use of active measures;
- Exposes its human rights violations on the world stage;
- Delegitimizes Russia's Government by revealing large-scale corruption; and,
- Embarrasses Putin and his inner circle". (McCarthy, 2019. P.53)

Considering, the unusual relationships established between president Trump and Putin in 2016, the GEC remained underfunded and under-utilised while OFI was activated as the Foreign Malign Influence Center only on September 23, 2022. Donald Trump rejected accusations circulating in the American press that he had clandestine relationship with Moscow since the 1980s. The FBI started the so-called 'Russia investigation' trying to establish whether the Kremlin helped to elect Donald Trump in the 2016 presidential elections. Considering that at the time President Trump was in office, the investigation was transferred to special prosecutor Robert Mueller in May 2017. The Mueller report (March 2019) concluded that the Trump pre-election campaign welcomed Russian interference in the electoral process but found insufficient evidence of a criminal conspiracy to charge the incumbent President with effectively what could be considered state treason. The very fact that the Kremlin managed to interfere into the American electoral system was a major achievement of the Russian information war efforts and signified at least a temporary victory of Russian 'special measures' or so called 'Moscow's black magic'.

6. "Information War is the main type of war"

> "Russia is waging the most amazing information warfare blitzkrieg we have ever seen in the history of information warfare"
> Gen. Philip Breedlove, NATO summit 2014

> "Russia is in a state of information war with Anglo-Saxons"
> Putin's spokesman Dmitriy Peskov, March 2016

There could be multiple reasons why the Kremlin under President Putin chose to believe that the Russian Federation is under attack by the West. The Soviet cultural legacy to view the world as a battle space of advanced 'imperialist' countries pitted against the development of the socialist world played a role in the background but cannot explain the political choices made by the Kremlin. Putin's KGB background and psychological make up was another factor as the KGB was at the core of creating and fighting conspiracies throughout the Soviet era. However, post-Soviet Russian governments embraced the capitalist market economy and Putin inherited the political system that served, first of all, the oligarchs including Yeltsin's close family. In fact, President Yeltsin chose Putin as a successor hoping that an effective relatively young technocrat with a KGB background would be able to safeguard the riches of the *nouveau riche* elite. Oligarchs embraced the Western lifestyle very quickly and gradually Russian foreign policy towards the 'near abroad' i.e. former Soviet republics, became reminiscent of imperialist patronage. If the new Russian ruling class wanted to model the RF in an American fashion, including its perceived economic domination of neighbours and post-colonial exploitation of natural resources, why did it create the narrative that Washington was waging an information war on Russia which was no longer Communist and therefore not a threat? This did not make sense considering that Washington turned a blind eye to Yeltsin's unconstitutional, violent disposal of the opposition-dominated parliament in October 1993 and supported his re-election in 1996. President Putin inherited not only a pro-Western oligarchic regime but also good political relationships with most Western governments. In fact, Putin initially played with the idea of joining NATO, so clearly did not perceive the North Atlantic military alliance as a threat to the RF. Moscow and Washington co-operated in pressuring Ukraine, Belarus and Kazakhstan throughout the 1990s into nuclear disarmament that favoured Russia. (In 2022, Moscow will use against Kyiv at least some of the strategic missiles that Ukraine surrendered under pressure from Washington). However, the Kremlin quickly figured out that the USA treated Russia as an equal only when it reflected American interests but was not willing to grant the Kremlin rights to split Eurasia into spheres of influence. The Kremlin's belief in such a right stemmed from the GPW myth, which was and is perpetuated by the Russian elite under Putin, and harks back to the Yalta peace conference that created the post-WW2 world order in 1945. This is where cultural mindset has played a trick on both the American and Russian political interlocutors since the end of the Cold War. The Russian mind likes to paint a holistic understanding of how the world works and then design actions / policies that would reflect such understanding. The Marxist-Leninist ideology reflected Russian cultural longing for an orderly worldview and the Soviet state policy was designed accordingly. This was first understood by some military theorists in Russia by the end of the Soviet era. Andrei Kokoshin was Deputy minister of defence during most years of Yeltsin's administration, and he described challenges to Russian-American relations during Gorbachev's rule in the following way:

"It is important to note that the changes in the military-technical dimension of Soviet doctrine, particularly in strategy and campaign tactics, were initially overlooked by the West... As a result, the unilateral reduction of the Soviet armed forces, declared by Mikhail Gorbachev on December 7, 1988, at the UN General Assembly, came as quite a surprise for many American Sovietologists. This was probably rooted in the peculiarities of the Western mentality, especially that of Americans. Whereas in Russia the traditional way of thinking is deductive (i.e., from the general to the specific), in the United States it is the opposite (i.e., from the specific to the general). In a way, these inverse approaches coincide with the decision-making process in these two countries. In the Russian system, the political and even philosophical conceptions of the leadership are essential to the development of practical measures." (Kokoshin, 1998, P.191-92).

In other words, the strategic vision culture in Russia and the West (first of all the USA) were reversed in their thinking process. Western approach looked at the positive, mostly economic aspects of co-operation with Russia and treated the RF as an ideal emerging market where to sell its value-added products and buy cheap raw natural resources. Military-political co-operation with Moscow evolved on ad-hoc transactional basis where and when it was considered appropriate. Washington and London were comfortable with such transactional approach reflecting their own strategic culture and lack of universal grand design for the world that would allocate Russia a decisive role beyond existing permanent seat on the UN Security Council. Admitting Russia to the largely symbolical G8 summits was meant to satisfy Russian sensitivities of a former rival to the US super-power. Yeltsin's administration played along and was largely busy with internal affairs until the Kosovo crisis in March 1999 made it clear to the Russian elites that they have lost a decisive say in the European affairs. The illusion maintained in the Kremlin that Russia is perceived by the West (NATO) as a military super-power was shuttered and so did the Russian understanding of the world order where Moscow should have played a decisive role. The Kremlin's 'holiday from history' ended with the first NATO air-strikes against the Federal Republic of Yugoslavia on 24 March 1999. While NATO considered the Kosovo campaign as a humanitarian intervention to avoid what President Clinton called a potential Holocaust of Kosovo Albanians, Russian perception was completely different and forced Moscow to re-think its relationship with the West. The old Russian paranoias about the 'imperialist' West dictated by the Soviet worldview were quickly restored and embellished with new Eurasianist (neo-imperialist) ideology gradually embraced by President Putin. Once the Russian elites created a new perception of the West as the enemy of Russia, the state policies responding to the imagined Western information war were put in place. The road to war with the West effectively started once President Putin overpowered the oligarchs by the early 2000s and officially voiced his opposition to the American dominated 'unipolar world' in his 2007 Munich speech:

...what is a unipolar world? However, one might embellish this term, at the end of the day it refers to one type of situation, namely one centre of authority, one centre of force, one centre of decision making. It is world in which there is one master, one sovereign... and this certainly has nothing in common with democracy. Incidentally, Russia—we—are being constantly taught about democracy. But for some reason those who teach us do not want to learn themselves. I consider that the unipolar model is not only unacceptable but also impossible in today's world" (Putin 2007)

Meanwhile most of the Western capitals were blissfully unaware of the fact that Moscow's slide on the road to war was for the same cognitive reasons that made them miss Gorbachev's decision for unilateral disarmament two decades earlier. Those Western experts and Eastern European politicians who sounded alarms were branded as 'Cold War warriors' or dismissed as anti-Russian nationalists. Western consideration between security and prosperity *vis-a-vis* Russia was deliberately skewed towards the latter. Western companies were desperate to sell more goods, including those of dual-purpose, to the Russian market while Moscow set out on the path towards re-armament and anti-Western subversion. The key effort of such subversion was the information war on the West carefully disguised by Putin's rhetoric about economic partnership, exploiting Western greed (prosperity) drive.

The evolution of Russian information warfare under Putin has changed from its Soviet origins of military deception to a strategic political war, taking its current shape since around 2011. The new information security doctrine elevated information warfare to the dominant form of New Generation Warfare where the traditional kinetic element was reduced to 10-20% or might be not required at all. In other words, this chapter describes how Russian understanding of information war evolved from supporting operations (to deceive and distract the enemy), to a strategic weapon aiming to defeat the enemy through so-called 'indigenous destructive ideas'. Information war therefore became the main type of war while kinetic high-precision weapons are kept as a deterrent and the 'doomsday' insurance to be used only as the last resort.

Soviet military doctrine traditionally used the term 'Information warfare' to cover what is now accepted as 'hybrid warfare' tactics. Information warfare would include elements of both '*obman*, *maskirovka*' (deception) as well as 'active measures' to create effects (events) on the ground that could be used to advance overall military strategy. In short, the ultimate objective for Russian Information Warfare strategy now became to Deceive, Distract and Destroy the adversary. The later element contrasts with Western (NATO) approach to information operations which are limited to military deception and influence of adversary's will to fight (NATO, 2010). The Crimean takeover (2014) and subsequent years of the armed conflict in Ukraine served as a test ground for the new Russian information warfare tactics. It had been years in preparation and it therefore helps to recreate accurately its planning timeline, preparation and execution stages. Analysis of the Russian 'Crimean campaign' and information warfare tactics against Ukraine in general allows us to establish the RF's information warfare methodology, media toolkit, impact on the target population as well as shortcomings that could be exploited in order to dispel deception elements of hybrid warfare, which amounts up to 80% of the hostile course of action.

Definitions of Hybrid Warfare vs Information Warfare

Russian literature mostly refers to the term 'hybrid warfare' when describing hostile actions by Western countries against Russian interests. Although one can argue that the 'hybrid warfare' term has been subsequently adopted by the Russian military thinkers, they still prefer to use the more traditional term 'Information war' describing their own tactics. NATO's *Handbook of Russian Information Warfare* underlines that in Russian military thinking 'Information warfare' is not limited to armed conflict and is considered to be ongoing in peace time: "The concept carries within it computer network operations alongside disciplines such as psychological operations (PsyOps), strategic communications, Influence, along with intelligence, counterintelligence, *maskirovka*, disinformation, electronic warfare, debilitation of communications, degradation of navigation support, psychological pressure, and destruction of enemy computer capabilities." (Giles, 2016, P.6) *Maskirovka* in this quote is used in more narrow (tactical) way, while some authors refer to wider strategic approach when "*Maskirovka* is in fact war that is short of war, a purposeful strategy of deception that combines use of force with disinformation and destabilisation to create ambiguity in the minds of Alliance leaders about how best to respond" (Julian Lindley-French, 2015). Both Russian and Western definitions seem to agree that 'hybrid warfare' includes conventional, irregular and cyberwarfare targeting of the enemy on the conventional battlefield, the indigenous population of the conflict zone, and the international community public opinion in order to achieve political objectives on the ground and avoid attribution of (military) aggression. Excluding cyberwarfare, no other element is entirely new, so the novelty of 'hybrid warfare' is primarily in the correlation of factors applied. While 20th century conventional warfare was fought mainly on the battlefield with some elements of information warfare, 'hybrid warfare' is mostly conducted in the information space (mass / social media) and cyber space (networks) with conventional battlespace being 'optional' or 'additional'. Some Russian authors have even suggested that ideally, information warfare alone can achieve political victory over adversary through the successful imposition of 'self-destructive information systems' on the target population which voluntarily disarms and gives up due to 'reprogramming' and subsequent loss of the will to fight (Rastorguyev, 1999). The Russian Ministry of Defence adopted such an approach by 2011 when it stated that new rules of international engagement required steering the adversary towards a self-destructive course of action at peace time via 'destabilizing the society and state, and forcing the state to make decisions in the interests of the opposing party (Oborony, 2011). In this respect information warfare signifies the return of what George Kenan defined[3] back in 1948 as a 'political war', when he encouraged U.S. leaders to disabuse themselves

---

3   The political war concept was defined in a May 4, 1948, memorandum produced by the State Department's policy planning staff under George Kennan: "Political warfare is the logical application of Clausewitz's doctrine in time of peace. In broadest definition, political warfare is the employment of all the means at a nation's command, short of war, to achieve its national objectives. Such operations are both overt and covert. They range from such overt actions

of the 'handicap' of the "concept of a basic difference between peace and war" and to wake up to "the realities of international relations—the perpetual rhythm of struggle, in and out of war" (Jones, 2018). When the Chief of the Russian General Staff presented the new Defence Doctrine in 2013, he emphasized the lessons learned from Western 'hybrid warfare' i.e. the Arab spring and other 'colour revolutions' in Eastern Europe. In Gerasimov's words, the modern military conflict "is an integrated application of military, political, economic, informational, and other powers by state and non-state actors to achieve their political goals" (Gerasimov, 2013). President Putin signed the new Russian Defence doctrine in December 2014 prompting conclusions that "for Russian military leaders warfare is '...*not continuation of politics by other (military) means*' but an integral part of politics" (Ermus, 2017). Ermus and Salum analysed differences and similarities between Gerasimov's "new generation warfare" and the US Special Forces unconventional warfare operations (See Figure 1) and arrived at conclusion that the Russian concept relies much more heavily on information operations.

---

as political alliances, economic measures (as ERP—the Marshall Plan), and 'white' propaganda to such covert operations as clandestine support of 'friendly' foreign elements, 'black' psychological warfare and even encouragement of underground resistance in hostile states".

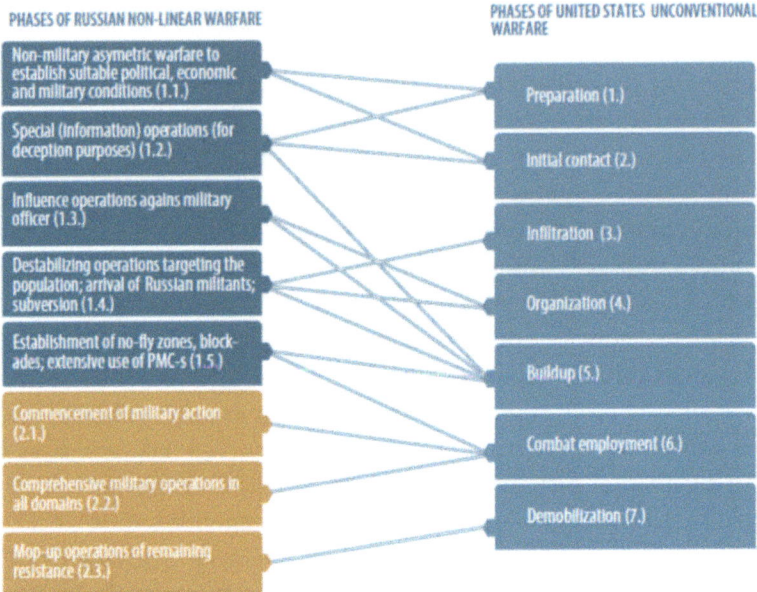

Figure 1. Comparison of the phases and sub-phases of the Russian new generation warfare and US phases of unconventional warfare.[136]

Evolution of post-Soviet Russian theory of information warfare and its likely objectives

Soviet information operations were at the heart of the USSR's internal and external policy as propaganda of communist ideology worldwide was an official foreign policy objective. During the Cold War, disinformation was part of 'active measures' conducted covertly by the KGB and overtly by the International Information Department in charge of Soviet broadcasting. KGB's 'black propaganda' — creating forgeries and creating rumours, however, was more tactical by its nature. For instance, the KGB created a wave of publications in Indian and then international media claiming that AIDS was invented by the American military as a biological weapon that got out of control. Although relatively successful, this campaign was not more than a distraction in the on-going Soviet-American confrontation. Strategic Soviet disinformation pushed through various cultural organisation and state press agencies essentially meant to create an agenda in the information space that would highlight deficiencies of the capitalist world and highlight benefits of the communist system. The CIA estimated that the USSR spent more than $4 bn a year on 'active measures' operations annually in 1980's and over 10,000 disinformation operations were conducted by the Soviet bloc over the course of the Cold War[4]. (KGB alone employed up to 15,000 officers engaged in psychological warfare and disinformation). However, by 1991 Russian elites gave up entirely on the Communist ideology and therefore the case for 'active measures' against the Capitalist Western world lost its *raison d'etre*. However, President Yeltsin's decade of infatuation with Western liberal capitalism and democracy proved to be no more than a creative break from the Cold War confrontation. Vladimir Putin's ascension to power in 1999 reinvented the ideological basis for geopolitical confrontation in the form of the Eurasian neo-imperial ideology and an alternative to the EU – the Eurasian Economic Union. Cold war disinformation warriors quickly jumped on the opportunity to justify their existence.

Most Post-Soviet Russian bibliography on information warfare associates the collapse of the USSR with clandestine psychological or information warfare operations designed by the West with deep infiltration, so that even President Gorbachev is often portrayed as a "Western agent of influence" (Kurginian, 1992). One of the key thinkers (Academician of the Russian Military Academy of Science) Igor Panarin concluded that "The USSR's defeat in the Cold War was defeat in the information-ideological war" (Panarin, 2003, P.40). What is more important, such war against Russia was perceived as ongoing long after the USSR demise: "Psychological wars never end and therefore we are still under the artillery barrage" (Pocheptsov, 2001, P.284). Russian statecraft elite widely shared this conclusion and attempted to safeguard the state "infor-

---

4 See Putin's Asymmetric assault on democracy in Russia and Europe: implications for US national security. In: A Minority Staff report prepared for Committee on Foreign Relations US Senate. US Government Publishing Office. Washington. 2018. P.36

mation security". President Yeltsin instructed newly appointed Defence Minister General-Colonel Rodionov (18 July 1996) that "Along with appropriate maintenance of the nuclear deterrent we should pay more attention in developing entire multitude of information warfare means". The Security Council of the Russian Federation developed a new Doctrine of Information Security of RF that was approved by President Putin in September 2000. The new Doctrine listed the key "external" threats: attempts by a number of foreign states to diminish national interests of the Russian Federation in the information sphere (both internally and internationally) and hostile information warfare development (both through mass media and cyber). Igor Panarin summed up the ultimate goal of the Russian information security strategy as securing effective functions of the societal information sphere in global competitions with leading nations and domination in the regions of key geopolitical importance for Russia. He defines these geopolitical areas in terms of neo-Eurasian ideology: "The Russian political elite should become *passionarnoy* (energetically active – OH) and develop new geopolitical doctrine based on *noosphere* matrix of Russian super-ethnos consciousness. This doctrine should protect *noosphere* matrix of consciousness from negative information influence from geopolitical adversaries in federal and regional elections" (Ibid., P.27). (For more information on the concept of new Eurasianism see: Hryb 2020).

Zavadski introduced one of the most quoted Russian definitions of information warfare:

> "Information warfare consists of actions taken to achieve information superiority of national military strategy through influencing adversary's information and information systems and, at the same time, defending your own information and information systems." (Zavadski, 1996).

Panarin distinguished two key elements in information warfare (*protivoborstvo*): info-technical (information systems or *sistemy sviazi*, telecoms and Electronic Warfare) and info-psychological (influencing public opinion and psychology of ruling elites). Interestingly, Panarin considered China as a world leader in information warfare and claimed that the term 'information warfare' appeared first in China back in 1985. The Chinese approach combines both ancient and modern. Panarin quotes Sun Tzu that the best policy in war is to capture a country intact as destroying it on the battlefield is 'too easy': "Ultimate excellence lies not in winning every battle, but in defeating the enemy without ever fighting". According to Panarin, modern Chinese military adopted information doctrine developed by the Soviet chief of General Staff Marshal Ogarkov (1977-84), which did not take root in the USSR but was adopted by the Chinese military thinker Wang Pufeng. According to Panarin, the toolkit for psychological warfare has not changed much in time and includes disinformation, gossip (*slukhi*), propaganda etc. What makes modern warfare different is the technical delivery means of global mass media and satellite TV when foreign leaders can address targeted population of other countries directly.

Zinoviev identifies *zapadnizatsiya* (westernisation) as a Western information warfare tactic which was employed in time of peace to promote superiority of Western way of life in order to subjugate non-Western people around the globe. He states that the West targeted the USSR as a Communist state but instead destroyed Russia:

> "The bomb of *zapadnizatsiya* detonated in Russia and caused unprecedented destruction not only in state structures, economy, ideology and culture but in the fabric of society. No conquest or weapon could have achieved so much in such a short period of time and on such a scale in the past. ...Communism was the target but Russia was killed. The West achieved the greatest victory in human history with this weapon defining, in my opinion, future social evolution for centuries to come". (Zinoviev, 1995).

Assuming that society could be understood as a self-learning information system, Rastorguyev suggests his own definition of information warfare as actions aiming at causing material loses through information application and gaining advantage in sharing limited material resources. Society as a self-learning information system can win the war if it can identify which incoming information or 'encoding' is useful and which would lead to destruction. Rastorguev suggests a wining algorithm that can ensure victory over adversary through mapping of information, which looks like a methodology of time-tested KGB 'reflexive control' technique adopted for the information age:

1. Identifying key basic elements of adversary's information system space;
2. Identifying key characteristics and potential of adversary's basic elements within the information system;
3. Modelling possible reaction of basic elements to different incoming 'coding' information;
4. Selection of the most desirable reaction of the basic elements;
5. Preparation of societal space where these basic elements of public opinion exist;
6. Execution of the most desirable scenario.

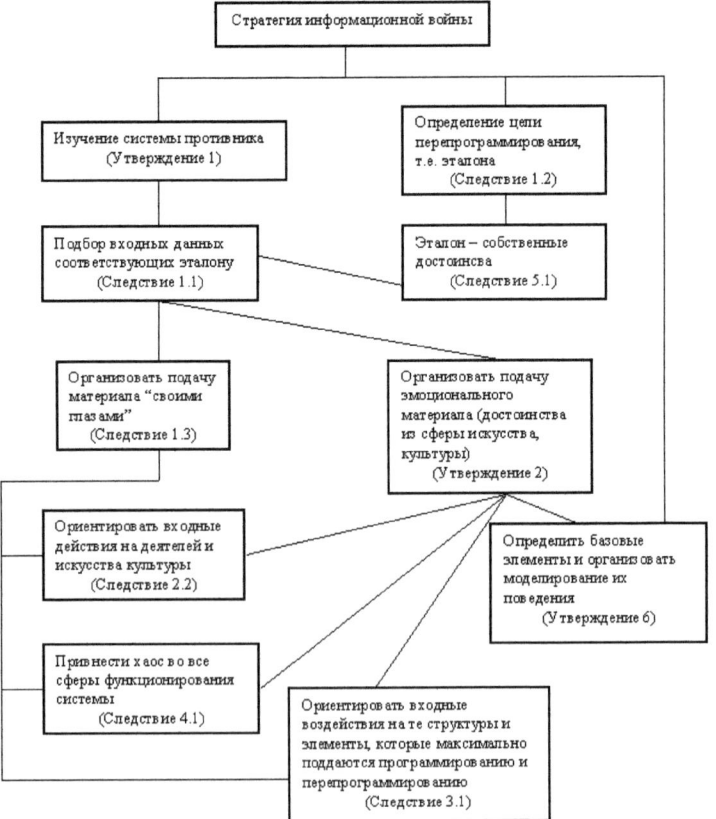

Rastorguyev's algorithm was designed for both information warfare planning as well as identifying whether the host society is under attack from an alien information system. However, his mathematical modelling shows that it is impossible to identify whether a society is under information warfare attack because incoming flow of information is constant. Therefore, he implies information warfare is perpetual and could be detected only from post-event results of destruction i.e. when it is too late to react. These results are similar to the aftermath of any war:

1. Death and emigration of local population;
2. Destruction of industrial base and reparations;
3. Loss of territory (at least partial);
4. Political dependence on victorious powers;
5. Rapid demilitarisation with either cuts in military personnel or ban on independent armed forces;
6. Brain-drain and loss of technological competitiveness.

Rastorguyev formulates defeat of society as an information system in algorithmic terms as following:

1. Steady loss of information system capacity, loss of societal structures and elements; degradation of system to the degree when it becomes harmless to the victorious power;
2. Society is engaged in activities in the interest of victorious power that were unnatural previously. In other words, society as a defeated information system, is responding to encoding information pre-programmed by the victor (like a computer might run a malware programme instead of a legitimate one);
3. Defeated information systems gradually become a functioning part of the superior system acting according to the algorithm of the victor;

Considering that outcomes of conventional war and information war are the same, i.e. forcing the victor's will on the target population, the latter is more economical and therefore could be waged permanently without much expense associated with traditional kinetic energy. Rastorguev agrees with Ovchinski that Western computer modelling techniques of potential social developments are, in fact, tools of information warfare (Ovchinski, 1997, P.69). The battlespace then is the mass media space conducted through active and convincing language. Society can lose the war in the mass media space when it abandons its own language and culture i.e. dies as an independent information system. So, what can such 'infected' societal system do if it is re-programmed for self-destruction? Rastorguev indicates that the only tactic to survive information warfare is in 'irrational behaviour' as a recovery strategy. In practical terms such irrational behaviour of defeated societies is causing permanent upheaval: "Irrational behaviour is chaos, aimless riot, it is terrorism". Considering that superior information systems depend on their digital economies, the most efficient terrorist attack should aim at data centres and first of all at digital banking platforms. Disrupting a major bank by hitting its data centre with "microwave radiation weapon can cause a systemic crisis of entire financial system of developed countries by destroying public confidence in contemporary technology of monetary market". However, the most effective offensive information warfare tactic, according to Rastorguev, is triggering self-destructive programmes (algorithms) within any given information system. This requires a number of steps:

1. Reconnaissance and mapping of mechanisms that activate already existing societal programmes
2. Identifying self-destruction programme (-s)
3. Developing a particular information weapon system suitable for the target
4. Deployment of information weapon system on the target

Rastorguev considers his information warfare strategy to be a universal algorithm in perpetual current war of civilisations where the West in general, and the USA in particular, are waging war against the rest of mankind for access to limited natural resources on the planet. Information warfare therefore is "always exclusively offensive and only offense can win the war". Rastorguyev's elaborated information warfare theory is widely referred in Russia as a key foundation work, especially due to extensive mathematical modelling supporting his arguments. His book *Information War* was recommended for publishing by the Security Committee of the State Duma of the Russian Federation and the Military technology department of the Russian Engineering Academy as "the most competent and comprehensive work on this subject". In return, Rastorguev acknowledged that it was "his duty to express gratitude to the staff of the Security Council of the Russian Federation, the Public Relations Centre of the Federal Security Service of Russia and the Security Committee of the State Duma of the Russian Federation" for their contributions and feedback on his earlier work".

The new edition of Russian Doctrine of Information Security signed by President Putin in December 2016, retained key assumptions from 2000 edition and provided additional legal and material foundations for information 'counter-measures' that were justified by increasing foreign 'offensive operations' against the Russian Federation (Putin, 2016). It also reflected experience from its ongoing campaign in Ukraine and envisaged improvement of the Russian Armed Forces' capacity for information warfare through perfection of "systems that ensure information security of the RF Armed Forces, other troops, military formations and agencies, including forces and means of information warfare", through regular training and exercises (the Doctrine, IV, 21 b). In February 2017, Defence Minister Sergey Shoigu reported to the Russian parliament that he added information warfare troops to the RF Armed Forces saying that "Propaganda should be smart, competent and effective". The head of a defence affairs committee in the Russian Duma, Ret. Gen Vladimir Shamanov, informed that troops' task will be to protect the national defence interests and engage in information warfare". (The Hill, 2017)

Ukrainian-Russian armed conflict (2014-) as a test case of Russian information warfare tactics

Putin's attempted annexation of Crimea in 2014 became a test ground of newly developed Russian information warfare and new generation warfare tactics and allowed recreating methodology, evolving application and preliminary results. Deceptive and distractive tactics of the so-called "little green men" successfully prevented the Ukrainian armed forces from resisting military invasion and the takeover of peninsula, prompted local Crimean population largely to submit to the annexation scenario and sufficiently deceived the international community into de-facto accepting fait accompli. Gen. Philip Breedlove addressed the NATO summit in Wales (September 2014) saying that "Russia is waging the most amazing information warfare blitzkrieg we have ever seen in the history of information warfare." Interestingly, Putin's spokesman, Dmitriy Peskov, admitted in March 2016 that Russia is in "a state of information war with Anglo-Saxons" and Western media (Peskov, 2018). According to a 2017 British intelligence parliamentary report, Russia continued conducting "information warfare on a massive scale" in Ukraine while denying it and pretending to be a party to peaceful settlement within the Minsk process (UK Parliament, 2017).

So, how did the Russian military do according to their own standards and methodology? Applying Rastorguev's model of information warfare would suggest that Kremlin successfully preplanned and executed five out of six stages that meant to achieve destruction of the Ukrainian state and its territorial partition in one form or another (Bender, 2014). Russian government-controlled media successfully introduced *casus belli* for invading Ukraine, starting in Crimea, by portraying post-Yanukovych government in Kyiv as a US sponsored right-wing junta persecuting the Russian speaking population in Eastern Ukraine. Between 70 and 90% of the Ukrainian Security forces and military personnel in Crimea defected to the Russian side, following their Commander-in-chief and Minister of Defence who both fled to the occupied Crimea and then Rostov in the RF. The Ukrainian army and security services were massively demoralised by infiltration from Moscow in previous years after Kremlin forced President Yanukovych to nominate Russian citizens in key security and defence posts.

Stage six meant to complete the division of Ukraine into a pro-Russian, industrialised *Novorosiya* and the predominately de-industrialised rest of Ukraine but the plan stalled everywhere else outside of Crimea. As former acting Ukrainian president Oleksandr Turchynov pointed out, the Russian military invasion in Donbas was repelled in early 2014 not by the regular Ukrainian army but civilian volunteers who took up arms and opposed Russian 'hybrid forces' taking advantage of post-Maidan security vacuum (Turchynov, 2018).

"Putin miscalculated. He thought he had destroyed the Ukrainian army, special services, the economy. But he did not think that a volunteer movement would be created in Ukraine, when lawyers, teachers, students from the Maidan would go to the front line. The creation of a voluntary movement at that time was a key moment that frustrated Putin's plans. It was the volunteers who kept Putin away and saved the situation, since they gave the army the time to recover, to buy bullet-proof vests, helmets, weapons," the Ukrainian National Security and Defence Council secretary said, recollecting, in 2018. As British military adviser Glen Grant pointed out, the Ukrainian Army's success in containing Russian aggression in Donbas owned more to the bravery of its soldiers and commanders on a tactical and operational level than the actions of the Ukrainian General Staff (Grant, 2018).

In Rastorguyev's terms, Ukrainian volunteers "rioted" against the self-destructive information system imposed by Moscow on the Ukrainian state during President Yanukovych years. Once 'Infowar blitzkrieg' proved to be insufficient in mainland Ukraine, the Kremlin escalated the conflict with more conventional warfare tactics, conducted via DNR / LNR proxies in Donbas and supported by Russian regular troops, 'complimenting' information warfare. Accordingly, the Kremlin had to complement its initial strategy to deceive, distract and destroy Ukraine as a state by constant denial of its actions in Donbas, presenting itself as a neutral party to the so-called Minsk process of peace-negotiations. Ultimately the Russian information campaign in Ukraine turned out to be only partially successful if victory is confirmed when "defeated information systems gradually become a functioning part of the superior system acting according to the algorithm of the victor". When it comes to the Ukrainian society as a 'self-learning information system', it has become much more unified in the face of Russian aggression and therefore remained undefeated by 'the new generation' warfare. By summer 2021, Moscow realised, that unless attacked by conventional armed forces on a massive scale, Ukraine would not come under Russian control in the immediate future. Ukrainian legislation referred to Crimea and parts of Donbas as "temporary occupied territories" and Russia as the "aggressor state", insuring bitter anti-Russian sentiment in Ukraine for generations to come.

Conclusions

Russian information warfare theory and doctrine emerged from the ruins of the USSR as a defensive tactic against perceived Western (largely US) clandestine war on the CIS countries. As soon as President Putin managed to rebuild confidence of the Russian military through successful campaigns in the North Caucasus, including Georgia (2008), Russian Information warfare doctrine was upgraded to the offensive form that was tested in Ukraine (2014), Syria (2015) and the USA during the 2016 presidential elections. The Syrian campaign crystallised also the new ratio of non-kinetic and kinetic elements of the military intervention as 4:1 with 4 being allocated to the Information warfare, including psychological operations, cyber warfare and propaganda[5] (Fainberg, 2017). Partially successful, Russian 'new generation warfare' was complemented with 'political war' tactics, continuously denied in the international public discourse. President Putin's announcement of a new range of nuclear super-weapons in March 2018 should be considered as part of evolving information warfare and escalated confrontation with the USA. Moscow's calculations that Russia cannot lose the war with the West (in Peskov definition with the "Anglo-Saxons") as long as it is undeclared and plausibly denied could lead to miscalculations and escalate the confrontation dubbed as Cold War 2.0. Looking at the success and failure of the Russian information warfare theory and application from its own point of view will help to

---

5 On Russian 'new generation warfare' in Syria see: Sarah Fainberg (2017) Russian Spetznaz, contractors and volunteers in the Syrian conflict. Notes de l'Ifri, Russie. Nei. visions. No. 105.

predict its likely evolution both in doctrinal terms and on a tactical / operational level. The key conclusion is that, in Russian military thinking, information warfare must be always offensive and therefore acquires perpetual character (both in cyber-physical and cognitive domains).

Such conclusion was supported by grim assessments of the likely Russian strategy in Ukraine where President Putin found himself "hopelessly entangled in his own web of deceit and appears to be stuck fast in eastern Ukraine, unable to either advance or retreat (Dickenson, 2017). He may no longer be able to win the war, but he dares not risk peace". Lt. Gen. Ben Hodges, former commander of U.S. European Command's Army component (2014 – 2017), predicted correctly in 2018 that Kremlin's objectives in Ukraine as partition and isolation: 'The next phase will probably be land and sea operations that would eventually secure maybe even Mariupol but continue to take the Ukrainian coastline and connect Crimea back up to Russia along the Sea of Azov. It's not going to happen in the next six months, but this is the direction they're taking until they completely own the Black Sea and they've isolated Ukraine." (Hodges, 2018).

Takeover of Ukraine, however, was only part of the grand strategy designed in Moscow to confront the West as per the new rather pessimistic Russian view of the world. The Kremlin developed a much more ambitious strategic plan to restore Russian super-power status in what Moscow viewed as new multi-polar world. As we can see from the following chapter, the Russian leadership published a number of strategic documents that indicated a major collision course with the West. Meanwhile, most Western capitals were still hoping to restore profitable business as usual and limited its response to the Russian takeover in Crimea with 'smart' but symbolic sanctions. (As AFU discovered in 2022 some French and German companies continued to supply military technology to the RF Armed Forces despite sanctions as was uncovered on captured Russian armour).

The misunderstanding of the causes of conflict on both sides would lead to further escalation despite mutual rhetorical calls for de-escalation.

The new Russian National Security Strategy (NSS), signed by President Putin on 2 July 2021, openly accused the West in interfering in Russian internal affairs "using indirect methods aiming to create long-term instability in the RF" and undermining Russian international image: "Information campaigns are undertaken in order to create a hostile image of Russia" (NSS, 2021, P.6).

A former acting Director of the Defence Intelligence Agency David Shedd observed that despite "defensive" NSS wording Russia is aspiring to become a cyber superpower and the US should adopt a holistic approach to information security in which both the Russian technical and cognitive components need to be addressed: "The Kremlin does not limit itself to hacking our computers — it also wants to hack our minds with the goal of disrupting our democracy, polarizing society, sowing fear and doubt" (Shedd, 2021).

7. Moscow's Black Magic or Reflexive Control in Russian Active Measures

Chapter 7 looks at the Russian reflexive control theory and its application in the so called 'active' or 'supporting' measures that are the substance of the Information war. While neither theory nor 'active measures' methodology are new and show clear continuation from the Soviet military science, their application to the contemporary Russian 'hybrid manoeuvre' represents a new development. In fact, there is almost no academic research on the application of the reflexive control theory in the contemporary Russian Information manoeuvre, so uncovering this Moscow's 'black magic' is important for understanding how the targeted societies could protect themselves.

Since 1960s, the Soviet General Staffs utilised application of reflexive control theory both for deception and disinformation purposes in order to influence and control enemies' decision-making process, for:

> "Control of an opponent's decision, which in the end is a formation of a certain behavioural strategy on him *through reflexive interaction*, is not achieved directly, not by blatant force, but by means of providing him with the grounds by which he is able logically to derive own decision, but one that is predetermined by the other side. This can be achieved:
> - By applying the pressure of force
> - By assisting the opponent's formulation of an appreciation of the initial situation
> - By shaping the opponent's objectives
> - By shaping the opponent's decision-making algorithm
> - By the choice of the decision-making moment
>
> (Lefebvre & Smolyan, 1968).

In other words, 'reflexive control' operators seek to cause "targets to act in the interests of propagandist without realizing they have done so" (Paul and Matthews, 2016). In practical terms, this method represents "a means of conveying to a partner or an opponent specially prepared information to incline him to voluntarily make the predetermined decision desired by the initiator of the action," (Thomas, 2004, P.237). On a tactical level, "actions may include transferring a particular framing of the situation to the target's mind, creating a goal for the target, and playing to what targets believe (or want) to be true in order to use their own responses to amplify the effect of an initial action" while strategically "the aim is not only to manipulate perception or to persuade an audience on a particular issue (as in traditional propaganda) but to influence opponents' entire framing of reality, distort their decision processes, and exploit their resulting actions" (Kilcullen, 2019 P.156).

The Five-Days war between the Russian Federation and Georgia (2008) could be a good example of using reflexive control on both a conventional, tactical and strategic level. Deep-shaping operations by the Russian military using South Ossetian proxies helped to frame the understanding of the Georgian leadership and prompted a potentially fatal predetermined decision i.e. starting a military incursion into a separatist territory in order to stop shelling by the separatists. After months of conflict escalation by the South Ossetia militia, President Saakashvili walked his armed forces into a trap at a time (7 August 2008) when his framing of reality *vis-a-vis* Russia and the West was distorted by means of Russian deception that encouraged over-confidence in dealing with South-Ossetian separatists. Once the tactical move by the Georgian forces provided *Casus Belli* for the Russian government, prepositioned 58th combined arms Army started to pour in via a mountain tunnel (8 August 2008) and achieved a sound political-military victory only in five days.

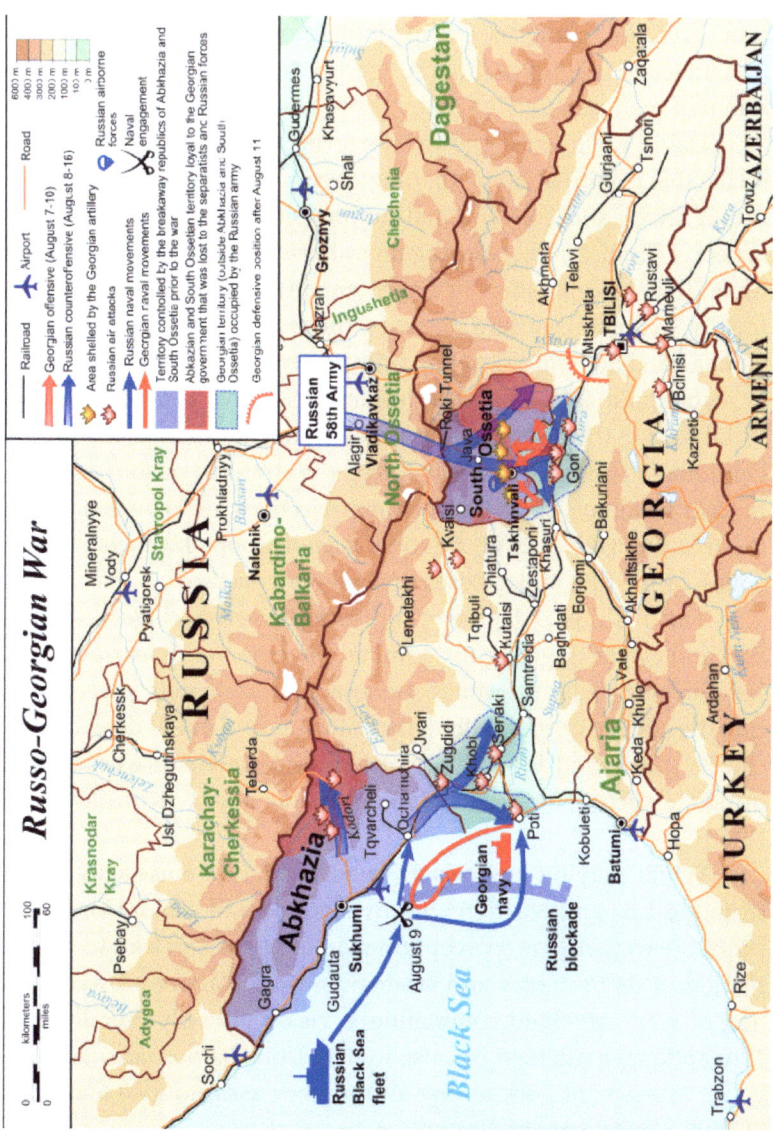

How could Russian deception be so effective, considering that Georgian leadership knew about potential threat? As the Russian scholar S.A.Komov explained 'reflexive control' aims at "distraction, overload, paralysis, exhaustion, deception, division, pacification, deterrence, provocation, suggestion and pressure, all with the intent of manipulation" (Komov, 1997, 18-22).

David Kilcullen suggested the term of 'liminal warfare' to describe this combination of shaping cognitive operations before the actual attack and conventional military invasion: "This temporal aspect of liminal manoeuvre again underscores the primacy of OPE (operational preparation of environment) or shaping operations. Ideally, in liminal warfare, actors on the ground (such as Ukrainian, Abkhazian and South Ossetian militias, Syrian refugees in the Arctic, cyber militias and patriotic hackers in Estonia and Georgia, and WikiLeaks in the case of US election hacking) act as adjuncts to conventional shaping by combat forces (or strategic posturing using nuclear weapons) so that campaign objectives are achieved before the first airstrike goes in, the first assault troops hit their landing zones, or the first tank crosses the line of departure".

This requires a degree of sophistication in intelligence collection and clever targeting as "Liminal phenomena sit astride a sensory or perceptual threshold. Actions that are barely perceptible, ride the edge of observability, or oscillate in and out of detectability can be considered liminal operations, and a style of warfare that optimize such operations is liminal manoeuvre." (Kilcullen 2020 P.150)

While playing enemies is ancient art that Russia inherited from the Tzars' interaction with Byzantine and Golden Horde empires, overreliance on 'perception management' can lead to confirmation of its own bias and strategic miscalculations as well. The 'fog of war' can cloud commanders' vision not only literally on a conventional battlefield but also in the virtual battlespace. If intelligence assessment goes wrong and the key assumptions about the enemy are fundamentally misconstrued, then all reflexive control interactions could lead to no more than self-deception. In 1980s, the Soviet leadership was seriously preoccupied with their assumption that the US is preparing to launch a pre-emptive nuclear strike against the USSR. Avoiding this misperceived threat became the main effort for the Soviet military machine that directed its misconceived 'active measures' towards a non-existing threat. It would not be surprising if the current Russian military leadership were in a similar confusion about American threat in the cognitive (*konstientalnyi*) battle space. Jonson observed that the "most central political elites and military theorists expressed the view that war was going through a fundamental transformation because non-military means were so effective that they should be considered violent, the boundary of war and peace was blurring. Non-military means were becoming four times as important as military means, representing their own form of warfare, and the effectiveness of non-military means constituted a cardinal change in the concept of war and its knowledge system." (Putin 2012; Gerasimov 2013; Gareyev 2013; Gerasimov 2013).

For instance, one of the key Russian information warfare theorists V.Lepskiy arrived at a conclusion that the American Government is playing its NATO partners using 'reflexive control' in order to 'programme' them to be passive executioners of decisions taken in Washington. According to Lepskiy, Nato is a good example how 'controlled chaos' technology is being used in Western hybrid warfare against the allies in order to destroy targeted societies as 'subjects of international order' and turn them into 'controlled objects'. The US, allegedly, deconstructed NATO and then re-created the organisation in such a way that member-countries have been relegated to a status of 'objects' serving a hidden American agenda. Lepskiy assumes that the US did what Russia would do i.e. it used 'reflexive programming' for imposition of pre-determined beliefs, points of view, opinions and psychological constructs leading 'subjects' to internalise and accept suggested new norms of behaviour. As a result of alleged 'programming', NATO countries were turned from founding members and, therefore, 'objects' of the international treaty, into 'passive subjects' that cannot develop on their own. "These considerations confirm that NATO evolved in the last 30 years in a totalitarian cult organisation with fundamental re-assembly of its subjects" (Lepskiy 2019). Lepskiy's article, *The problem of assembly of subjects in Information wars*, was published in a new peer review specialist journal, *Information wars* (*Informatsionnye voiny*) — established specifically to perfect Russian understanding of information warfare theory and must be symptomatic of a conspiracy mindset of its editors. Lepskiy specifically refers to the veteran Soviet mastermind of reflexive control theory Vladimir Lefebvre's concept of 'controlled confrontation' when two leading subjects of confrontation conspire to create a secret virtual union ('collective subject') that would always win against third party subjects. The later simply cannot see this virtual union (effectively conspiracy) and can only plan against two visible original subjects of information confrontation. Third party subjects of information confrontation become victims of reflexive control as they do not realise the objectives of the secret 'virtual collective subject', existence of which they do not acknowledge. Lepskiy claims that such 'controlled confrontation' model was proposed by Russia to the US in 2000 against third party terrorist threats but it was not accepted. In other words, creation of conspiracy between Moscow and Washington to control unsuspecting partners and competitors was suggested, so that the USA can 'save face' at the time when unipolar world is changing into a multipolar one for the sake of achieving "harmony for international community". But why would not Washington enter into such a conspiracy with Moscow as proposed, allegedly back in 2000? Lepskiy implies that the US administrations preferred to employ the 'controlled chaos' methodology to the rest of the international community members independently. Therefore, Russia should propose "asymmetrical response to 21 century's information wars and facilitate re-assembly of subjects of international development" in order to liberate countries from American control. It is assumed that the mankind is ready for such a "meta-system civilization shift" as Western technology-based civilization exhausted its development based on chasing capitalist profits in a consumer-oriented society, which is destructive to human and bio-environment. This Western civilizational crisis also became the main cause of all information wars. Hence, Russia can lead to a new world order based on socio-humanitarian civilization where humanity will become a subject of its own destiny. "The suggested approach represents Russia's asymmetrical response to information wars of the 21st century. It will ensure Russian leadership of planetary social change enabling to re-assemble subjects of international development and create conditions of dynamic and secure development of Russia as well as the international community" (Lepskiy 2019 P.7.) Although such an argument is well elaborated and supported by scientific method of analysis with references to the existing in Russia body of knowledge, the findings might simply have nothing to do with reality as recognised in the West. In other words, Washington could have refused the Russian approaches to enter into a conspiracy (assuming they took place) because two parties lack common understanding of the realities of international globalized society. Or as Angela Merkel summarized the results of her conversations with President Putin regarding RF's invasion in Ukraine: "He is (lives) in another world". (The Week, 8 Jan 2015) As Vladimir Putin is fluent in German and Merkel is fluent in Russian this was not a language issue but culturally determined worldview problem. As Johnson suggested "A key insight from the field of strategic culture points out that communities with different cultures and values can look at the same thing but interpret it very differently" (Jonson 2020). Likewise, "strategists and their institutions cannot be accultural and hence will continuously perceive and interpret the material realm culturally" (Poore 2003, P.282). Russian cultural mindset is inclined to explain the outside world through the prism of conspiracies that partially could be explained by Russian historical experiences e.g. Rasputin and the Romanov's family, Lenin's conspiracy with the German General staff, Stalin's obsession with Trotskists conspirators and Jewish "doctors-saboteurs" (*vrediteli*), Khruschev's coup against notorious Stalin's henchman Beria, Brezhnev's coup against Khruschev, GKChP putsch against Gorbachev, Prigozhin's mutiny against the Kremlin etc. Likewise, Russian understanding of the outside world being significantly influenced by conspiracies also translates into Russian understanding how the international community is organized. Russian culture as many others is self-referential and the Russian worldview paradigm is "idiosyncratic, reflects a strong cultural imprint, and needs to be analysed in the context of its strategic culture" (Adamsky 2018, P.35). Considering that Russian military strategists believe that they are in a state of information war with the Anglo-Saxon West, the culturally conditioned perception of cognitive "*konstientalnaya*" struggle becomes paramount. As Berzins argued "the Russian view of modern warfare is based on the idea that the main battlespace is the mind and, as a result, new generation wars are to be dominated by information and psychological warfare, in order to achieve superiority in troops and weapons control, morally and psychologically depressing the enemy's armed forces personnel and civilian population" (Berzins 2014, P.5). Reflexive control of the enemy's mind is the principle Russian weapon in this battlespace, so it is only natural for the Russian ruling elite to assume that Washington is using the same weapon as well. The battle of minds therefore takes place among "smoke and mirrors" where images of adversarial actions are often perceived through imagined shadows. Just like "beauty is in the eyes of the beholder", so are the adversarial hostile acts in the eyes of reflexive control operators. As a result, they end up living in a world of their own, as observed by Angela Merkel.

As a consequence, Bartles concluded that "now the Russian military is seeing war as being something much more than military conflict", so, for instance when it comes to sanctions "while the West considers these non-military measures as way of avoiding war, Russia considers these measures as war" (Bartles 2016, P.34). As stated by Valeriy Gerasimov the "line between peace and war is blurring" and that "non-military forms and means of struggle have received an unprecedented technological development and acquired a dangerous and sometimes violent nature" when "hybrid actions are actively used by the US and NATO countries in the international arena". In other words, Russian military elite perceives that emphasis in methods of confrontation is shifting toward the use of political, economic, diplomatic, information, and other non-military measures implemented with the inclusion of the protest potential of the population" (Gerasimov 2017). If the West is fighting this "hybrid war" and Russia fights back in a similar way, then it is only natural to assume that from the Russian point of view not using reflexive control would be an obvious weakness for Washington and hence the conclusion that it does. Retrospectively, the US Strategic Initiative (SDI), nicknamed in 1980s as the "Star

Wars" programme, is now perceived in Russia as an example of Washington using reflexive control against the USSR. For instance, the head of the Security Council Nikolay Patrushev stated in an interview that, once the CIA identified the Soviet Union's economy as its weakest link, the US Government designed a two-pronged approach to reduce the USSR's income from foreign trade and to increase its expenditures; SDI was a key initiative in the later aspect. The USSR was manipulated to enter the arms race, exhausted its economy and collapsed (Yegorov 2014).

The Russian elites must understand that "trickery and lies" in war could lead only to a destructive spiral for all parties. And it is in this context the West should have seen proposals from President Putin to sign an agreement with Washington on information security and cyber (Kremlin Website September 2020). This was not the first proposal for Washington from Moscow to come up with a strategic framework that would introduce transparent rules in "information space" similar to those that the US had with the USSR in nuclear armaments. One of the reasons why both parties so far were unable to agree even on the terms of such agreements is again cultural: "information space" in the Russian understanding includes the cognitive sphere, which it does not in the Western understanding (Giles and Hagestadt 2013, P.7). In other words, the Russian understanding includes the content of information, whereas the Western focuses on the infrastructure for its transmission (Giles, 2012, P.27). In the absence of such agreement with the US, Russian military planners can only continue plotting new stratagems in the mind battlespace as suggested for example by Lepskiy.

Application of Reflexive control in the Russian information manoeuvre in Ukraine

While Russian-Georgian Five-Days war was a good example of Russian reflexive control in a conventional armed conflict, the role of reflexive control in information manoeuvre is better understood in case of Ukraine where Russian-Ukrainian war is ongoing since 2014. While Crimean takeover was clearly well-prepared military operation (with medals minted before troops move) Moscow still needed a Casus Belli for invading a "brotherly" state of Ukraine which sovereignty and territorial integrity Moscow guaranteed under the Budapest Memorandum signed when Ukraine agreed to give up its Soviet nuclear arms arsenals in 1994. Once President Yanukovych fled Kyiv in January 2014 and the speaker of Ukrainian parliament became a temporary head of state organizing a new presidential elections, the Kremlin activated its invasion plans following a classic justification when war is presented as "peace enforcement". The Washington Post provided quotes suggesting how "Putin's attack on Ukraine echoes Hitler's takeover of Czechoslovakia" while Russian liberal opposition TV Rain station screened detailed documentaries with both Russian and German experts comparing similarities in Putin's and Hitler's rhetoric justifying military aggression as "defence" (TV Rain 2022, Current Time 2022, Radio Liberty 2022).

Just like Czechs never threatened ethnic Germans in historical Sudetenland, Ukrainians never threatened Russians in Crimea, and especially could not discriminate Russian language usage. If anything, ethnic Ukrainians that constituted approximately one fourth of the population could not exercise their own right to be educated in Ukrainian language as only one school offered teaching in Ukrainian for a population of two and half million residents in 2014. Similar situation was in many Donbas towns where for instance in Donetsk also only one school taught in Ukrainian before the conflict started. Therefore, the Casus Belli did not have justification and the "threat" had to be invented using "active" or "supporting measures" based on reflexive control during covert stage of developing "hybrid war" scenario. This was effectively achieved by perception management. Once Russian flags appeared on the streets and squares of Eastern Ukrainian cities, they naturally provoked negative reactions from Ukrainian radical right organizations that until then struggled to achieve any significant support in Ukrainian society.

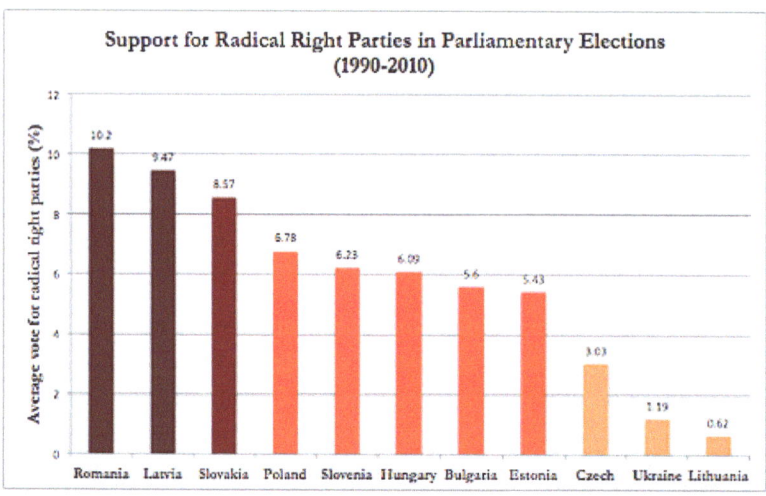

Support for Radical Right Parties in Parliamentary Elections (1990-2010)

"Svoboda" and similar right-wing organizations active during the Revolution of Dignity in Kyiv managed to organize transportation of its supporters to Symferopol (capital of Crimea) to show support for local activists objecting to pro-Russian separatists organized there by covert Russian operatives. Ukrainian nationalists traveling from Lviv to Crimea was a perfect picture to support Russian narrative about Neo-Nazi junta from Western Ukraine taking over Kyiv and over cities, hence justifying Russian intervention to "protect" ethnic Russians. The strange tendency for Ukrainian "nationalists" to turn up in the right place, at the right time and in the right kit (e.g. carrying inflammatory slogans and fire torches) where Russian TV crews prepositioned their cameras became a subject of commentary in the Ukrainian press since 1990's. It was an open secret that Ukrainian radical right organizations were penetrated and manipulated by the Ukrainian (and likely Russian) security services. This fact was partially confirmed by one of the Ukrainian Security Heads Valentyn Nalyvaichenko who recognized that SBU supported "Trysub" organization (Fakty, 2015). Culturally, Ukrainians almost expected KGB successors organizations to behave in such way, as fighting Ukrainian "bourgeois nationalism" was an enduring Soviet propaganda cliché. In fact, creating fake front organizations was well publicised and celebrated in Russia as a KGB method since its inception in 1920's as VChK:

> "The fake White Russian counterrevolutionary organization (Trust) would serve, throughout the entire Cold War, as a towering example of an intelligence tactic with a bright future: a way to subvert, support and exploit political activists, "like a sticky fly strip attracting insects", as the official SVR history put it (Rid, 2020 P. 32)

This partially explained low public support to the Ukrainian right-wing organizations as citizens simply expected a trap in any organization openly proclaiming ideas of Ukrainian "nationalism" to recruit members. For example, 2014 parliamentary elections, that took place when the country was already at war, showed that only 1% of population in Ukraine voted in support of right-wing organisations, which is significantly less than in many EU countries in peace time.

Press reports suggested that Viktor Yanukovych even sponsored radical right "Svoboda" in the parliamentary elections of 2010, so he could run for presidency using presence of right-wing MPs in the Ukrainian parliament as a manufactured threat to rally Russophone Ukrainians in his support (Zaxid.net, 2011). In other words, this was a known political strategy used by both Russian and Ukrainian politicians to manipulate feelings of ordinary citizens in order to create artificial strife in society and then offer themselves as "guarantors" of civil peace. Svoboda and the Right Sector activists did not let Yanukovych down in March 2014 and turned up on time in front of the Russian TV cameras anticipating arrival of Ukrainian "Neo-Nazis" as was promised. Agent provocateurs on both sides organized conflicting meetings and pushed for violent clashes carefully recorded on Russian TV and used to create, develop, and amplify the narrative of fear about Ukrainian Neo-Nazi junta taking over Ukraine and Crimea.

The most brazen and well covered case of a Russian propaganda fake was documented by the EU counter-disinformation centre and known as a crucified boy story run by the Russian state TV1 in July 2014. Journalists interviewed a local resident from temporary occupied Ukrainian town Sloviansk who pretended to be an eyewitness of a heart-breaking story about a three-year-old child being crucified by Ukrainian nationalists in front of his mother's eyes on the main town square. Journalists from Russian Novaya Gazeta debunked the story within 24 hours, and the Ukrainian Stopfake.org think-tank provided evidence as well but fake news travelled faster: "The story was one of the peaks of the Kremlin-orchestrated campaign targeted at inciting hatred against Ukrainians. Sadly, none of the stories that proved that the story was a fake could have reached such a massive audience as a TV channel with supposedly 250 million viewers worldwide" (EUvsDisInfo July 15, 2016).

Simultaneously with the "Nazi" narrative, Russian propaganda does not shy away from using antisemitic attacks against the Ukrainian leadership and personally President Zelensky. Ex-president of the RF Dmitriy Medvedev compared Volodymyr Zelensky with WW2 Jewish Nazi collaborators. High ranking Russian official implied that Ukraine's head of state resembled a Jewish Sonderkommando, a reference to those incarcerated Jews forced on pain of death to dispose of gas chamber victims during the Holocaust. According to CEPA analysis "Russia plays antisemitic card in Ukraine" revealing the real face of its leadership:

> "The Putin regime has once again consciously sought to instrumentalize Russian and Ukrainian antisemitism for its own purposes, as Medvedev's article makes all too clear. Indeed, there is no more odious attack on a person of Jewish origin, like Zelenskyy, than the accusation of Nazi collaboration. The fact that one of Putin's inner circle reaches for language from the ancient armoury of hate to indicate the strength of the Russian state's emotions simply underlines the flaming antisemitism at the heart of the country's government and the nature of its representatives" (CEPA, 2021).

This was also classic KGB style "active measures" using well tested method of fake anti-semitism and neo-nazi activism employed against NATO countries in Europe during the Cold War. Both KGB and Stasi treated Germany's WW2 past as "an open wound that presented a prime opportunity: by portraying West Germany as riddled with neo-Nazis, the Soviets could weaken

Bonn, alienate it from its French, British and American allies and occupying authorities, delay or prevent German rearmament, paralyze the political debate, and drive a wedge into NATO". Sergey Kondrashev, who later briefly headed the KGB's active measures shop, recalled that Russian intelligence instigated right-wing "hate sessions against Jews" and arranged the desecration of Jewish grave sites. Another former senior KGB officer, Oleg Kalugin, who served in New York in the early 1960s, recalled in his memoirs how his agency executed the operation, and specifically referred to smearing swastikas on three synagogues: "My fellow officers paid American agents to paint swastikas on synagogues in New York and Washington. Our New York station even hired people to desecrate cemeteries," he wrote, referring to American Jewish leaders," Kalugin added... describing the activity as "maintaining anti-Semitism" (Jonson, 2020 P.132).

In October 1985 KGB conducted also a similar operation against Jewish and Ukrainian diasporas in the US code-named "Operation Payback". Liubomyr Lutsiuk published documents confirming how "often repeated allegations about "thousands of Nazi war criminals" from Ukraine hiding in North America were nothing but a ruse, one intended to foment friction between these two communities" (Luciuk, 2021, P.9).

Portraying Ukraine as a neo-fascist state since 2014 played another important role — managing perception of international opinion and demobilizing international support to the real victim of the armed aggression. While international journalists were struggling to distinguish truth from fiction, in a country that few previously visited before, Russia created enough confusion to achieve new facts on the grounds i.e. occupy Crimea and legitimize its take-over by organizing a fake referendum. By the time the fog of cognitive warfare settled down, President Putin was firmly in charge of Crimea as "liberator" without Ukrainian troops firing a shot. As Kilcullen observed acting on the edge of perceptual threshold between covert and over action is key in information hybrid or "liminal" manoeuvre:

"Russia's ability to ride the edge, operating right on the detection threshold—taking sufficiently few and ambiguous actions to achieve core political objectives, but not enough to trigger a military reaction—is an example of what I earlier called a "liminal manoeuvre"... Liminal phenomena sit astride a sensory or perceptual threshold. Actions that are barely perceptible, ride the edge of observability, or oscillate in and out of detectability can be considered liminal operations, and a style of warfare that optimize such operations is liminal manoeuvre (Kilcullen 2019 P.150).

Casus Belli in Crimea became only an opening move in the Russian-Ukrainian war taking place in the cognitive battlespace since 2014. Open Source Intelligence think tank Belingcat's investigation found out that "Azov"—one of the Ukrainian voluntary battalions fighting Russian aggression in 2015—was penetrated by "esoteric" Russian neo-Nazi organization Wotanjugend whose leaders 'fled' Russia to 'fight' Putin's regime in Donbas.

In other words, while Russian Cossacks in Crimea perpetuated the narrative of fighting neo-fascists in Ukraine their Russian neo-Nazi colleagues engaged in 'false-flag' neo-Nazi activities in Ukraine.

In January 2019, a convicted Russian neo-Nazi Levkin described Wotanjugend as mostly an online entity, one that was "way too hardcore to be represented in the public sphere" as an active physical organization. In its place, Levkin argued that "there's already a movement that deserves support…I'm talking about [Azov's] National Corps". https://www.bellingcat.com/news/uk-and-europe/2019/09/04/the-hardcore-russian-neo-nazi-group-that-calls-ukraine-home/

Alexey Levkin seemed to belong to a new breed of professional "elite neo-Nazi avant-garde" offering services on-demand who, according to Bellingcat, travelled around Europe with his Wotanjugend band and sold songs on various online platforms. Similarly, the Azov movement leader Andriy Biletsky did his MA thesis on the history of Ukrainian insurgency army before joining Tryzub in his native Kharkiv and becoming a nationalist leader / politician himself (DSnews.ua , Accessed on 10 Jan 2023).

Injecting Neo-Nazi poison into Ukrainian resistance movement where was little or none, of course, is essence of reflexive control manipulation method. The real significance of infiltrating a para-military Ukrainian formation was not its subversion (as in conventional armed conflict) but its exploitation in the information war i.e. in cognitive battlespace. When Ukrainians, weary after six years of armed conflict, elected President Zelenskiy in June 2019, his key campaign promise was ending the war in eastern Ukraine. Since assuming office, Zelenskiy has embarked on a plausible, but politically risky strategy to break the stalemate. In the hope of finding a solution, the president agreed in late September to a simplified version of the 2015 Minsk peace accords. As a result of Minsk group negotiations, troops pullback in a frontline village of Zolote and two other towns in Luhansk region were agreed under so called Steinmeier formula with Russian led separatists on 1 October.

Almost immediately, several dozen veterans from Ukraine's Azov battalion, made their way down to Zolote to protest against Mr Zelensky's "confidence-boosting" measures on the front line. Acting in front of the TV cameras, Azov veterans set up an impromptu "last checkpoint" in the town, claiming that they would not abandon it, hence, stopping the Ukrainian troops pullback. President Zelensky felt compelled to travel to Zolote to confront the veterans in person and their encounter was filmed covertly with footage released online. (Independent, 2019)

https://www.independent.co.uk/news/world/europe/east-ukraine-zelensky-honeymoon-impeachment-trump-latest-a9176536.html

In an emotional standoff, Mr Zelensky appeared struggling for arguments with war veterans and agitated. The whole episode seemed to be staged in order to discredit the Ukrainian leadership and reinforce the new Russian narrative: the new President is weak and real power in Ukraine still lies with out-of-control neo-Nazis.

Online channel "Russia Insight" commented: "Ukrainian Neo-Nazi Azov Militia Refuses To Listen To Orders Of Zelensky and Reject Minsk Peace Deal And Promises There Will Be no peace in Donbas".

The deliberate and almost immediate video "leak" online, illustrates how decades old reflexive control technique can be boosted on a much bigger scale thanks to the internet technology:

> "The internet facilitated acquiring and publishing unprecedented volumes of raw files at a distance and anonymously. Automation helped to create and amplify fake personas and content, to destroy data, and to disrupt. …And the darker, more depraved corners of the internet offered teeming petri dishes of vicious, divisive ideas, and guaranteed a permanent supply of fresh conspiracy theories. All this took place while many reporters, worn down by breakneck news cycles, became more receptive to covering leaked, compromising material of questionable provenance, and as publishers recycled unoriginal, repetitive content. The end effect was that a significant and large portion of the disinformation value-creation chain was outsourced to the victim society itself, to journalists, to activists, to freelance conspiracy theorists, and to a lesser degree, to researchers". (Rid, 2020 P.434).

In case of Crimea and Donbass, reflexive control operators affected not only the unsuspecting war veterans to act in a pre-determined manner but also international media workers to report it—perpetuating the required narrative and making them part of the (Russian) information warfare effort. GRU campaign to influence 2016 elections in the US used the same technique on American audiences. An anti-Hillary Clinton Facebook advert featuring images of Devil and Jesus wrestling over the US elections campaign is a good example that was covered in the US Congress official report (Data source: "Social Media Advertisements," US House of representatives, Permanent Select Committee on Intelligence, May 10, 2018; the "Satan v Jesus" ad is at (US House of representatives, 2018).

The actual Facebook post placed by the St Petersburg based Research Internet Agency generated only 14 clicks and its impact was negligible. However, once American mainstream media "uncovered" the story—the ad became a sensation that delivered intended result of dividing public opinion along political lines:

> "The New York Times ran a front-page piece that described the Satan vs. Jesus arm-wrestling image, and scores of news outlets, national and international, picked up the illustration from there. (The online headline was "Russia-Financed Ad Linked Clinton and Satan"; the print issue story was headlined, "Congress Scolds Tech Companies over Russia", The New York Times, November 2, 2017, p.A1). The ad had become an icon—but not for effective disinformation. The ad epitomized how mainstream press coverage *generated* the actual effect of disinformation operation. ...Social media had actually *increased* the significance of traditional journalism as an amplifier of disinformation operations (Rid, 2020, P.408).

Both examples from Ukraine and the US also illustrate the New Generation Warfare principle of perpetual character of information war. Similar Russian techniques were used in the US 2020 elections when FBI identified that both Russian and Iran obtained data of American voters to improve civilian audience targeting. American media reporting still helps Russian reflexive control operatives to obtain access to hearts and minds of US voters:

"Any random five-minute segment on virtually any US cable news network since 2016 elections illustrates this process in action: the American news media have deepened, extended, and amplified the destabilizing effect of what was, at best, a modest Russian influence operation as described in the 2017 US intelligence assessment, the 2018 indictments of the IRA and other Russian actors, and the Muller report. (Office of the Director of National Intelligence, "Assessing Russian Activities"). Cable news personalities have prattled on for literally thousands of hours about what they frame as a past Russian information operation from 2016—whereas, seen from Russia, the operation is ongoing and is now self-sustaining thanks to these same news personalities. This is classic reflexive control: the very commentariat that endlessly laments the operation has now itself *become* the operation". (Rid quoting Diane Choticul, The Soviet Theory of Reflexive Control in Historical and Psychocultural Perspective: A Preliminary Study, technical report (Monterey, CA: Naval Postgraduate School, 1986), https://apps.dtic.mil/dtic/tr/fulltext/u2/a170613.pdf.)

The armed conflict in Eastern Ukraine have been kept simmering just below the perceived threshold of conventional war in the "separatist" enclaves in order to avoid additional international sanctions, while also allowing the time for a full-blown covert information warfare across entire territory of Ukraine to achieve the desired outcome in defeating Ukrainian sovereignty. Russian conventional forces in and around Donbas represented a conventional threat that complemented the battle in cognitive space in Kremlin's hope to win the war without sending tanks in:

"And ideally, if critical objectives can be achieved before conventional operations begin—if the purpose of combat becomes merely to consolidate gains already won by a liminal warfare (e.g. by a resistance movement, cyber militia or subversion) campaign coordinated with political warfare and conventional shaping—then conventional combat operations are no longer decisive and may never need to occur. If an enemy can be beaten before the first tank rolls, the tanks may never need to roll at all (Kilcullen, 2019, P. 160).

Russian approach to liminal or hybrid war in Ukraine shows on the one hand a long-term strategy on behalf of the aggressor but on the other, Moscow's relative weakness against surprising resilience of the Ukrainian society. Moscow's "active measures" employing reflexive control over Ukrainian political groups, deep infiltration of Ukrainian security structures and systematic shaping actions provided enough leverage to maintain the pressure, so Kyiv could not end the war on its own terms. However, that leverage was not enough to impose its own political will on Kyiv. In this respect, cognitive fight in information battle space yields results in the real world:

> "Active measures will shape what others think, decide and do—and thus change reality itself. When victims read and react to forged secret documents, their reaction is real. When the cards of an influenced parliamentary vote are counted, the result is real. When social media users gather in the streets following a bogus event invitation, the demonstration is real. When readers start using racial epithets offline, their views are real. These measures are active, in the sense that operations actively and immediately change views, decisions and facts on the ground, in the now" (Rid 2020 P. 429).

The key conclusion from this chapter suggests that the reflexive control method in Russian information warfare cannot be underestimated as something ephemeral, restricted to the Russian "near-abroad" and, therefore, not very relevant for the West. This point was made with a military precision by Chief of British Army Defence Staff General Mark Carleton-Smith:

> "Mistaking hybrid warfare as an ancillary branch of twentieth century conflict misses the scale of the challenge. Beginning with the click of a mouse, from cyber-attacks to disinformation campaigns, the adversary is manoeuvring across multiple domains uncontested. Failing to recognise and respond to these realities not only risks strategic defeat before the first shots are fired, it has the potential to upend the international order" (RUSI 2018).

At the same time, Russian failure to take over Ukraine using hybrid warfare between February 2014 and February 2022 clearly showed the limits of the information manoeuvre on its own against well informed and anticipating adversary and prompted a full-scale invasion on 24 February 2022.

8. The Full-Scale Invasion of Ukraine and Lessons Learned for NGW

Chapter 8 brings together all elements of the Russian New-Generation Warfare to see how they were applied in Ukraine in order to estimate the measurement of success from the Russian point of view. It shows that despite close historical ties with Ukraine, military strategists in Russia miscalculated Ukrainian resistance potential, which ironically suggests a lack of cultural understanding and intelligence-assessment failure. The very fact that Russia instigated a full-scale military intervention in Ukraine and still could not win in this armed conflict after a decade illustrates the limitations of "hybrid warfare". It also suggests that relative success of the takeover in Crimea is only possible if the targeted society is not prepared for a hybrid scenario and the decision-making time for politicians to react is disastrously long, allowing the aggressor to accomplish the occupation almost without firing a shot. In other words, deception on such a scale was possible only by abusing the benefit of the doubt in international opinion, a benefit that is no longer extended to the Russian Federation leadership.

When Russian Chief of General Staff Valery Gerasimov declared in 2016 that the nature of the New Generation Warfare waged by the West has changed, he gave the following reasons: "The rapid development of science and technology is changing the nature of armed struggle" wherein "the main way to achieve the goals is remote, contactless impact on the enemy due the massive use of high-precision weapons from air, sea, and space", while "colour revolutions' are used as the main means [...] to a non-violent change of power". In other words, he indicated the two pillars of the NGW: precision weapons, representing Regular Warfare (RW), and Information War leading to nonviolent change of political regimes representing Unconventional Warfare (UW). Russian CGS thinking indicates acceptance of previous assumptions made by Gen Slipchenko about NGW as the Sixth-Generation warfare: "In sixth-generation warfare there is only one goal: directly destroy the enemy's economic potential and to do so from a distance. The information component and high-precision weapons were the two pillars of noncontact warfare" (Slipchenko 2002). A major innovation of Slipchenko's thought in Russian military science was his view that "information had become a destructive weapon just like a bayonet, bullet or projectile" (Slipchenko 2005, P. 33), while considering the nature of war to be constant, he suggested adding a component that traditionally has been seen as nonviolent—information—as a destructive weapon.

The current ruling Russian elite is convinced that the West is at war with Russia, which is non-kinetic at this stage but nonetheless is as potentially destructive in its consequences. It does not mean that the Russian ruling elite expects a new Blitzkrieg of NATO forces towards Moscow. As Maj. Gen Vladimir Slipchenko, deputy head of the Academy of Military Science, indicated, the new generation of warfare (the sixth) has evolved: "no one is ever going to come to us by land again" (Slipchenko 2005, p. 13). He saw that if war reached Russia, it would be via "aerospace and the strike will come from precision weapons" and that "this strike will not be against the armed forces, if they are still in the old generation, but against the national economy".

President Putin developed his conspiratorial view of the warring West and justified his latest invasion in Ukraine as a legitimate pushback to the Anglo-Saxon subversion:

> "The United States and its vassals grossly interfere in the internal affairs of sovereign states by staging provocations, organising coups, or inciting civil wars. [...] But a model of this sort can only be retained by force. Therefore, the collective West is deliberately undermining the European security system and knocking together ever new military alliances. NATO is crawling East and building up its military infrastructure. They need conflicts to retain their hegemony. It is for this reason that they have destined the Ukrainian people to being used as cannon fodder. They have implemented the anti-Russia project and connived at the dissemination of the neo-Nazi ideology. Under these circumstances, we have taken the decision to conduct a special military operation in Ukraine, a decision which is in full conformity with the Charter of the United Nations [...] to ensure the security of Russia and its citizens and protect the residents of Donbas from genocide. (Putin's speech at the 10th Moscow Conference on International Security, Kremlin.ru, 16 August 2022).

Putin's conviction was echoed by other senior officials in his administration. Deputy Head of Putin's Administration Sergey Kirienko mentioned to the Voice of America: "We understand very well that we fight in Ukraine not with Ukraine, and of course, not with the Ukrainians. The entire NATO block is fighting with Russia on the Ukrainian territory using Ukrainians" (Voice of America, 11 Aug 2022). Former President Medvedev reinforced such a view by implying that the West is at war with Russia: "Russia is conducting a special military operation in Ukraine and is attaining peace on our terms. The (Western) goal is the same: to destroy Russia" (D. Medvedev, Deputy chairman of Russia's security council, Sky interview on 8 Aug 2022).

Any Western attempts to 'defuse' Russian warmongering by giving reassurance of peaceful intent to the current leadership in the Kremlin would be rejected as military deception. As Russian Defence Minister Sergei Shoigu said back in 2019, Russia was once deceived by the West in the early 1990s and Moscow's slow realization of this deception cost it dearly: "We failed to understand it in time, and for a very long time we did not understand the essence of what was happening around us. The task that they (the West) set for themselves — the task of destroying and enslaving our country. Like what has in fact been done with the 'Young Europeans' and former Soviet republics" (Defence Minister Sergei Shoigu, Moskovskiy Komsomolets 22 Sep 2019).

Numerous representatives of more conspiratorial minded Russian elites, including in academia, claimed since the mid-1990s that information weapons equal to a devastating bomb had been used to destroy the USSR, and the RF was a collateral "kill" (Zinoviev, 1995). In other words, Unconventional Warfare in the form of an "Information Weapon" is presented as much more powerful and long lasting than the outdated and ineffective 5th-generation conventional weapons of Regular Warfare, including nuclear bombs.

Russian ruling elites chose to draw such conclusions from the demise of the USSR and therefore their belief in the changing nature of war is based on their social and political experience, albeit wrongly interpreted. The Russian Ministry of Defence devised a response to the perceived threat by 2011 by adopting a counter-information war strategy when it stated that new rules of international engagement require steering the adversary towards a self-destructive course of action during peacetime via "destabilizing the society and state, and forcing the state to make decisions in the interests of the opposing party (Oborony, 2011)" — a classic reflexive-control approach but applied as an information manoeuvre. In this respect information warfare signifies the return of what George Kenan defined back in 1948 as a "political war", when he encouraged U.S. leaders to disabuse themselves of the "handicap" of the "concept of a basic difference between peace and war" and to wake up to "the realities of international relations — the perpetual rhythm of struggle, in and out of war" (Jones, 2018). When the Chief of the Russian General Staff presented the new Defence Doctrine in 2013, he emphasized the lessons learned from Western "hybrid warfare" i.e. the Arab Spring and other "colour revolutions" in Eastern Europe. In Gerasimov's words, the modern military conflict is an integrated application of military, political, economic, informational, and other powers by state and non-state actors to achieve their political goals (Gerasimov, 2013). According to General Kartapolov, Conventional Warfare amounts to no more than 10% of the NGW and victory could be achieved without a shot fired. The latter conviction is partly based on the Russian army's experience in the occupation of Crimea in 2014 and therefore informs both their doctrine and practice. The fact that the Russian reinvasion of Ukraine in February 2022 was not designed as a 5th-generation operation in Conventional Warfare but as a "special military operation" conducted in an Unconventional Warfare form only confirms such thinking.

    The Royal United Services Institute concluded in their 'Preliminary lessons in conventional Warfighting from Russia's Invasion of Ukraine: February-July 2022' that "Russia's strategic objective in its invasion of Ukraine was the subjugation of the Ukrainian state. This plan was formulated first and foremost by Russia's special services and a core group within the presidential administration, supported by senior officials in the Ministry of Defence" (RUSI, 2022, p. 7). Data, provided to RUSI analysts by the Ukrainian General Mykhailo Zabrodsky, suggested that:

the Russian military suffered from major errors of judgement made by the Russian leadership, special services and the presidential administration. The force also suffers from structural weaknesses in its force design and training system that created specific operational and tactical frictions. It was also a force designed for 'active defence' strategic military operations, not for a large-scale attack on another sovereign country without full wartime mobilisation. (Ibid., p. 46)

Despite partial success of the Russian deception plan as to where the main effort would be, overall intelligence assessment about the Ukrainian military and civilian resistance potential were completely flawed. RUSI arrived at a conclusion that the tiny pool of personnel involved in informing Putin's key decisions contributed to a range of false assumptions that appear never to have been challenged and which subsequently unravelled the Kremlin's initial plans because of a successful Ukrainian defence of the capital. Once a lightning takeover of Ukraine failed, the Russian military realised that they were not prepared for a conventional war against a Western-supported AFU on such a scale and were forced to withdraw so as to refocus their efforts on a smaller scale in southeastern Ukraine.

How does all this inform Western (NATO) perceptions of Russian militarism and their response strategy? NATO General Secretary Jens Stoltenberg expected Russia to be on a long-term collision course with Europe:

> "The regime in Moscow wants a different Europe. It wants to control neighbouring countries, and it sees democracy and freedom as a threat. This puts Russia in a position of constant conflict with the West. So even if this war ends, the problems in our relationship with Russia persist. The Ukrainian forces have inflicted heavy losses on Russia in Ukraine. But Russians have once again shown a willingness to take great risks and endure great human losses. They have already mobilized 200,000 extra troops. In addition, we know that they can acquire a lot of new material. And perhaps most importantly, there is no indication that Russia's ambitions have changed" (Stoltenberg, 2023).

Long-term confrontation with Russia affects NATO's broader de-escalation strategy, which is based on applying pressure to the RF by non-military means. The UK's Integrated Operating Concept25 (IOpC25) provided a conceptual framework of operating in the era of Constant Competition: Protect, Engage, Constrain and Fight (PECF) against peer-like nation-state competitors (https://assets.publishing.service.gov.uk/government/uploads/system/uploads/attachment_data/file/1014659/Integrated_Operating_Concept_2025.pdf).

However, the nature of war is considered to be constant and refers predominantly to Regular Warfare, i.e. mass violence inflicted on the opposing armed forces after declaration of an openly armed conflict. Therefore, the main concern within the IOpC25 framework is to avoid escalation of the conflict to the fighting stage (i.e. RW) on the assumption that such can quickly progress towards a nuclear confrontation with Russia. Information manoeuvre within IOpC25 is based on a traditional understanding of information operations as a supporting function to RW during armed conflict, i.e. in 'wartime'. However, in theory IOpC25 allows engaging the enemy in view of constraining and deescalating (off-ramping) in 'peacetime', yet no relevant permissions are available as NATO's PsyOps doctrine does not permit adversarial targeting in 'peacetime'. This represents a conceptual misalignment of Western information manoeuvres as deescalation tools applied in peace time when the Russian main effort is waging a 'pre-emptive' Information War against the West. This conceptual NATO weakness vis-à-vis Russian subversion is not new and was observed by Evgeniy Messner back in the 1960s when he wrote that the West relies on traditional technological superiority over its adversaries and therefore cannot win the Soviet subversive war:

> "SHAPE (The allied HQ in Europe) conducts only military intelligence against possible adversary and does not possess departments for psychological, political and social etc. intelligence. As long as SHAPE commanders perceive war as merely a war they will inevitably be defeated as they miss the point. Future war will be either mutiny growing into a subversive war, or war changing into a subversive war or simply mutiny but never only a war". (Messner 1960, p. 132)

Such conceptual misalignment could lead potentially also to a Western wasted effort by countering the Russian RW element that might not be in Russian plans at all. In other words, NATO's response aims at preempting fighting the last (Cold) war of the 5th generation, while Russia has already been fighting a war of the 6th generation. This potentially provides Russia with comparative advantage as the Kremlin can save resources required for a 'total war' with the West and get better returns on investment from an Information War and/or subversion. A declassified US intelligence report alleged that Russia has covertly spent more than $300m (£260m) since 2014 to influence politicians in more than 24 countries (BBC, 14 Sep 2022), including in the USA where the Kremlin tried to influence the 2020 presidential election:

> We assess that Russian President Putin authorized, and a range of Russian government organizations conducted, influence operations aimed at denigrating President Biden's candidacy and the Democratic Party, supporting former President Trump, undermining public confidence in the electoral process, and exacerbating sociopolitical divisions in the US. (US National Intelligence Council, 15 March 2021)

With the exception of the US, most NATO members can ill afford simultaneous funding of both pillars of 6th-Generation warfare: Regular Warfare high-precision weapon platforms and Unconventional-Warfare information tools / resources. Western understanding of war as mostly regular kinetic warfare determines the prioritisation of expensive RW projects leaving minimal funding for UW and Information Warfare. In other words, Moscow can overmatch NATO in information manoeuvres because it is the Russians' main effort while NATO underinvests in Information Warfare and cannot use it efficiently due to artificial cognitive (conceptual) and legal constraints of using UW in 'peacetime'. As Natalya Bugayova indicated: "Russian President Vladimir Putin's center of gravity is increasingly his ability to shape perceptions and create the projection of a powerful Russia based on limited real power" (Bugayova, 2022, P.9).

Messner's insights informed by his military service on both the Russian (WW1) and German (WW2) sides retain their relevance half a century later as NATO has not changed its doctrine in principle from the 1960s. He believed that the USSR used conventional forces as a deterrent but conducted its war with the West using unconventional tactics. "Red Moscow keeps a large army just in case.

They have much more flexible arms than a regular army — the mutiny i.e. implementation of Mao's military theory." Following the dissolution of the USSR, the West simply declared victory in 1991 but failed to learn the lessons from the Cold War, even though the Soviet Union remained undefeated militarily. The Kremlin gave up the fight in 1991 following internal ideological logic — it was not coerced by the adversaries. In other words, the West did not impose its will on Russia (a clausewitzian concept of victory) but rather the Kremlin lost its will due to lack of self-belief in the Soviet socialist economy model.

Meanwhile, Putin's Russia simply picked up the fight where Gorbachev left it after Perestroika. According to Messner, both Moscow and Beijing historically benefited from Western cognitive aberrations that explained the tremendous success of Mao's military theory. In other words, a 'decadent' West and especially the US, misperceived "co-existence" as some sort of peace not war and therefore did not resist such "peace". "The East and all other destructive forces engage, with the same seriousness, in conducting co-existing forms of warfare that the West understands as peace. Carl Jaspers failed to improve Western cognitive ability when he wrote that "the Soviets conduct 'Cold war' under disguise of co-existence". Marshal Vasilevsky once said that "The Cold war is a continuation of war by other means (i.e. continuation of the Great Patriotic War from 1941-45)" (Messner 1960, P.155). The 2022 Russian manual for mobilised soldiers going to fight in Ukraine openly states that the special military operation is the Great Patriotic War 2.0 against NATO (Razumov 2022, p. 8).

If the lessons for NATO were identified sixty years ago, were they actually learned? Bugayova's report was published by the US funded Institute of Studies of War in 2022:

> The West's partial effectiveness in countering the Kremlin reflects blind spots in the West's conception of the Russian challenge — rather than Putin's strengths. Putin is resilient in a number of ways, but weak in others. The converging global crises of 2020 have worsened Putin's weaknesses. He often achieves gains by slim margins. His behaviour is sometimes counterproductive to his own objectives. He nevertheless remains on a trajectory to gain more influence in his core theatre and beyond. The West misperceives Putin's areas of strength and weakness, as well as his threat perceptions. As

a result, Western states periodically and inadvertently empower Putin or miss opportunities to counter him. Putin is thus gradually winning a war of wills that many in the West do not even recognize is occurring. (Bugayova, 2022. p. 15)

According to Messner, Mao's principle of swarm mosquito tactics was always at the core of the Mutiny (subversion) war: "You must attack like mosquitos attack a giant—bite, poison; suck the blood out until he will collapse". This goes back to the Sun Tzu theory that good commanders win the war without engaging in a battle, take cities without a siege and destroy kingdoms without fighting on battlefields. The West did not comprehend this war while Mao excelled at such a reversed warfare: "You must confuse the enemy's commanders in order to achieve victory—make them death and blind, polluting their eyes and ears. These are methods of psychological warfare". And this is how such war proceeds according to Messner: "Western military and political leaders stay deafened and blinded. They can only sigh observing multiplicity of 'criminal cases' and do not understand that this is a subversive war, the mutiny war" (Messner 1960). Here is Bugayova's take on it from 2022: "The West's tendency to ignore Russia's trivial activities is another major opportunity for Putin. Slow, under the radar creep, often at the tactical level, is generally how the Kremlin sets conditions for strategic gains" (Ibid, p. 9).

In other words, despite all costly mistakes the only reason why Russia, like the USSR, gets away with its subversion of the West is reluctance of the latter to adopt its military posture adequately, known as "defence pretence". What could be, however, an adequate NATO response? According to the NATO Secretary General there are three lessons from the Russian invasion in Ukraine:

- First, we need to invest even more in defence. [...] With troops at higher readiness. Modern equipment. And well-trained soldiers. It costs money.
- The second lesson is that it is dangerous to depend on authoritarian regimes. It was not long ago that many believed that buying gas from Russia was purely a commercial matter. The reality is that it is a political issue. It is about our

safety. Business is also politics. We must not repeat this mistake with other authoritarian regimes. Not least China. We must not make ourselves vulnerable by becoming too dependent on critical raw materials and products. We must not export technology that can, in turn, be used to threaten us. We must not lose control of critical infrastructure, which is essential both for civil society and for military activity. Like ports, railways, telecommunications—5G networks. We will still trade with China. But it must be done in ways that do not undermine our security. It is a shared responsibility. The authorities have a responsibility to establish rules and frameworks. But the companies also have an independent responsibility to exercise due diligence. We cannot take as a starting point that every profitable project should be carried out—just because it is profitable. Short-term economic interests cannot trump fundamental national interests. It is often said that war is too serious to be left to generals. Similarly, we can say that business activities are too serious to be left to business leaders alone.

- The third lesson is that authoritarian regimes have increased their cooperation. A couple of weeks before Russia's invasion of Ukraine, President Putin and President Xi met in Beijing. They announced a strategic partnership with 'no-limits'. Russia and China train and operate more together militarily. They have an increasing economic cooperation. And China has not condemned Russia's invasion of Ukraine. On the contrary, they promote the Russian narrative, which puts the blame on NATO. And China has for the first time backed Russia's demand that NATO closes its door to new member states. Not only is the cooperation between Russia and China strengthening, but Russia is also building closer ties with other authoritarian regimes, such as Iran and North Korea. These are different regimes. But they have in common that they promote an alternative world order. They advocate values that violate our belief in freedom and democracy. In a more dangerous world, it is all the more important that we, who believe in freedom and democracy, stand together. (Stoltenberg, 2023)

Let us consider how Putin's regime achieved its tactical victories in Ukraine by 2022 and what NATO could learn from Russia's strategy since 2014. First, Western 'smart' sanctions clearly failed to deter Putin from a full-scale invasion of Ukraine in 2022. Even though Russia is the de-facto most-sanctioned country-in-the-world, Russian state budget revenues in 2022 increased in comparison with 2021. It was not difficult for Moscow's planners to predict that any major war scenario in Europe would spook Western markets and as a result the price of energy resources and food stocks would go through the roof. According to Sergey Aleksashenko, former deputy chairman of the Russian Central Bank in Yeltsin's governments, despite economic setback the Kremlin still has enough money for war in Ukraine:

> according to the Russian government and the Central Bank Russia's GDP fell by 3% in 2022. However, overall Russian budget revenues from oil and gas sales increased by 34% in comparison with 2021. Gazprom's and the Russian budget became net beneficiary in terms of cash flow: rapid price increase on the European markets (460% in comparison with 2021) increased revenues so much that the government introduced a windfall tax (for three months) taking 1,25 trillion roubles from Gazprom that increased the annual state budget by 5% (in 2022).

Despite all the blast and fury from NATO countries, the Kremlin's line that sanctions harmed the West more than Russia might be plausible at least in the short term. The RF's real military spending could have benefited from the energy prices hike:

> Continuing warfare caused a fast increase in Russian military expenditures. Ministry of finance estimated in September 2022 that they will increase by 1,45 trillion Rubbles (45% increase to what was planned) by the end of 2022. Considering that all defence expenditures in the Russian budget are classified it is impossible to trace how the money were allocated, […] so we should not be surprised if eventually overall military expenditures related to the aggression in Ukraine would turn out to be even higher. (Aleksashenko, 2022)

The Russian budget passed by the Duma on 26 October 2023 boosted defence spending in 2024 by 70%, which constituted a third of overall spending, which in turn is three times more than Russia spent on defence in 2021. As President Putin boasted, the Russian budget showed a surplus of 660bn roubles in the last quarter of 2023—all fuelled by energy exports and internal military industry growth. Russia is shifting successfully to a long-term war economy with the finance ministry projecting GDP growth in 2024 at 2.3% (*The Economist*, 2023).

Meanwhile, despite unprecedented solidarity and economic support, Ukrainian GDP fell by 30,4% in 2022, according to the Ukrainian ministry of economy (me.gov.ua 2023). Considering that most of the actual fighting and destruction takes place on Ukrainian territory, the losses to the Ukrainian economy run into trillions of dollars, while the Russian economy is relatively intact. Taking into account that the Russian government benefitted from the full-scale war in Ukraine economically, the strategy to engage and constrain Russia through sanctions could be said to have backfired.

Another lesson from 2022's invasion is that the Western policy of soft 'smart sanctions' was not complemented by sufficient military posture that would deter Moscow. President's Biden outright refusal to engage Russia's militarily in Ukraine meant that the West also lost the benefit of strategic deterrence, giving the Kremlin guarantees that it can act with impunity.

Perhaps the most unexpected lesson for both Russia and the West was dogged Ukrainian determination to mount effective defence despite perceived Russian military overmatch and Western reluctance to come to the aid of Kyiv militarily. One of the reasons why Ukraine withstood Russian invasion and successfully counter-attacked is that the Ukrainian General Staff managed to keep its defence plans secret from both foes and allies, and this provided Kyiv with the benefit of surprise. President Zelensky's refusal to flee Kyiv as suggested by the Americans in the opening days of a Russian blitzkrieg seemed to be a surprise for both Washington and Brussels. Former UK Prime Minister Boris Johnson admitted that all his defence intelligence assessments suggested that Ukraine would surrender within days, and that assumption was widely shared within the EU:

> When the 115 battalion tactical groups were assembling on the border, it was a horrific scenario. I was getting daily reports from defence intelligence in

the UK. I have to tell they were not optimistic about Ukraine's ability to hold on. To be absolutely frank, they thought they told me that it would be over in a matter of days! [...] My people kept saying 'It's going to be over soon.' I kept saying 'Yeah, but you don't understand that Ukraine will fight'. I had this argument with other European friends and colleagues. (Johnson, 2023)

For Moscow, Zelensky's standoff and the AFU's successful counterattack around Kyiv and south-eastern Ukraine was a total surprise they could not comprehend. What was meant to be a Special Military Operation, i.e. a special forces operation, turned into conventional warfare they did not plan for. Western military and financial aid coupled with Ukrainian mass mobilisation and effective military command meant that by the end of summer 2022 the AFU could launch a successful counteroffensive liberating most of Kharkiv and Kherson regions i.e. nearly half of the territory captured since February 2022. Ukrainian defence forces were fighting a truly 'total war' with massive popular support. Such determined resistance triggered cognitive dissonance of the Russian invading force when Russian troops realised that they are not perceived as 'liberators' but as unwelcome enemies. Hence, what was meant to be a triumph of the Russian 'military glory' turned very quickly into gruesome killing, raping, and pillaging. Considering that war in Ukraine was covered by mainstream and social media 24/7 the large volume of the war crimes committed was often recorded and broadcast in real time. CCTV footage of Russian soldiers looting shops, corporate premises and private dwellings went viral around the world and the Russian narratives of 'liberation' were quickly discredited, at least among Ukrainian and Western audiences. Even the Russian 'fifth column' in Ukraine—the Ukrainian Orthodox Church under Moscow Patriarchy—had to distance itself from Russia rather than embrace the *"Russkiy Mir"*, declaring its formal independence from the Russian Orthodox Church in May 2022.

Kyiv easily won the information manoeuvres in 2022, turning the tables on Moscow and setting preconditions for a counterattack in summer 2023. This, of course, came at a terrible price for Ukraine with 15 million citizens becoming IDPs and refugees scattered in various countries of Europe and North America. Both the Russian and Ukrainian armies suffered over 100,000 casualties each, killed and injured by the end of 2022 (BBC 19 Nov 2022). This figure more than doubled to half a million killed and injured on both sides by the end of summer 2023 (*New York Times*, 2023) and reached a million by 2024 (WSJ, 2024).

However, overall Ukrainian human, economic and welfare losses were disproportionally higher. Russian missiles and drone attacks against Ukrainian national critical infrastructure and civilian areas literally struck Ukrainian towns and villages into darkness. The very same missiles that Kyiv handed over to Moscow as part of a Budapest memorandum agreement on nuclear disarmament in exchange for security assurances were used to bombard Ukraine in 2022-23.

In this respect, RF Armed Forces followed the logic of sixth-generation warfare where missile strikes were aimed first of all against the national economy in order to undermine popular support for the national government. The problem for Moscow tuned out to be with the Ukrainian population's resilience and determination coupled with patriotism regarding the military command that all combined to outperform typical government resilience. Relatedly, as per the subversion scenario, Ukrainian governmental structures and security services were compromised with Russian infiltration and subversion long before the full-scale invasion. After all, subversion of the Ukrainian government must have been a main effort for the Kremlin that ran extensive networks in preparation for the Special military operation. Putin's personal friend, Viktor Medvedchuk, a former head of Ukrainian presidential administration under President Kuchma, was effectively Russia's unofficial ambassador / governor in Ukraine until his arrest in 2022. Security services of Ukraine published a video statement from Mr Medvedchuk suggesting that some of his subversive activity in Ukraine was in collusion with the previous presidential administration of President Poroshenko (Security Service of Ukraine, 2022). The Kremlin's strategy since 1991 was always to subvert first the top leadership in Ukraine either by joint oil and gas schemes or direct infiltration of presidential administrations. President Zelensky's administration did not seem to be an exception considering allegations of direct collusion between top officials in his administration and the Russian intelligence services in so-called "Wagnergate" (Sukhankin, 2021). RUSI's 2023 report on the RF's unconventional operations provides a good insight into Russian penetration of top government channels, including via some key generals in the security service of Ukraine (RUSI 2023).

It is not impossible that President Zelensky did not flee Kyiv because he could not, due to the protective constraints placed by the top military command who had learned from experience in 2014 when the defection of the Ukrainian commander-in-chief caused a paralysis of national defence and security forces. RUSI confirm that decapitation of the Ukrainian leadership as well as regional levels was in the plan of the invading Russian force:

> The assumption appears to have been that Ukrainian government officials would either flee or be captured as a result of the speed of the invasion. It was also anticipated that shock would prevent the immediate mobilisation of the population, and that protests and other civil resistance could be managed through the targeted disintegration of Ukrainian civil society. To manage these protests Russian forces would be supported by Rosgvardia (Russian National Guard) and riot control units. Meanwhile the FSB was tasked with capturing local officials. The Russian counterintelligence regime on the occupied territories had compiled lists that divided Ukrainians into four categories:
> - Those to be physically liquidated.
> - Those in need of suppression and intimidation.
> - Those considered neutral who could be induced to collaborate.
> - Those prepared to collaborate.
>
> For those in the top category, the FSB had conducted wargames with detachments of the Russian Airborne Forces (VDV) to conduct kill-or-capture missions. (Ibid., p. 14)

Zelensky admitted in 2023 that no dialogue is possible with Putin's regime, which plotted to kill him personally and his family. According to the Presidential adviser Mykhailo Podolyak, President Zelensky had survived more than a dozen assassination attacks (CNN, 2023). More than four hundred Wagner mercenaries were reportedly in Kyiv in February 2022 with orders to kill Zelensky as part of Russian 'decapitation strategy' (Guardian, 2023).

This is another lesson for countries in the immediate neighbourhood with Russia such as Georgia, Moldova, Hungary, Poland, the Baltic States and Finland, that reveal the real face of 'Russkiy mir'. Once the 'liberator' troops roll over the border, the death squads follow. It would not matter if citizens caught up in the 'liberation' have previously loved great Russian literature, enjoyed Bolshoy ballet, and like the Pope Francis did, believed that the Russians are not capable of cruelty as they suffered so much in WW2 themselves. The death squads might not even speak classic Russian, might be unlikely to have read *War and Peace* and would not conduct interviews identifying political loyalties. They could speak any of the 35 regional official languages recognised in Russia, have hostile views of European 'satanic' culture in principle, or could be even guards of ex-jihadist Chechen warlords like those who tried unsuccessfully to hunt down President Zelensky in February 2022. Death squads rape and kill first and ask questions later—a clear continuity of practice from the 'Great Patriotic War' as this was much experience of WW2 in the Polish, Baltic and German populations during the invasion by the Red Army. Painful memories of civilians were repressed under Communism but never really erased from collective memory. Hence, it is not surprising that in 2022 the Polish government picked up on lessons from Bucha and acted on them immediately by changing its defence posture with rapid defence procurement programmes and the creation of new combined arms divisions on its Eastern borders.

That takes us to another important lesson from the AFU experience, namely that lessons must be learned rather than just identified, and adequate policies implemented. The AFU learned in 2014 that they should expect the Ukrainian leadership and security services to be penetrated by Russian intelligence and potentially be subverted when the enemy strikes. So, in anticipation of the 2022 invasion the defence preparations were ongoing despite President Zelensky appearing oblivious of imminent invasion in his speech on New Year's Eve 2021. He repeated his reassurances to the Ukrainian citizens that no war was to be expected a week before the large-scale invasion, and they should plan barbeques for the Easter celebration in 2022 (Ukrainska Pravda, 2022). There is no reason to doubt that Zelensky was sincere in his 'no war' belief, so was he a victim himself of successful Russian military deception? This might indeed be the case, considering that the Head of Ukrainian military intelligence Kyrylo Budanov stated (in October 2023) that he correctly predicted the day and time of the RF invasion and therefore the military were ready to fight (Budanov, 2023); Zelensky subsequently dismissed the head of Ukrainian Security Service Ivan Bakanov and the Prosecutor General Irina Venediktova citing high levels of penetration and treason within their departments that could explain Russian success in occupying large parts of Southern Ukraine unopposed. President Zelensky explained the dismissals in his video address on 17th July 2022: "651 criminal proceedings have been registered regarding treason and collaboration activities of employees of prosecutor's offices, pretrial investigation bodies, and other law enforcement agencies" (CNN 2022). Given such high levels of law-enforcement penetration and subversion, why did the "special military operation" has not been more successful and failed in its main objective to capture Kyiv and decapitate the Ukrainian leadership in February 2022?

In this respect Ukrainian military tactics, ironically, followed advice from Russian theorist Rasstorguyev, who claimed that the only way to win the clandestine subversion war against a superior enemy force is to do the unexpected, e.g. to engage in decentralised defence or to go on a riot creating chaos that the invading force cannot control or predict. Following such logic, the Ukrainian defence strategy incorporated arming of the civilian population — which had the underappreciated advantage of democratic societies that governments are not afraid of their own populations. Indeed, the Ukrainian volunteer army coupled with determined and well (partly Western) trained armed forces compensated for the security services' failures to prevent Russian subversion of the Ukrainian government that led to the rapid takeover of the entire region of Southern Ukraine including Kherson city. Ukrainian mass-resistance in the first weeks of the full-scale invasion allowed the AFU to regroup / redeploy and for Western aid to arrive, halting the Russian advance on the capital. Moscow's plan to stage a victory parade in Kyiv by the end of February 2022 backfired and led to a humiliating retreat from North-Eastern Ukraine as well as Kherson city.

The best the Russian government could hope for by February 2023 was to hold on to parts of the Luhansk and Donetsk regions as well as the left bank of the Dnipro River in Kherson, and Zaporizhia regions that could potentially constitute the Novorossiya—a separatist project promoted in 2014-2015. The Kremlin remained flexible with its plans in Ukraine as officially the "special military operation" only meant to "liberate" the people of Donbas. So, what are the lessons that the Kremlin could have learned from its 2022-23 full-scale invasion?

The answers to this question can inform our baseline understanding of how Russian military thinkers define their approach, preferably from a doctrinal point of view, which in turn will allow better understanding of lessons learned from this episode of the Cold War 2.0. Unsurprisingly, Ukrainian success on the battlefield using high-precision Western weapons and target acquisition capabilities confirmed Russian pre-existing fears that the USA and NATO are fighting in Ukraine using the new generational approach to war. On a strategic level, Russian analysts concluded that the traditional theory of deterrence, which had defined NATO's approach to the USSR for decades, has been replaced by the theory of preventive use of force (теорией упреждающих силовых действий). 'Global strike' is the key US concept underpinning this theory that envisages targeting of pariah states by high-precision non-nuclear weapons within an hour of identifying the target and committing to destroy it anywhere around the globe. Bespalov & Tikhonov published their "Analysis of concepts by leading states with regards of use of non-nuclear means of destruction" in the official General Staff *Military Thought* publication in November 2022, where they conclude that the USA aims to "strike targets anywhere, anytime in a global battle space" (Bespalov & Tikhonov, 2022, p. 9). The authors conclude that:

> in the medium perspective, the USA will strive to own strategic non-nuclear weapon systems with a short flight time to strike the target that formally are not limited by any bilateral or international constraints, capable to achieve strategic offensive objectives, destroying large number of Russian nuclear

forces before the RF Commander-in-chief can make a decision of a counter-strike. This would have extremely negative consequences for the RF national security and will require active counteraction to emerging threats from the political leadership of the RF. (Ibid., p. 12)

In other words, defeat on the battlefields of Ukraine prompted the Kremlin to escalate the military-technological response to the American challenge with an announcement of new *Wunderwaffen* that previously had been mentioned but not necessarily fully developed or deployed. So, President Putin said goodbye to frigate Admiral Gorshkov in January 2023, announcing the new hypersonic missile system (the Zircon) as a "unique weapon" without "equivalent in any country in the world" that will "protect Russia from potential external threats and will help ensure the national interests of our country" (*NZ Herald*, 8 Jan 2023).

At the same time, Aleksandr Bartosh, a senior member of the Military Academy of Science, demanded to update the Russian doctrines with new concepts in his article "The Gray Zone is the battlespace of 21 century. American spider net is taking over the world" (Bartosh, 2022 in Nezavisimoye Voennoye Obozreniye, 27 October). He argues that the USA are using the Gray Zone (GZ) to force countries to adhere to American national interests without conflict or adversarial reaction. In his view the Russian doctrine should feature definitions of "hybrid war and its instruments such as proxy-war, information-psychological war and colour revolution". Bartosh arrives at conclusion regarding the USA that could equally apply to how Russia sees itself: "The prospect of strategic defeat of our adversaries poses the choice between escalating the military preparations (that could lead to the global confrontation) or using 'the fog of uncertainty' in the military-political sphere by combining deterrence instruments in terms of flexible military and political-diplomatic strategies of forcing and containing by means of denial" (Bartosh, 2022).

General-Colonel Leontiy Shevtsov, adviser to the director of Rosgvardiya, reflected on Bartosh's theory of hybrid war in his article "Hybrid war and the special military operation in Ukraine. The role of theory in context of the latest combat practice". The author notes that Russia's geopolitical adversaries widely use such instruments of hybrid warfare as cognitive war and proxy war that could be years or even decades in preparation: "Hybrid war is designed as a pivotal point on the escalation ladder at which parties can decide to move from non-violent forms of confrontation to increasing of armed actions up to a global conflict". Shevtsov listed a number of factors that define the character of hybrid war that the USA and NATO are waging against Russia:

- the global geopolitical nature of the conflict, since the USA strives to defeat Russia as one of its main geopolitical opponents, as being the only one that can destroy America by means of armed conflict;
- the civilizational nature of the conflict, as the USA seeks first to weaken Russia, China and Iran as their most significant opponents, who, within the framework of their own cultural and worldview paradigms, oppose the American projects of globalization and liberalization;
- the permanent and universal nature of the conflict, which is due to the use of a strategy of attrition in a hybrid war, which provides for a gradual transition from nonviolent actions in the political, economic, information and psychological spheres to military-force operations. The strategy is designed for a long time and is being implemented with varying intensity in specially created "gray zones" as theatres of hybrid warfare;
- the diffused nature of the military conflict, which uses all known non-nuclear means and methods of war, including the technologies of the "colour revolution" as a catalyst for operations in order to accelerate the collapse of the state. The use of a colour revolution as a catalyst is a synthesis of a strategy of attrition and crushing;
- the indirect nature of the conflict through the use of proxy warfare as a tool to disguise the aggressor state (Shevtsov 2022).

Both Bartosh and Shevtsov therefore view Russian aggression in Ukraine as a proxy war between the RF and the USA / NATO that is taking place according to the laws of hybrid war using various hybrid threats and instruments to escalate / de-escalate the conflict. Both agree on the implications of such hybrid warfare for Russia and the list of strategies available to the Kremlin and its international allies. Accordingly, Russia can:

- Discuss the Gray Zone (GZ) scenarios with key allies and partners to better understand their concerns, responses and needs, and develop a common strategy of confrontation;
- formulate a set of criteria for determining the most dangerous American strategy in the GZ, which should be counteracted with the help of inter-state efforts;
- give priority to countering the United States in disputed territories in Europe, the Indo-Pacific Region, the Middle East and via responding to Washington's geopolitical international and economic strategy;
- utilize an interagency body of the RF to develop action plans against the GZ, similar to existing military operational plans, but focused on responding to a number of possible escalation scenarios for US actions in the GZ. This last task is of the greatest relevance for Ukraine, Belarus, Serbia, the Arctic, Transcaucasia and Central Asia, and Africa. Joint planning in the Indo-Pacific region requires for this purpose a close cooperation with China, North Korea and other partners if necessary.
- continue to create a global intelligence infrastructure covering the territory of Russia and partner countries in the mentioned regions, in order to increase intelligence sharing and analysis, improve regional cyber-defence capabilities, raise general awareness of the actions of the United States and NATO, and provide advanced information coverage of such actions in order to prevent strategic suddenness of subversive operations from the GZ. (Bartosh 2022)

We can conclude that these military analysts are indeed in unison with Russian politicians mentioned earlier who believe that Russia has not invaded a sovereign state of Ukraine (an international point of view as per the UN resolutions) but indeed is confronted by the USA and NATO and therefore is engaging in self-defence. There is truly a cultural or 'civilizational' abys between the two points of view that make them nearly impossible to reconcile. Sadly, opinion polls suggest that majority of the Russian population share the Kremlin's worldview even if support for the actual war efforts in Ukraine is gradually decreasing (Politico 2023). So, what are the potential implications of such cultural / civilizational contrast in interpreting the same reality of war in Ukraine for the future relationship between Russia and Ukraine as well as Russia and the USA / NATO?

An American based academic network PONARS Eurasia suggests preparing for Russia's coming retrenchment:

> Russia's full-scale war on Ukraine is a direct threat to European security. Likewise, there is no guarantee that Russia will abandon its hostility to Europe once the war is over. The enormous sacrifice the Ukrainians have made to protect their country has given time for Europe to prepare for the possibility of a hostile Russia that is fully adapted to sanctions and other levers of pressure. For the years to come, Moscow will undertake a reconstruction of its economy and military adapted to survive under sanctions, along the lines of Iran and North Korea. This reconstruction will take years but not decades, and Europe will have to be ready for whatever emerges. (Klyszcz, 2022)

This is an optimistic scenario that envisages that somehow the current conflict would not escalate out of control and some sort of peace agreement would be achieved between Russia and Ukraine with international mediation. A less optimistic scenario would mean initial Ukrainian defeat and subsequent war involving Russia and the USA, admitted General Mark Milley, who has completed a four-year term as chairman of the US Joint Chiefs of Staff: "If Ukraine loses and Putin wins, I think you would be certainly increasing if not doubling your defence budget in the years ahead. And you will increase the probability of a great power war in the next 10 to 15 years. I think it would be a very dangerous situation if Putin's allowed to win." (Milley, 2023)

From the Kremlin's point of view this is after all a long-term struggle with the USA / NATO, not Ukraine per se. So, what are the possible options on the road to peace considering completely opposite perception of reality between Moscow on the one hand and Kyiv, Brussels, Washington on the other?

9. Roadmap to Peace?

This final chapter looks at the real and perceived military threats and aggression justification narratives directed towards Russia from both a Russian and Western point of view. It exposes contradictions in the Russian approach perpetuating a 'besieged fortress' approach to the security community dilemma but also a lack of cultural understanding on behalf of the 'Anglo-Saxons' that could at times reinforce Russian fears. It considers three likely scenarios of peaceful coexistence that are culturally acceptable to both Russia and the collective West. The choice is ultimately in the hands of the Russian ruling elite that can eventually achieve a true "European security zone from Lisbon to Vladivostok" but only on mutually acceptable terms of a "no war security community". These terms could be based on a common cultural understanding of "just war theory" essentially a Christian ethical concept accepted by Moscow and wider European Judeo-Christian civilization.

Quoting the Kremlin's spokesman Dmitriy Peskov, "all wars end in peace and the war in Ukraine will be no exception". The question is, of course, peace on whose terms, considering that Moscow believes to be fighting the US and NATO rather than Ukraine. Initial Kremlin demands to Kyiv to de-Nazify, demilitarize and cede territory became a simple land grab by summer 2022 turning the "special military operation" into a war of attrition with indiscriminate missile strikes on Ukrainian cities when the Kremlin hoped to bomb the Ukrainians into submission. The Ukrainian Armed Forces managed to mobilise and reinforce by September 2022 and counterattack, liberating around half of the Russian occupied territories in the East and South of the country. Emboldened by military victories and international support, Kyiv set pre-conditions for peace talks with full Russian withdrawal from all Ukrainian territory, acceptance of Russian reparations and punishment of all war criminals. The West and, first of all, the US government, reassured Ukraine of continuing military and economic assistance for as long as it would take to liberate Ukrainian territories. What was meant to be a three-day victorious operation at the end of 8 years of hybrid armed conflict became for Moscow a full-scale conventional war that required partial mobilization of all fighting age Russian citizens and inevitable mass casualties known in Russian social media as the "meatgrinder". Pro-Kremlin propagandists gradually changed the narrative from SMO to "Russia is fighting against NATO" or even "Satanic" forces in Ukraine. Negotiating positions became entrenched and all parties started to plan for a long-haul confrontation. For President Putin this war is a matter of personal survival as historically the Russians do not forgive their leaders lost wars. For the Ukrainians it is an existential struggle to survive not only as a nation-state but also as a people with its own identity. As the Ukrainian Minister Reznikov indicated at the start of 2023, Russian state policy to steal thousands of Ukrainian children from the occupied territories reflected a clear genocidal intent (Reznikov, 2023). Indeed, on 17 March 2023, Pre-Trial Chamber II of the International Criminal Court (ICC) issued warrants of arrest for President Vladimir Putin and presidential ombudsman for children's rights Maria Lvova-Belova on suspicion for war crimes against civilians in Ukraine and specifically forced deportations of Ukrainian children:

> Mr Vladimir Vladimirovich Putin, born on 7 October 1952, President of the Russian Federation, is allegedly responsible for the war crime of unlawful deportation of population (children) and that of unlawful transfer of population (children) from occupied areas of Ukraine to the Russian Federation (under articles 8(2)(a)(vii) and 8(2)(b)(viii) of the Rome Statute). The crimes were allegedly committed in Ukrainian occupied territory at least from 24 February 2022. There are reasonable grounds to believe that Mr Putin bears individual criminal responsibility for the aforementioned crimes, (i) for having committed the acts directly, jointly with others and/or through others (article 25(3)(a) of the Rome Statute), and (ii) for his failure to exercise control properly over civilian and military subordinates who committed the acts, or allowed for their commission, and who were under his effective authority and control, pursuant to superior responsibility (article 28(b) of the Rome Statute). (ICC statement, 2023)

For the West, Russian victory in Ukraine would mean the end of the world order dominated by a single American superpower and a precedent when international borders in Europe can be changed by force of will. Initially reluctant to get involved, Western governments were prompted to act more decisively by public opinion of Europeans shocked by mass war atrocities uncovered after RF armed forces withdraw from Bucha, Irpin, Hostomel and other towns around Kyiv. Millions of Ukrainian refugees, overwhelmingly women and children, flooded Europe and reminded of the horrors of WW2, which the continent never imagined seeing ever again. Finland and Sweden broke their traditional (since the Cold War) neutrality and applied to join NATO, which in turn suddenly rediscovered its sense of purpose. Governments on both sides of the Atlantic were desperate to deny suggestions that World War Three was on the cards or in fact is ongoing as suggested by Pope Francis at the start of 2023. However, the sense of peace has disappeared, and experts suggest that a new way of war in a form of persistent world powers' competition is here to stay: "Our present notions of war, as something formally declared and ended, fought largely on the battlefield, where laws are meant to protect non-combatants and define the acceptable forms of force, are becoming less and less relevant. Instead, war is outsourced and sublimated, fought as often through culture and credit, faith and famine, as direct force of arms." (Galleotti, 2022, P.14)

Out of three international actors mentioned as parties of the conflict, NATO is in a better position as its member states are not directly affected by fighting a war. Ukraine is bleeding but the will of the people to fight until liberation of all occupied territories did not seem to subside after a full-scale invasion and was going strong throughout 2023-24 counteroffensives. The ultimate prize for Ukraine is not only sovereign territory but also membership in the EU / NATO's security community that can provide long-term security irrespective of whether or not all Ukrainian territory will be recovered from the Russian occupation. Moscow can retain some captured territory but can no longer return to business as usual with the West.

Therefore, the Kremlin will face three principal options: 1) continue NGW efforts actively opposing Ukrainian alignment with the EU and NATO perpetuating its subversion war against the West. That would mean effectively creating a new "arch of evil" in Eurasia (Iran, Russia and the North Korea); 2) accept the loss of

Ukraine and transition to a new form of "peaceful co-existence" that would merely mean continuation of Cold War 2.0. This might include a "no peace—no war" transition period, Intermarium Buffer zone with A2/AD on both sides from the Baltic to the Black Sea; "air-gap" in cyber and information flows with "sovereign internet" in Russia etc; 3) accept military defeat, reparations, a war-crime tribunal and strive to forge peace and reconciliation with Ukraine, spiritual healing and return to Europe with disarmament of its Western borders and some sort of integration with the European Union—a true "European security zone from Lisbon to Vladivostok". This final is the least achievable option in the immediate future but might be the most desirable long term, so must not be discounted.

As we could see in the previous chapter, the most likely scenario that awaits Europe is a retrenched Russia that is defeated in Ukraine strategically but full of resentment for as long as Putin's circle is in charge. Irrespective of whether Ukraine will liberate all its occupied territory or will be forced to cede some territory, the new political-military division will be firmly entrenched on the Eastern borders of Ukraine. "Ukraine's future lies in the European Union, our community of freedom, and it will soon stretch from Lisbon to Luhansk" suggested German Foreign Minister Annalena Baerbock at an informal EU summit in Kyiv (Quoted from Eurointegration.com.ua 2 October 2023). The New Iron Curtain 2.0 might even take the form of a wall if Kyiv were to construct a fence on its border with Russia like the one Poland constructed with Belarus in 2022 (this was the intent of PM Yatsenyuk's government in 2014 but for various reasons it was abandoned, with corruption / subversion charges investigated by the Ukrainian courts ever since). The EU and NATO membership for Kyiv will likely follow as Ukraine is the only country in Europe that had to fight a war for the right to join. As the president of the Council of Europe Charles Michele told the Ukrainian parliament in January 2023: "A brighter future awaits you all. A future within the European Union. There can be no independent and safe Europe without an independent and safe Ukraine. There can be no free Europe without a free Ukraine. Our future is bound together. Slava Ukraini! Vive l'Europe!" (Michele, 2023)

Moscow might be 'pacified' if some international sanctions would be lifted, making a symbolical gesture of good will towards the Kremlin. The Russian economy will stagnate and sooner or later a new leadership in Moscow will open up to the West as happened every century in the last 500 years. As Vladislav Surkov, one of the Kremlin's ideologists, predicted, Russia should be ready for another 100 years of "mixed race (half-blood) solitude" (*odinochestvo polukrovki*) between Europe and Asia:

> Solitude does not mean complete isolation. Unlimited openness is also impossible. [...] Without a doubt, Russia will trade, attracts investments, exchange knowledge, wage war (as warfare is a form of engagement), take part in pacts, be a member of international organisations, compete and collaborate, attract fear and hatred, cause curiosity, sympathy and admiration. However, all that would be without false goals and self-denial". (Surkov 2018)

Future transition from President Putin to the new incumbent in the Kremlin will not take that long, considering his age, and the new ruling elite might change its mind on confrontation with the West and choose the second-best options in relationship with the West, 'peaceful coexistence 2.0'. This phase might indeed last decades. In the past few centuries, Russia used to open for 20-30 years absorbing European culture and technology only to embrace isolation for the rest of each century. The West confused Russian 'opening' under Gorbachev and Yeltsin as "the end of history" while it was only a short spell before Putin followed in the steps of Ivan the Terrible, Alexander III, and Stalin. It is unlikely that these decades of Russia's "solitude" will be splendid for the majority of the Russian population, so there is hope that reconciliation with Europe is not ruled out in principle. However, what would be required for Russia to live in peace with itself and the West?

The concept of a security community envisages a situation among participating states where no party is preparing for a war with any other. This is ultimately what the EU / NATO is as a collective security community considering that NATO covers 96% of the EU countries. While Ukraine is aspiring to join such a security community, Russia considers itself at war with NATO now and will lack trust to stop preparing for war in the near future. The causes of mistrust are cultural / emotional more than rational as NATO never invaded Russia and most countries bordering Russia simply lack military capability to do so. Isaiah Berlin explored the Soviet / Russian mind in his book on Russian culture under Communism just after WW2 and his explanations stand valid now showing the enduring nature of the Russian culture:

> The general reasons for Russia's mistrust of the West is familiar: that she has never for long been part of Europe, has not mingled frequently with the European nations, and, in consequences, feels dangerously inferior. It is interesting to note that, with the possible exception of Turgenev, there is no great Russian writer who did not suffer from xenophobia, amounting at times to acute hatred of the West. There is a permanent neurosis resulting from this uneasy position which Russia feels occupied — "Scythians" belonging neither to East nor West". (Berlin, 2004, p. 90)

Lack of trust based on cultural neurosis has not changed with the fall of Communism even though it briefly subsided under President Yeltsin. Berlin also explained why dialogue with Russians does not dispel potential cultural misunderstanding: "It is necessary to remember that the Russians do not believe a word we say, because they think they understand us more clearly than we do ourselves" (Berlin, 2004, P. 96).

There were enough efforts, since 1946 when these words were written, for the Russians to learn more about the West, especially after the Iron Curtain fell in 1989. The Russian ruling elites travelled freely to the West and often moved their families to European capitals for education and careers. However, the more those worldly Russians understood the West the more suspicious some of them became of the West. The chief editor of Russia Today Margarita Simonian, who studied in the US, explained in 2018 why "We no longer respect the West":

> We no longer want to live like you do. In the past 50 years we secretly or openly craved to live like you but no longer do. We no longer respect you. [...] It is all your own fault. Western politicians and analysts, journalists, and spies. Our people can forgive a lot in principle. But we cannot forgive arrogance. (Simonian, 2018)

The arrogance Simonian referred to is most likely related to the Russian attempt to establish equal superpower relationships with the USA after the collapse of the USSR. Such attempts were both public and clandestine but, in both cases, unrealistic. Washington responded with a face-saving diplomatic formula calling the American-Russian relationship at the turn of the 21st century a "mature strategic partnership", but that upset the Kremlin even more, explained leading American geopolitical thinker of the 20th century Zbigniew Brzezinski:

> While the concept of 'mature strategic partnership' was flattering, it was also deceptive. America was neither inclined to share global power with Russia not could it, even if it had wanted to do so. The new Russia was simply too weak, too devastated by three-quarters of a century of Communist rule, and too socially backward to be a real global partner. In Washington's view, Germany, Japan, and China were at least as important and influential. Moreover, on some of the central geostrategic issues of national interest to America — in Europe, the Middle East, and the Far East — it was far from the case that American and Russian aspirations were the same. Once differences inevitably started to surface, the disproportion in political power, financial clout, technological innovation, and cultural appeal made the "mature strategic partnership" seem hollow — and it struck an increasing number of Russians as deliberately designed to deceive Russia. (Brzezinski, 2016, P. 101)

Perceived Western deception and conspiracy against Russia are exactly the reason why Vladislav Surkov believes that Russia has failed to integrate with Europe since the end of Cold War:

> At the end of last century our country got bored of "really existing socialism in one country" and we begged to get back to Europe. Someone decided that we are too big to fit in Europe as size matters, grandiosity was threatening. Hence, we had to downsize, cut territory, population, economy, army, ambitions, so we would fit the parameters of a middle ranking European country and could become one of them. We downsized. We believed in Hayek as ferociously as in Marx before. We halved our population, industry, military potential, parted with Soviet republics and started to part with federal republics... However, even such downsized and belittled Russia could not fit in the West. Finally, we have decided to stop downsizing and humiliation. More than that — we have claimed our rights. What happened in 2014 became inevitable. (Surkov, 2018)

As a result of Surkov's and other Eurasianists efforts, the Kremlin's response was to double down on anti-American sentiment, compensating for cultural insecurity with a pseudo-scientific Eurasianist ideology that proclaimed a unique Russian civilization and the destiny-right to "protect" Eurasia from the decadent West. President Putin declared his adherence to Eurasianism on many occasions, stressing his believe in a special Russian mission:

> I believe in *passionarnost*, in the theory of *passionarnost*. Both in nature and in society there is development, peak, and decline. Russia has not reached its peak. We are on the march, on the march of development. The country went through the most difficult trials in its history in the 1990s and early 2000s, but it is on the march of development. There are many problems, but, unlike other old or rapidly aging nations, we are still on the rise. (Meduza, 2022, quoted from https://meduza.io/feature/2022/11/14/kazhetsya-putin-i-pravda-dumaet-chto-mozhet-pobedit-zapad-pochemu)

Putin's Eurasionism was based on theories of a Soviet maverick historian Lev Gumelev and a self-confessed "white" Russian fascist Ivan Illin both of whom the Russian president quoted on numerous occasions in his public speeches. As Russian analyst and former Soviet general Dmitrii Trenin admitted, Putin believes in Eurasionism and his mission given by the God. The most prolific contemporary Russian theorist of Eurasionism and apologist of Russian destiny to wage end-of-the world war on the "Satanic" West is Aleksandr Dugin, who is sometimes called "Putin's brain". Dugin openly called for the killing of all Ukrainians who refuse to consider themselves a part of the Russian World, believing that Ukrainians and Belarussians are constituent parts of the Russian people. A full-scale invasion of Ukraine in February 2022 amounted therefore to what Timoty Snyder called "Russia's eugenic war" of genocide:

> When Vladimir Putin says that Russians and Ukrainians are one people, what he means is that Ukrainians will agree when force is applied. Russian war planning assumed that Ukrainian identity was a superficial implant, to be extirpated by a quick military strike that would physically eliminate a foreign-backed elite. That **form of genocide** proved to be impossible, because it was based on an erroneous assumption. Ukrainian self-understanding is spread wide and deep through the population of Ukraine, to the point where people take initiative themselves to help their country win the war. In this sense, Ukrainian identity is far easier to observe in this war than is Russian identity. (Snyder, 2022, 2023, https://snyder.substack.com/p/russias-eugenic-war)

Eurasianism became a semi-official Russian ideology, but it is far from being universally accepted by the Russian cultural elite. In fact, according to the Russian-American philosopher Mikhail Yampolsky, war in Ukraine exposed a complete lack of meaning in all the words used by the Kremlin and therefore did not resonate with the Russian people, who refused to mobilize for the war efforts:

> the more illusory the order, the greater the number of words produced for its false preservation. It is common knowledge that corruption is the core of the Russian state. However, the greater the depth and brazenness of corruption, the more patriotic the remarks of crooks and bribe-takers. Like Novorossiya or the Russian Empire, linguistic junk creates a facade of social fiction. The extreme persistence with which the Russian Federation's leadership has refused to label the conflict a war is indicative of this. War necessitates mobilisation and a shift in the way of life. And this is precisely what marginal radicals such as Girkin desire. But those in power are well aware that society lacks the capacity for mobilisation. […] This incapacity to mobilise its population is a fundamental distinction between the Russian state and the truly totalitarian regimes of Stalin and Hitler. They were able to wage war and to mobilise their people. (Yampolsky, 2022)

Yampolsky argues in his article "Regime of imperial paranoia: war in the age of empty rhetoric" that Russia's attempt to oppose Western economic expansion, by the use of its ultimate and only remaining credible power — the army — is a "Russian revolt against the universal rules of the world order". In Yampolsky's words, the Kremlin chose a military solution to the problem of its own (relative) economic decline, and the use of Eurasianist rhetoric is a meaningless justification due to the lack of credible ideologies in the world of the 21st century.

While Putin's Eurasianism might indeed be meaningless, the consequences of his genocidal war are real. The Ukrainian government is pushing for creation of a UN tribunal for the crime of aggression against Ukraine that is likely to investigate allegations of war crimes. A similar recommendation was passed by the EU parliamentary Assembly in January 2023 after receiving full support from governments of Germany, France, the UK and the Netherlands. MEPs decided that a special international tribunal is needed to deal with the crime of aggression against Ukraine and fill a legal vacuum in international criminal justice: "MEPs urge the EU, in close cooperation with Ukraine and the international community, to push for the creation of a special international tribunal to prosecute Russia's political and military leadership and its allies" (EU Press-release, 19 Jan 2023).

Sadly, it is not for the first time that Moscow inflicted genocidal policies on the Ukrainian people. It is not a coincidence that during the ongoing Russian "special military operation" the EU parliament recognised the Soviet Holodomor (1932-33) as genocide of the Ukrainian people. The EU press release explicitly stated that "current Russian crimes in Ukraine [are] reminiscent of the past", so the EU "call on all countries and organisations to also recognise the Holodomor as genocide" as the "Russian regime manipulates historical memory for the purpose of its own survival" (EU press release, 15 Dec 2022).

Similar Holodomor recognition declarations have been passed by the US (2018), Canada (2003) and Australia (2003) in the past, so there is a clear consensus on this issue in the West. As long as the Russian ruling elites continue to deny Kremlin's responsibility (past and present) for acts of genocide against the Ukrainians, and other people in Europe, no security community in Europe would be possible. The only reason post-WW2 Germany was readily accepted in the EU/NATO security community was that the German people accepted historical responsibilities for the horrors of WW2 and the Holocaust. Therefore, should Russia want to be part of Europe it will have to recognise that it is in the Russian national interest to co-operate with the UN Tribunal, hand over suspected war criminals to the courts, pay compensation to the victims, demilitarize its foreign policy, condemn the racist ideology of Putin's Eurasianism, and choose a genuine form of democratic government that would preclude revanchist tendencies from seeking to recreate the Russian empire under a new guise.

First of all, Russia needs reforms that would change the system of power with checks and balances rather than just condemn one political leadership or a single ideology. A comprehensive attempt to imagine such a Russia was published by Mikhail Khodorkovsky—a former oligarch and political prisoner who became an anti-war exile in London. The title of his monograph, *How do you slay a dragon? A Manual for Start-up Revolutionaries*, hints that replacing one "dragon" with another is not a real solution. Khodorkovsky first-hand learned how quickly even a well-intentioned politician in Russia, such as Yeltsin in his early presidential years, could gradually drift towards authoritarianism, such is the system and culture of the Russian state. Hence, the UK-based opposition activist suggests deep reform of Russia, turning it into a parliamentary republic of federal entities not based on ethnic principle but arranged around large mega-policies, centres of economic growth. Khodorkovsky goes as far as to offer the right of determination for the 83 Russian regions that constitute the Russian Federation. Those republics that decide to stay will be dedicated to the new democratic, economically dynamic Russia where strong regions will counterbalance any imperial tendencies from the centre. In short it would be a democratic devolution of state power to the regions while Moscow would retain control over law enforcement, foreign policy, and defence. Khodorkovsky warns Western politicians who argue that Russia should be allowed to save face after defeat in Ukraine, or even receive security guarantees from the West. He suggests that without profound reforms that would turn the Russian empire into a modern nation-state, Russia will be condemned to fall into an authoritarian vicious circle:

> The Russian autocratic system in any medium term has a pronounced militaristic profile. This practically does not depend on the format of the initial ideology and the personality of the national leader. At the stage of maturity, the ideology is transformed into a radical nationalist one, and the leader becomes a military leader. Making a choice in favour of an autocratic (static) civilization, the West makes a choice in favour of an inevitable relapse of the crisis, followed by aggression directed against the West itself. At the same time, each next crisis will be larger than the previous one and overcoming it will create the threat of an uncontrolled slide into a nuclear conflict. This would cause a phenomenon of bad historical infinity (consistency), where each next version of Russia turns out to be worse than the previous one. (Khodorkovsky, 2022)

Khodorkovsky believes that without profound reforms and a return to Europe, Russia will remain isolated economically, socially and will end up in a civilizational dead-end. Hence, his call is for a revolution and not necessarily a peaceful one. Khodorkovsky is realistic enough to admit that no change of Putin's regime is possible until Russia would suffer a military defeat in its criminal war with Ukraine. In his words, only a military defeat and its acceptance by the new transitional government could be a precondition for Russian reconciliation with Ukraine and Europe. Any compromise between the Russian regime and the West would only perpetuate new cycles of Russian militarism.

It is difficult to predict how long it might take for Russia to switch from a subversion war on the Western "Satan" to a transition government of "no war—no peace" without a revolution as professed by Khodorkovsky. It is not even clear if the Russian people want to return to Europe should the new ruling elites choose so. Opinion polls suggest that two thirds of Russians (64%), especially young people (71%), do not consider themselves European (RFI Levada, 2021). Increasing cultural isolationism suggests that Russian society is closing to the West again, repeating a familiar pattern from previous centuries.

This is often misunderstood in Europe as Europeans are accustomed to meet those representatives of the Russian elite known as "*zapadniki*", or Westernisers. Firm European belief in 'good Russians' is a stereotype based on interactions with a wealthy, educated elite from Russia that has little resemblance with "*glubinnyi narod*" or the heartland Russians. Some of these 'good Russians' often travel across European capitals, charm their no less elitist counterparts with cultural sophistication, impress with careless 'Russian generosity' spending on luxury properties, donating to the 'right' elitist charities and investing in 'sacred' Western institutions such as football clubs. They were also instrumental in offering unscrupulous Western politicians lucrative positions in the boardrooms of Russian corporations, with generous renumeration for very little amount of work. Who would not love 'good Russians' with whom one can do such good business indeed? Sadly, there are currently few statesmen in the West who, like the late senator John MacCain, could look in the eyes of a certain 'good Russian' and see the three letters summarising it all, K.G.B.

One would hope that Western academia with its well-developed schools of Slavonic studies would understand the mysterious Russian soul—its primary subject of scholarly interrogation through literature, history and philosophy. However, mainstream academia was largely oblivious to rising authoritarianism in Moscow until 2014 and ignored those Eastern European academics who tried to warn the world of the risks coming from Moscow. Polish, Ukrainian and Georgian intellectuals were consistently ignored as not 'sophisticated' enough to understand enigmatic Russia, or perhaps were too 'nationalist' or otherwise prejudiced. "No guilty people in the world?" asks Ukrainian philosopher Oksana Zabuzhko in her essay on how to read Russian literature after Bucha. She points to the large volume of books published in the West on Russia that missed the biggest development in that country in the last 20 years: "Without them, it will be impossible to understand how the West could have become so culturally disorientated that, for more than twenty years, it stubbornly ignored a textbook example of the growth and ripening of a new totalitarianism in Russia and repeated the very behavioural patterns of the 1930s that encouraged Adolf Hitler" (Zabuzhko, 2022). The reason for such cognitive bias among the academics could be that they followed the example of politicians—all looking for 'good Russians', sophisticated, generous, and understanding. (See How Russia penetrated the heart of UK power and academia in *The Times* (2019), the UK parliament report on "Moscow's Gold: Russian Corruption in the UK" 2018 and Moscow on the Thames by Kidd, 2022). On the academic debates see Taras Kuzio (2020) "Crisis in Russian Studies? Nationalism (Imperialism), Racism and War." *Europe-Asia Studies*, 74(6), pp. 1097-1098.

A small minority of authors dared to be different. Simon Pirani compared "Putin's Russia" trajectory with that of Mussolini (Pirani, 2010). Alexander Motyl consistently wrote about "Putin's fascist dictatorship" (Motyl, 2017). Edward Lucas wrote "The New Cold War" (2008) and "Deception: Spies, Lies and How Russia Dupes the West" (2012) while working as a journalist for the Economist Intelligence Unit (Lucas, 2008, 2013). Lucas draws attention to the Kremlin's deadly games with the West and Russia's "useful idiots" — intellectuals or political activists who advocated a special relationship with Moscow. Traditionally, "useful idiots" came from the left who believed in the Soviet model of socialism and supported the USSR for whatever they believed it was and not what the USSR did. They ignored even Soviet military interventions into other socialist countries such as Hungary and the Czech Republic, always finding something to justify Moscow. However, since 1991, pro-Russia sympathisers increasingly came from business circles and were political lobbyists who supported Moscow for money and not so much for love. In Germany, such useful idiots were known as Russland-Versteher — people who "understand" Russia. The German tendency to "understand" whatever Russia does usually is linked with a special historical sense of 'guilt' for war crimes from WW2. However, as Timoty Snyder pointed out, most of the Wehrmacht war crimes were committed on the territory of Poland, Belarus and Ukraine, so the sense of guilt was misplaced. Even though President Steinmeier admitted that German foreign policy towards Russia was wrong in the last 20 years, German government reluctance to allow exports of German-made Leopard tanks for the defence of Ukraine in 2022 left a "bitter aftertaste" in the EU. Deputy Minister of Foreign Affairs of Poland Pawel Jablonski threatened that Poland would take unilateral decisions if Berlin continued to hesitate. Answering the question of where such resistance on the part of Germany stems from, Jablonski replied that German "sympathy" towards the RF was built on the Russian money that benefited both politicians and businesses: "These are sympathies in which Russia has invested a lot of money. Today, of course, these people will not openly say that they support Russia, there are many who are ashamed of this. But in reality, they act in such a way as not to cause great harm to Russia" (Ukrinform, 20 Jan 23). Indeed, President Putin was always defiant between 2014 and 2022, pointing out that no major Western businesses left Russia after the takeover of Crimea despite so-called smart sanctions. The situation did change with a mass exodus of disappointed Western businesses from Russia in 2022 but many Western companies and especially financial institutions continued to provide services to the RF. A French company in Moscow was sending Christmas food parcels to the Russian soldiers on the Ukrainian front line while an Austrian bank provided such soldiers with repayment holidays on personal loans. Lenin's principle that the "capitalists will sell us the rope that we will hang them with" worked for Putin just as well a hundred years later. What looks to the West as a delicate balance between "security and prosperity" in relationship with Russia, from the Kremlin's point of view appeared as an opportunity to exploit Western "fear and greed".

It is safe to predict that the Kremlin's money will continue flowing to the West in the form of charitable donations that will make friends and influence people. The next Dragon in the Kremlin will continue, with a wry smile, pretending that he does not exist, practising the subversion war with a "weaponization of everything" that will go on, and the meatgrinder of the proxy wars will continue to grind for a foreseeable future.

So, is Russia lost for Europe? Hope springs eternal goes the English saying or, as they say pessimistically in Russia, hope dies last. Considering the mutual lack of trust and Russian disappointment with Hayek and Marx as European "subversive ideologists", what can stop the opposing parties from sliding into a Hobbesian world of perpetual conflict?

Perhaps, it is worth looking at a common denominator between Russian and Western cultures that could kickstart the "inter-civilizational dialogue". What makes Russian culture compatible with Europe is a belief system based on Christian values, if they are to be stripped of so-called "political orthodoxy", also known as "Orthodox Stalinism". The later term refers to a clan of Russian Orthodox Church leaders who openly support the war in Ukraine, and bless the troops and armour promoting the Russian World as a key pillar of the Eurasianist ideology. So, any dialogue with the current Patriarch of the Russian Orthodox Church, whom Bulgarian vice PM Simeonov once called a second-rate KGB agent and a cigarette smuggler, of course would be futile:

We have to tell people clearly who Patriarch Kiril is. He did not descend from heaven. He is not a messenger from Jesus Christ who came from Paradise. Patriarch Kiril is a known as cigarette *mitropolit* of Russia. […] He is not an Eastern-Orthodox priest. He is a

Soviet KGB agent Mikhailov — a second-rate Soviet agent'. (Focus, 2021) (On Patriarch Kiril's KGB past see *The Guardian*, 1999, Faktor.bg 2021, Sonntagszeitung 2023).

Yet, 68% of Russians consider themselves Orthodox Christians although most of them do not actually attend church services. 77% of Russians believe in God, which is astonishing for a post-Communist society (Izvestia Levada, 2013). Could the belief in Christian values of love to their neighbour save the Russian World and make it compatible again with Europe?

Using eschatological verses, so dear to the heart of the "*Russkiy Mir*" proponents, the smog of the unholy information war could be dispelled indeed as we struggle not against the people but against a proverbial Kingdom of Darkness, mentioned by St Paul in his letter to Ephesians: "Our struggle is not against flash and blood but against the rulers, against the authorities, against the powers of this dark world and against the spiritual forces of evil in the heavenly realms" (Eph 6:12).

In a modern interpretation, as Dallas Willard suggests, these powers and forces are spiritual agencies that work with the idea-systems of evil that are "their main tool for dominating humanity. Christian spiritual reformation is a matter of recognizing in ourselves the idea-systems of evil". After all, this understanding of war as a set of essentially evil belief systems has direct resemblance in classic Russian literature, which still forms the core of modern Russian culture.

> But what is war? What is needed for success in warfare? What are the habits of the military? The aim of war is murder; the methods of war are spying, treachery, and their encouragement, the ruin of a country's inhabitants, robbing them or stealing to provision the army, and fraud and falsehood termed military craft. The habits of the military class are the absence of freedom, that is, discipline, idleness, ignorance, cruelty, debauchery, and drunkenness. And in spite of all this it is the highest class, respected by everyone. All the kings, except the Chinese, wear military uniforms, and he who kills most people receives the highest rewards. (Tolstoy, *War and Peace*, Part Ten, XXV, P. 725)

If anything, the "hybrid" war practiced by the Kremlin since 2014's annexation of Crimea was entirely based on the "trickery and lying" that passed for a military strategy. What could be more ungodly than to declare the Ukrainian people as brothers only to invade their country, kill resisting citizens, rape women, steal children and bomb entire cities to the ground? It might take a while before 70% of Russians who supported the "special military operation" (Vedomosti VTSIOM, 2022) in Ukraine would come around and see it as an unjust war or indeed a war crime from a Christian point of view. It is unlikely but not impossible, so might be important to maintain cultural and interfaith dialogue across the Cold War 2.0 divide. In this new type of war, the wider world has an important role to play as "in asymmetric warfare, the responsibility to judge the war, to join the arguments about how it is being fought, extends more widely. The world's judgements are important, and if the "world" get things right, the war will probably end with justice done" (Walzer 2015. P.XXII).

Pope Francis offered his mediation service to stop the "senseless war" in Ukraine as "a crime against God and Humanity" lamenting in his 2022 Urbi at Orbi that the icy winds of war continue to buffet the mankind: "Our time is experiencing a grave famine of peace also in other regions and other theatres of this third world war" (Al Jazeera, 2023). Western realization of armed conflict in Ukraine as a global event is gradually sinking in, as suggested by a collective work of war strategists, *The Eastern Front of World War 3*, edited by Phillip Petersen:

> This volume connects the dots that so many refuse to recognize, or at least are prohibited from acknowledging. If majorities in the United States and the liberal democracies are denied political equality and social justice so that Vladimir Putin may undermine support for collective defense of international legal norms—as was done during the Trump Administration—then no amount of kinetic warfare capabilities will be sufficient to bring strategic stability and security to the liberal democracies. (Petersen, 2023)

Once conventional confrontation will peak with all Russian 'Bulavas' and American 'Tomahawks' primed on global targets manifesting MAD reality, suddenly talking God might appear as the least irrational option in world capitals. Hence, the Holy See's plea might still ring true: "May the Lord inspire us to offer concrete gestures of solidarity to assist all those who are suffering, and may he enlighten the minds of those who have the power to silence the thunder of weapons and put an immediate end to this senseless war!" (France 24, AjJazeera, 25 Dec 2022)

Conclusions

The decade long Russian-Ukrainian war became the most significant armed conflict at the beginning of the 21st century that will define the geopolitics of Eurasia for decades to come. The West underestimated Russian neo-imperial ambitions and will have to review its security architecture in Europe. In turn, Russia underestimated the ability of the EU and NATO countries to stand up for their values in defence of political and economic alliance interests when challenged in Ukraine. Both the West and Russia underestimated the ability of Ukraine to stand on its own feet at a time of existential and genocidal threat. Neither Russia nor the West can afford to lose in Ukraine, so the confrontation will have to end in a compromise with most (if not all) of Ukraine joining the security community of the EU and NATO. Historically, Russian expansion in Central Europe was always contained by the major powers and this bloody episode of European history will not be an exception. Should Russia manage to retain part of the internationally recognised Ukrainian territory, e.g. Donbas or Crimea, the Cold War 2.0 will replay in Ukraine as it did in Germany during the Cold War that ended in 1989 with German reunification. The difference is that Communist ideology of the USSR was essentially internationalist and did not aim at ethnic cleansing of the entire Eastern Germany of Germans by turning them into Russians as is the case under the Russian occupation in Ukraine. In that respect, Russian state policy is more akin to the Third Reich policies in the occupied Poland when the local population perceived Germans (*Volksdeutsche*) was privileged at the beginning of the WW2 and then removed from Slavic territories in a German retreat. Just like Nazis removed hundreds of thousands of Polish children considered to be *Volksdeutsche* in 1945, the Russian government removed thousands of Ukrainian children under the same pretext of 'saving' them. It is unlikely that without a military defeat like the German one in WW2, the Russian authorities will admit to its crime voluntarily and co-operate with international institutions such the UN or the International Criminal Court. Even if a proposed International Tribunal for the crimes of Russian aggression in Ukraine will become a reality, an undefeated and unrepentant Moscow authority will not likely co-operate. Therefore, the Cold War 2.0 will be ideologically even more uncompromising. A neoliberal EU/NATO security community including Ukraine will face off against an unreformed, authoritarian, gerontocratic Russia clinging to the racist imperialist ideology of Putin's Eurasianism. Considering that traditional Russian opening up to the West played out at the turn of the last century, the rest of the 21st century will most likely continue in confrontation. It does not help that the Russian understanding of the nature of war shifted to perpetual information confrontation that would inhibit dialogue with the West and decrease chances for reconciliation. The next couple of decades might see the competitive nature of major powers taking the form of an information war on the verge of conventional conflict, shifting in and out of a grey zone with occasional flare up of proxy wars in countries which cannot benefit from membership in the European security community under NATO's collective defence umbrella. In this respect, hot conflict on the fringes of Europe might shift to the Caucuses where Russian expansionism will clash with European aspirations regarding Georgia as well as the Turkish strategy of "one people – two states" towards Azerbajan. Depending on the peace settlement in Ukraine, Moldova's best chance to resolve the cancerous separatist wound created by Moscow in the dying days of the USSR (i.e. the Trans-Dniestrian "republic" PMR) is to join the EU and realign its defence forces with Romania, a NATO member. The so called PMR problem could be resolved with returning the territory on the left bank of the Dniester River to Ukraine where it belonged before Stalin decided to create a Moldovan SSR at the beginning of WW2. Ukraine and Romania created a similar precedent of territorial settlement on mutually agreeable terms thus reformatting old Soviet borders. Moldova and Ukraine can do this even easier if both would become members of the EU. However, if the Russian military presence in the PMR will not be resolved under the peace settlement with Ukraine then this unrecognised republic could also remain a hot spot of confrontation with Moscow.

However, one of the most contested areas affecting the security of Europe is in the Arctic. A Russian Arctic bid to the UN submitted in 2015 extends as far as the North Pole, and, thereby, Russia

CONCLUSIONS 193

is currently a revisionist power claiming up to 1.7 million square kilometres of Arctic Sea shelf extending more than 350 nautical miles from the shore. This could lead to either conventional armed conflict or, most likely, a covert and asymmetric (hybrid) competition over a disputed sea shelf, already in the next decade.

The arms race between Russia and the West will aim at creating and deploying weapons systems based on the new technological principles such as direct energy (laser) or quantum cyber. This would move mankind into the brave new world of seventh-generation warfare as designated by Russian theorists. Considering that Western sanctions will slow down the Russian military-industrial complex, the West might rearm slightly sooner than Moscow, providing a leading edge sufficient for an effective deterrence. However, the new arms race will require rethinking defence policies and business models in Brussels as well as Washington. Western defence procurement might need to change from benefiting the defence industry to prioritising armed forces' requirements. Otherwise, China might leap technologically ahead of the West giving Russia a sheltered space, and crucially time, to rearm. Until then the NATO/Russia confrontation will take place mostly in the information and cyber-physical space that poses two relatively new challenges in comparison to the Cold War.

The first challenge relates to the cyber-physical space which is currently unregulated even though cyber targeting of national critical infrastructures could bring down civilization as we know it. In this respect, there should be enough incentive for all cyber war capable parties to treat cyber weapon systems as WMD and achieve mutually acceptable international restrictions on their use. The ability of the USSR and the USA to reach a compromise on nuclear weapons suggests that a similar compromise could be achieved in the cyber space. This time, however, any similar WMD accords should also involve China. Otherwise, no major powers would want to limit their choice of weapon system if Beijing would stay out of such a weapons-reduction framework. Until now, Moscow was open to such negotiations as there was realization in the Kremlin that Russian national critical infrastructure is just as vulnerable as that in the West.

The second challenge is related to Russian successes in subverting the top political leadership in the West. It was impossible to imagine someone like Donald Trump, with his shadow dealing with Russia, being elected President of the USA during the Cold War era. It was impossible for the USSR to recruit a state leader of West Germany to become Moscow's lobbyist and a salaried board member of the Soviet ministry of oil and gas. Gazprom's strategy of "schrederezation" of Europe became possible only because post-industrial, post-religious and post-ideological neoliberal Western elites lost a sense of moral compass that electoral democracy awarded them during the Cold War's confrontation with Communist authoritarian regimes. The moral relativism of some Western politicians was identified as a clear exploitable weakness by the Kremlin and lucrative offers of Moscow's Gold started to flow in. Considering that there is currently no democratic mechanism guaranteeing that unscrupulous Western politicians would be able to resist the temptation to get rich with Moscow's help or in fact get elected to the highest office, NATO's collective defence should be reconfigured. Policing corrupt politicians is clearly too important to leave it to generals of local national security agencies. Creating a NATO counter-intelligence agency might help with timely exposure of political subversion if not prosecution.

Russian militarism as a method to resolve political and economic challenges by military means will not disappear unless there is political reform in Russia that would remove unlimited powers from the head of state. Whether it is a parliamentary republic, or a confederation is up to the Russian people to decide. However, a successful reform in Germany post-WW2 with policies of de-Nazification, demilitarization and re-education is not a bad example to follow. Only truth about victims of genocidal policies conducted by the Kremlin in the 20th and 21st centuries will bring about that cultural change which can put Russia on a path of reconciliation with Europe. That truth will make Russians free and if that truth is formulated in terms of traditional Christian ethics, still widely shared in the Russian Federation, the reconciliation dialogue might get off to a good start.

Bibliography

Acherson, N. (2015) *Black Sea: Coasts and Conquests: From Pericles to Putin.* Kindle Edition.

Adamsky, D. (2018) From Moscow with Coercion: Russian Deterrence Theory and Strategic Culture. In: *Journal of Strategic Studies* 41 (1-2), pp. 33-60.

Aleksashenko, S. (2022) Enough money to keep the war going. https://re-russia.net/en/analytics/039/

Al Jazeera (2022) Pope urges end to 'senseless' Ukraine war in Christmas message. 25 Dec https://www.aljazeera.com/news/2022/12/25/pope-urges-end-to-senseless-ukraine-war-in-christmas-message

Al Jazeera (2023) Pope says Ukraine war 'a crime against humanity' in annual speech. 9 Jan.

Arctic Council (2019) http://council.gov.ru/media/files/VAzBy5r749G uzRCQD6zKQ6N0UzKAICAg.pdf

Applebaum, A. (2017) *Red Famine: Stalin's War on Ukraine.* Anchor Books.

Applebaum, A. (2022) The U.S. Is Naive About Russia. Ukraine Can't Afford to Be. In: *The Atlantic* https://www.theatlantic.com/ideas/archive/2022/01/ukraine-russia-kyiv-putin-bluff/621145/

Bartles, C. (2016) Getting Gerasimov Right. In: *Military Review.* January-February, pp. 30-38.

Bartosh, A. (2022) The Gray Zone is the battlespace of 21 century. American spider net is taking over the world. In: *Nezavisimoye Voennoye Obozreniye*, 27 October.

BBC. (2022) Ukraine war: US estimates 200,000 military casualties on all sides, 19 November. https://www.bbc.co.uk/news/world-europe-63580372

Belobrov, Yu. (2019) NATO naraschivayet voyennuye aktivnost v Severnoy Atlantike. In: *Mezhdunarodnyaya zhizn'*, Moskva, August.

Berlin, I. (1949) *The Soviet Mind. Russian Culture under Communism.* Brookings Institution Press: Washington, D.C. (2004 Edition).

Bender, J. (2014) REPORT: Putin Offered Poland's Prime Minister the Chance to Join Forces and Partition Ukraine. In: *Business Insider* https://www.businessinsider.com/putin-offered-to-partition-ukraine-with-poland-2014-10?IR=T

Berzin, J. (2014) Russia's New Generation Warfare in Ukraine: Implications for Latvian Defence Policy. National Defence Academy of Latvia Center for Security and Strategic Research. April 2014

Bespalov, Ya. & Tikhonov, M. (2022) Analiz konseptsiy veduschikh gosudarstv po primeneniyu perspektivnykh neyadernykh sredstv porazheniya. In: *Voyennaya mysl'*. Vypusk 11.

Bever, A. (2012) *The Second World War*. Orion Publishing Group.

Booth, K. (1981) The Military Instrument in Soviet Foreign Policy. In: *Soviet Strategy*, Edited by J.Baylis and G.Segal, pp.75-101. London: Croon Helm.

Boulègue, M (2019) Russia's Military Posture in the Arctic. Chatham House. Research Paper. Online version: https://www.chathamhouse.org/2019/06/russias-military-posture-arctic

Brezhnev, L. (1970) The Great Victory of the Soviet People. In: Brezhnev, L. I. The Leninist Course. Speeches and articles. Volume 1. Publishing House of Political Literature.

Brzezinski, Z. (2016). *The Grand Chessboard. American Primacy and its Geostrategic Imperatives*. Basic Books: New York. (First published 1997).

Budanov, K. (2023) Ukraine's intelligence chief recalls first few days of full-scale invasion. In: *Ukrainska Pravda*, 16 October https://www.pravda.com.ua/eng/news/2023/10/16/7424364/

Bugayova, N. (2020) Putin's offset: The Kremlin's geopolitical adaptations since 2014. In: *ISW Military learning and the future of war series*. September 2020

Bulganin, N. (1950) Stalin and the Soviet Armed Forces. Quoted from https://www.marxists.org/archive/bulganin/1949/12/21.htm

Byl li Lenin nemetskim agentom. (2017) In: *diletant.media* online https://diletant.media/articles/35587130/

Byl li Lenin nemetskim shpionom? (2020) In: *Radio Sputnik* online 21 Feb 2020 https://radiosputnik.ria.ru/20200221/1565002161.html

Carleton-Smith, M. (2018) Foreword to *Defence Global* https://edition.pagesuite-professional.co.uk/html5/reader/production/default.aspx?pubname=&edid=fc50d232-0df5-4759-bfaa-05e5761e5701

Carter, N. (2019) Speech at a RUSI conference https://rusi.org/event/dynamic-security-threats-and-british-army

CEPA. (2021) Russia plays the antisemitic card in Ukraine. https://cepa.org/article/russia-plays-the-antisemitic-card-in-ukraine/

Cherushev, N. (2018) Sovetskaya voyennaya nauka 30-yh godov 20 veka. In: *Oboznik* online http://oboznik.ru/?p=27108

Christofer, P. and Miriam, M. (2016) The Russia "Firehouse of Falsehood" Propaganda Model: Why it Might work and Options to Counter it (Santa Monica, CAL RAND Corporation), 1. https://www.rand.org/pubs/perspectives/PE198.html

Choticul, D. (1986) *The Soviet Theory of Reflexive Control in Historical and Psychocultural Perspective: A Preliminary Study*, (Monterey, CA: Naval Postgraduate School, 1986), https://apps.dtic.mil/dtic/tr/fulltext/u2/a170613.pdf.

CNN (2022) Zelensky suspends top officials over staffers' 'collaboration' with Russia. 18 July https://edition.cnn.com/2022/07/17/europe/zelensky-fires-top-officials-intl/index.html

CNN (2023) Ukraine says it's foiled assassination plot against Zelensky. 7 August https://edition.cnn.com/2023/08/07/europe/zelensky-assassination-plot-intl/index.html

Cogan, Ch. (2014) 'You Have to Understand, George. Ukraine Is Not Even a Country'. In: *Huffington Post*, 16 March https://www.belfercenter.org/publication/you-have-understand-george-ukraine-not-even-country

Conquest, R (1986) *The Harvest of Sorrow: Soviet Collectivization and the Terror-Famine*. Oxford University Press.

Current Times (2022) https://www.youtube.com/watch?v=eIDQrRBapJ4

Davies, N. (2007) *Europe at War 1939-45: No Simple Victory*. Viking Press.

Dickenson, P. (2017) Why Putin Cannot Risk Peace in Ukraine. November 12 https://www.atlanticcouncil.org/blogs/ukrainealert/why-putin-cannot-risk-peace-in-ukraine/#.WgmVdz9VU4U.twitter

Dixon, N. (1976) On the Psychology of Military Incompetence. (Quoted from Basic Book 2016 edition).

DOD Arctic Strategy (2019) https://media.defense.gov/2019/Jun/06/2002141657/-1/-1/1/2019-DOD-ARCTIC-STRATEGY.PDF

Dugin, A. (2017) Brexit is a victory for humanity. In: *Katehon* Online version https://katehon.com/article/brexit-europe-falling-abyss

DSNews.ua (2021) Andriy Biletsky https://www.dsnews.ua/ukr/dosie/andrey-bileckiy-05092021-435990

Ermus, A. (2017). Russian Information Warfare Against the Ukrainian State and Defence Forces: April-December 2014. ENDC Occasional Papers, No.7, p. 58.

EU Parliament (2022) Holodomor: Parliament recognises Soviet starvation of Ukrainians as genocide. EU Press-release, 15 Dec. https://www.europarl.europa.eu/news/en/press-room/20221209IPR64427/holodomor-parliament-recognises-soviet-starvation-of-ukrainians-as-genocide

EU Parliament. (2023) Ukraine war: MEPs push for special tribunal to punish Russian crimes. EU Press-release, 19 January. https://www.europarl.europa.eu/news/en/press-room/20230113IPR66653/ukraine-war-meps-push-for-special-tribunal-to-punish-russian-crimes

EUvsDisinfo. (2016) Anniversary: "The crucified boy" turns two. https://euvsdisinfo.eu/anniversary-the-crucified-boy-turns-two/

European Pravda. (2023) EU Will Stretch from Lisbon to Luhansk—German Foreign Minister. 2 October 2023 https://www.eurointegration.com.ua/eng/news/2023/10/2/7170581/

Fainberg, S. (2017) Russian Spetznaz, contractors and volunteers in the Syrian conflict. In: *Notes de l'Ifri, Russie. Nei. visions.* No. 105.

Faktor. (2021) Temida: posechenieto na ruskiya partiarkh Kiril prez 2018 g ye politichesko, Valeri Simeonov ne ye obidil moskovskiya gost. 12 April https://faktor.bg/bg/articles/petak-13-temida-poseshtenieto-na-ruskiya-patrirah-kiril-prez-2018-g-e-politichesko-valeri-simeonov-ne-e-obidil-moskovskiya-gost

Fedotov-White, D. (1936) Soviet Philosophy of War. In: *Political Science Quarterly* 51 (3), pp. 321-53

France 24 (2022) Pope Francis pleads for end to 'senseless' Ukraine war in Christmas message. 25 December. https://www.france24.com/en/europe/20221225-pope-francis-pleads-for-end-to-senseless-ukraine-war-in-christmas-message

Fridman, O. (2018) *Russian "Hybrid Warfare"*. London: Hurst & Company.

Frunze, M. (1921) (1982) Armiya I revoliutsiya. In: *Scott and Scott, Soviet Art of War*, pp. 27-30.

Focus (2021) Sud v Bolgarii stav na storonu vice-premiera? Yakyi nazvav patriarkha Kirila "agentom KGB". In: Focus.ua 14 April. https://focus.ua/uk/world/480037-sud-v-bolgarii-vstal-na-storonu-vice-premera-nazvavshego-patriarha-kirilla-agentom-kgb

Galeotti, M. (2022) *The Weaponization of Everything: A Field Guide to the New Way Of War*. New Haven and London: Yale University Press.

Gareyev, M.A (2013) Predchustvovat izmeneniya v kharaktere voiny. In: *Voyenno-Promyshlennyi Kuryer* 20 (488) http://vpk-rews.ru/articles/16089

Gareyev, M.A. (1998) *If War Comes Tomorrow? The Contours of the Future Armed Conflict*. Edited by J.W.Kipp. London: Frank Cass.

Gerasimov, V. (2013) Tsennost nauki v predvidenii. "Value of science is in foreseeing. New challenges dictate necessity to reconsider forms and means of warfare". In: *Voyenno-Promyshlennyi Kuryer* 8 (476) 26 Feb.

Gerasimov, V. I. (2017) Mir na graniakh voiny. In: *VPK* 10 (674) https://vpk-news.ru/artciles/35591

Giles, K. (2012) Russia's Public Stance on Cyberspace Issues. In: *2012 4th International Conference on Cyber Conflict*. Online version: http://www.conflictstudies.co.uk/files/Giles-Russia_Public_Stance.pdf

Giles, K. (2016) *Handbook of Russian Information Warfare*. Nato Defence College.

Giles, K. (2019) The Moscow Rules. Online edition: https://icds.ee/en/the-moscow-rules-ten-principles-for-working-with-russia/

Giles, K., and W. Hagestad (2013) Divided by a common Language: Cyber Definitions in Chinese, Russian and English". In: *2012 5th International Conference on Cyber Conflict*, edited by NATO Cooperative Cyber Defence Centre of Excellence, pp. 413-29. https://ccdcoe.org

Grant, G. (2018) How Ukraine can build an army to beat Putin. In: *Kyiv Post* online: https://archive.kyivpost.com/article/opinion/op-ed/glen-grant-ukraine-can-build-army-beat-putin.html

Grant, M and Ziemann, B. (2018) Introduction: The Cold War as an imaginary war. Manchester University Press. Quoted from https://manchesteruniversitypress.co.uk/wp-content/uploads/2018/07/Sample-978178499440.pdf

Grechko, A.A. and N.V. Ogarkov (1993) *The Soviet Military Encyclopaedia: Abridged English-Language Edition*. Boulder, CO: Westview.

Gogun, A. (2016) *Stalin's commandos: Ukrainian Partisan Forces on the Eastern Front*. I.B.Tauris.

Hodges, J. (2018) Why Russia is Swallowing the Black Sea. In: *Military Times* online https://www.militarytimes.com/news/your-army/2018/12/31/why-russia-is-swallowing-the-black-sea-and-wont-stop-until-it-has-choked-out-ukraine/?fbclid=IwAR1tsWRBDelv-ICp3KofhjPQcaFSBk2dmp_JiSMWItAgZ5k9UHnXGyikXEY

Hosa, J. (2018) Has Russia Already Won the Scramble for the Arctic? In: *The Maritime Executive* online: https://www.maritime-executive.com/editorials/has-russia-already-won-the-scramble-for-the-arctic

Hurska, A. (2021) Demographic Transformation of Crimea: Forced Migration as Part of Russia's 'Hybrid' Strategy. In: *Eurasia Daily Monitor*, volume 18, issue 50 https://jamestown.org/program/demographic-transformation-of-crimea-forced-migration-as-part-of-russias-hybrid-strategy/

Hryb, O. (2019) Evolution of Russian Information Warfare. In: *British Army Review*. Special Report: Culture in Conflict, pp. 74-89.

Fakty (2015) Nalyvaychenko rozkryv tayemnytsiu finansuvannia "Pravoho Sectoru" (video) https://fakty.com.ua/ua/ukraine/suspilstvo/20150410-1547865/

Entsyklopedia pobedy. (2010) Entsyklopediya Pobedy. Spravochnik dlia obuchayuschihsya gudarstvennyh obrazovatelnyh uchrezhdeniy po istorii Velikoy Otechestvennoy Voiny 1941-1945 g.g.» M.: Izdatelstvo "Armpress".

Isserson, G. (1940) Novyye formy borby. Moskva, Voyengiz, 1940. Quoted from http://militera.lib.ru/science/isserson/index.html

International Criminal Court. (2023) Situation in Ukraine: ICC judges issue arrest warrants against Vladimir Vladimirovich Putin and Maria Alekseyevna Lvova-Belova. *Press Release*: 17 March.

Izvestia. (2013) Rosiyanie schitayut siebya veruyschimi no v tserkov nie khodiat. 24 December, https://iz.ru/news/563084

Jones, S. (2018). The Return of Political Warfare. In: *CSIS* online https://www.csis.org/analysis/return-political-warfare.

Johnson, B. (2023) I Believe That Ukraine Will Retake Crimea and Donbas, but Russia Will Not Dissolve. In: *Ukrainska Pravda*. 18 January. https://www.eurointegration.com.ua/eng/interview/2023/01/18/7154388/

Jonsson, O. (2019) *Russian Understanding of War*. Georgetown University Press.

Julian Lindley-French, C. F. (2015). NATO: Countering Strategic Maskirovka. Julian Lindley-French, CDFAI Fellow, NATO: Countering Canadian Defence and Foreign Affairs Institute (Policy Paper, p. 7).

Kaczynski, A. (2017) 80 times Trump talked about Putin. In: *CNN* online https://edition.cnn.com/interactive/2017/03/politics/trump-putin-russia-timeline/

Kaftan, V. (2019) Sotsiogumannyye tehnologii sovremennoy informatsionnoy voyny: spetsifika, tendentsii razvitiya I napravleniye optimizatsii. Federalnoye kazennoye vyssheye uchebnoye zavedeniye "Voyennyy universitet" Ministerstva oborony RF. Moskva (na pravakh rukopisi).

Kalugin, O. (2007) Inside the KGB. In: *CNN* Archive https://web.archive.org/web/20070206020316/http:/www.cnn.com/SPECIALS/cold.war/episodes/21/interviews/kalugin/

Kamenir, V. (2014) The Bloody Triangle along WWII's Eastern Front. In: *Warfare History Network* https://warfarehistorynetwork.com/article/the-eastern-fronts-bloody-triangle/

Kantor, Yu. (2016) Rasstrelyannaya armiya. In: *Lenta.ru* online https://lenta.ru/articles/2016/03/19/redarmy/

Karaganov, S. (2019) In: *Rossiyskaya Gazeta*, 26 December.

Khodorkovsky, M. (2022) *How do you slay a dragon? A Manual for Start-up Revolutionaries*. Online version https://dragonbook.khodorkovsky.com/

Khruschev. (1959) On peaceful coexistence. In: *Foreign Affairs*, 1959 October. https://www.foreignaffairs.com/articles/united-states/1959-10-01/peaceful-coexistence

Kilcullen, D. (2020) *The Dragons and the Snakes: How the Rest Learned to Fight the West*. Hurst & Company, London. Kindle Edition.

Kerrigan, M. (2018) *Russia. Crime and Corruption in the Kremlin*. Amber Books Ltd: London.

Kirienko, S. (2022) Interview with *Voice of America*, 11 August.

Kidd, P. (2022) Moscow on the Thames. How was a member of the House of Lords allowed to moonlight as the multi-millionaire head of oligarch Oleg Deripaska's energy company? Online version: https://airmail.news/issues/2022-4-2/moscow-on-the-thames

Klimov, M. (2019) Realnye ugrozy v Arktike: is-pod vody i s vozdukha. In: *Topwar.ru* https:\topwar.ru\157104-byt-gotovym-v-arktike-k-realnym-ugrozam-s-vozduha-i-iz-pod-vody-lda.html

Klyszcz, I. (2022) Prepare for Russia's Coming Retrenchment. In: *Ponars Eurasia* https://www.ponarseurasia.org/prepare-for-russias-coming-retrenchment/

Kofman, M. (2020) Russia's armed forces under Gerasimov, the man without a doctrine. In: *Riddle*, online version https://ridl.io/russia-s-armed-forces-under-gerasimov-the-man-without-a-doctrine/

Kokoshin, A. (1998) *Soviet Strategic Thought: 1917-91*. Cambridge, MA: Belfer Center for Science and International Affairs.

Komov, S.A. (1997) About Methods and Forms of Conducting Information Warfare. In: *Military Thought*, July-August, pp. 18-22)

Kremenyuk, V. (2022) Uroki Kholodnoy Voiny. Aspekt Press, 2015. https://russiancouncil.ru/library/library_rsmd/uroki-kholodnoy-voyny/

Kurginian, S. (1992) *Sedmoy Stsenariy*. Moscow.

Kuzio, T. (2020) Crisis in Russian Studies? Nationalism (Imperialism), Racism and War. In: *Europe-Asia Studies*, 74(6), pp. 1097-1098.

Lefebvre, V.A. and Smolyan, G.L. "Algebra Konflikta", Moscow 1968 (Accessed online on October 4, 2017) http://sbiblio.com/BIBLIO/archive/levefr_algebra/02.aspx

Lenin, V. (1916) The Military Programme of the Proletarian Revolution. In: *Jugend Internationale* 9-10, pp. 1-8.

Lenin, V. (1919) Address to the Second All-Russia Congress of Communist Organisations of the Peoples of the East. In: *Collected works*, Vol. 30, pp.151-62. Moscow: Progress Publishers.

Lepskiy V. (2019) The problem of assembly of subjects in Information Wars. In: *Informatsionnye voiny*. No.4 (52).

Lider, J. (1977) *On the Nature of War*. Farnborough, UK: Saxon House.

Light, M. (1988) *The Soviet Theory of International Relations*. New York: St. Martin's.

Lucas, E. (2008) *The New Cold War. Putin's threat to Russia and the West*. London: Bloomsbury. Quoted from Kindle 2014 Edition.

Lucas, E. (2013) *Deception: Spies, Lies and How Russia Dupes the West*. London: Bloomsbury.

Lucas, G. (2009) Anthropologists in Arms. In: usna.edu https://www.usna.edu/Ethics/_files/documents/Ethics and Military Anthropology Case WesternUniv 29 March 2009.pdf

Luciuk, L. (2021) *Operation Payback. Soviet Disinformation and Alleged Nazi War Criminals in North America*. Kingston: The Kashtan Press.

Luciuk, L. (Editor) (2008) *Holodomor. Reflections on the Great Famine of 1932-33 in Soviet Ukraine*. Kingston: The Kashtan Press.

Ludendorff, E. (1924) *Moi vospominaniya o voine 1914-1918*, Moscow.

Martin, M. (2019) *Why We Fight*. Hurst & Company. London.

McCarthy, M., Moyer, M., Brett, H. (2019) Deterring Russia in the Gray Zone. US Army War College. https://press.armywarcollege.edu/monographs/379/

Melvin, M. (2017) *Sevastopol's Wars: Crimea from Potemkin to Putin*. Oxford: Osprey Publishing.

Me.gov.ua (2023) Minekonomiky poperednio otsinuye padinnya VVP v 2022 rotsi na rivni 30,4%. https://www.me.gov.ua/News/Detail?lang=uk-UA&id=4470bafb-5243-4cb2-a573-5ba15d9c8107&title=MinekonomikiPoperedno

Messner, E. (1960) Miatezh — imia tretey vsemirnoy. In: *Miatezh Voina* 2005 *Russkiy Voyennyi Sbornik*. Voyennyy universitet. Moskva. Issue 21.

Medvedev, D. (2022) Interview with *Sky TV*, 8 August.

Meduza.io (2021) Kazhetsia Putin I vpravdu dumayet, chto on mozhet pobedit' Zapad. Pochemu? Vozmozhno potomu chto verit v teorii Lva Gumeleva. 14 Nov 2022 https://meduza.io/feature/2022/11/14/kazhetsya-putin-i-pravda-dumaet-chto-mozhet-pobedit-zapad-pochemu

Michele, C. (2023) Speech by President Charles Michel to the Verkhovna Rada in Kyiv. Press Release, 19 January. https://www.consilium.europa.eu/en/press/press-releases/2023/01/19/speech-by-president-charles-michel-to-the-verkhovna-rada-in-kyiv/

Milley, M. (2023) Gen. Mark Milley: The 60 Minutes Interview — CBS News, 8 Oct https://www.cbsnews.com/video/general-mark-milley-interview-60-minutes-video-2023-10-08/

Millard, R. (2020) BP's long and complicated relationship with Russia returns to the spotlight. In: *Daily Telegraph* online version: https://www.telegraph.co.uk/business/2020/02/19/bps-long-complicated-relationship-russia-returns-spotlight/

Mirovalev, M. (2023) Russia's atrocities in Ukraine, rehearsed in Chechnya. In: Al Jazeera online https://www.aljazeera.com/news/2023/1/20/russias-atrocities-in-ukraine-rehearsed-in-chechnya

Morozov, A. 20 Jan 2020, BBC Monitoring.

Moss, Ed. (2019) "Theological warfare: an aspect of information warfare between Russia and European powers". In: *The Naval Review*. Vol. 107 May, pp.126-134.

Mova kozakiv. (2016) In: *Spadok.org.ua* https://spadok.org.ua/mova-i-pys emnist/mova-kozakiv-yakoiu-bula-ukrayinska-400-rokiv-tomu

Mukhin, V. (2020) Na Zemliu Frantsa-Yosifa desantirovalis s 10-ni kilovemtrovoy vysoty. In: *Novaya Gazeta* 26 April 2020. Online version: http://www.ng.ru/armies/2020-04-26/2_7853_army.html

National Security Strategy. (2021) O strategii natsionalnoy bezopasnosti In: pravo.gov.ru, online: http://publication.pravo.gov.ru/Document/View/0001202107030001?index=6&rangeSize=1

NATO (2010) Bi-SC NATO Information Operations Reference Book In: *Publicintelligence.net*. Online version: https://info.publicintelligence.net/NATO-IO-Reference

Nato Parliamentary Assembly. (2023) United and Resolute in support of Ukraine Declaration 482*. *Press-Release*. Online version: https://www.nato-pa.int/download-file?filename=%2Fsites%2Fdefault%2Ffiles%2F2023-05%2FDECLARATION++482+-+UKRAINE+.pdf&__cf_chl_tk=5xT5sWgSfRe2bKdcBT52ICnzfOZAK1MvzlJ5KleHoQc-1689091366-0-gaNycGzNCxA

Napriach vse sily, navesti massovyy terror, rastreliat' (2021) In: *Novay Gazeta* online No.41 16 April https://novayagazeta.ru/articles/2021/04/12/napriach-vse-sily-navesti-massovyi-terror-rasstreliat

"Ne bylo nenavisti: Vladimir Putin rasskazal o podvige I semeyonoy tragedii" (2015) In: *Lenta.ru*, online: https://m.lenta.ru/articles/2015/04/30/putin_family/

New Zealand Herald. (2023) 'Like a fireball': Vladimir Putin unveils new weapon to threaten the world. 8 January, online version: https://www.nzherald.co.nz/world/like-a-fireball-vladimir-putin-unveils-new-weapon-to-threaten-the-world/7INXZGHZKJCJBOZC464LSA4GHY/

Nikulin, N. (2005) Vospominaniya o voynie. In: *Litres.ru*, online version: https://www.litres.ru/book/nikolay-nikulin-8709137/vospominaniya-o-voyne-18504104/chitat-onlayn/

Oborony Ministerstvo. (2011) Conceptual Views Regarding the Activities of the Armed Forces of the Russian Federation in the Information Space [Kontseptual'nye vzglyady na deyatel'nost' Vooruzhennykh Sil Rossiyskoy Federatsii v informationnom prostrantsve]. Ministerstvo Oborony.

Ofitsiyno pereimenuvaty "Rossiya" na "moskovia". In: *Ukrinform*, 2023. https://petition.president.gov.ua/petition/170958

Orwell, G. (2010) *Homage to Catalonia*. Penguin.

Osnovy gosudarstvennoy politiki Rossiskoy Federatsii v Arktike na period do 2020 goda I dalneyshuyu perspektivu. In: Rossiyskaya gazeta. 27 November 2009 (Russian Arctic strategy 2008-2020). https://rg.ru/2009/03/30/arktika-osnovy-dok.html

Ovchinski, A. (1997). Informatsionno-psikhologicheskaya sfera protivodejstviya organizovannoy prestupnosti. In: *Informatsionnoye obschestvo*. No.1.

Panarin, I. (2012) Vtoraya mirovaya informatsionnaya voina: Voina protiv Rossii. Moscow.

Panarin, I. (2003) Informatsionnaya voina i vybory. Moscow.

Panarin, I. (2010) Pervaya mirovaya informatsionnaya voina: Razval SSSR. Izdatelskiy Dom Piter. Moskva, 2010.

Paul, C and Matthews, M. (2016) "The Russian 'Firehose of Falsehood' Propaganda Model. RAND (blog) Santa Monica, CA: RAND Corporation, 2016. https://www.rand.org/pubs/perspectives/PE198.html.

Petersen, Ph. (2023) *The Eastern Front in World War 3*. Volume I. Kindle Edition.

Peskov, Dmitriy (2018) "Russia is in a state of information war with Anglo-Saxons" In: *BBC News*. https://www.bbc.com/russian/russia/2016/03/160326_peskov_russia_image

Pirani, S. (2010) *Change in Putin's Russia*. London: Pluto Press.

Pocheptsov, G. (2001). Teoriya Komunikatsii. Moscow.

Politico. (2023) Appealing to Russians to end the war on Ukraine is wasted breath. 20 January 2023 https://www.politico.eu/article/commentary-ukraine-war-russia-vladimir-putin-invasion-end/

Polonskiy, I. (2019) Arkticheskiye ambitsii SSHA. Vashington mechtayet o Severnom morskom puti. In: *Topwar.ru* https://topwar.ru/163753-arkticheskie-ambicii-ssha-vashington-mechtaet-o-severnom-morskom-puti.html

Poore, S. (2003) What is the Context? A Reply to the Gray-Johnston Debate on Strategic Culture. In: *Review of International Studies* 29 (2), pp. 279-84.

BIBLIOGRAPHY 205

Pravoslavie.ru (2014) Putin says that the Crimea where Prince Vladimir took baptism has sacred meaning for Russia. December 5. https://ort hochristian.com/75734.html

Prymachenko, Yu. (2017) The Soviet foundations of Russia's Great Patriotic War. In: *Euromaidan Press*, online: https://euromaidanpress.com/2017/05/09/the-soviet-foundations-of-russias-great-patriotic-war-myth/

Putin blames Poland for WWII and says Soviet occupation "saved lives" (2019) Notes from Poland https://notesfrompoland.com/2019/12/23/putin-blames-poland-for-ww2-and-says-soviet-occupation-saved-lives/

Putin, V. (2007) Putin's Prepared Remarks at 43rd Munich Conference on Security Policy. In: *Washington Post*, February 12, online: https://www.washingtonpost.com/wp-dyn/content/article/2007/02/12/AR2007021200555.html

Putin, V. (2012) Byt' silnymi: Garantii natsionalnoy bezopasnosti dlya Rossii. In: *Rossiyskaya Gazeta*, February 20, https://rg.ru/2012/02/20/putin-armiya.html

Putin, V. (2016) Ukaz Prezidenta RF or 05.12.2016. No.464 Ob utverzhdenii doktriny informatsionnoy bezopasnosti RF. Online: http://kremlin.ru/acts/bank/41460

Putin, V. (2020) On Ukraine (TASS interview). Online publication: http://kremlin.ru/events/president/news/62835

Putin, V. (2021) "On the Historical Unity of Russians and Ukrainians" Online version: www.kremlin.ru http://en.kremlin.ru/events/president/news/page/264

Putin, V. (2022) Speech at the 10th Moscow Conference on International Security, Kremlin.ru, 16 August. http://en.kremlin.ru/events/president/news/69166/videos

Putin, V. (2023) Speech at the "Just multipolarity: how to achieve security and development for all" Valdai discussion. http://kremlin.ru/events/president/news/72444

Radchuk, V. (2000) Ukrainska I rosiyska rozbihayutsia na 38%. In: *Derzhavnist ukrainskoyi movy I movnyy dosvid svitu*. Materialy Mizhnarodnoi konferentsii. Kyiv, P.362-374 Quoted from: https://ukrajinciberlinu.wordpress.com/2009/11/19/

Radio France International. (2021) "Levada": dve treti rossiyan nie schitayut Rossiyu Yevropoy. 18 March.

Radio Liberty. (2022) "Ya pytalsia dobitsia peremen mirnym putem" https://www.youtube.com/watch?v=E7N6Z8Wuzp8

Rauss, E. (1995) Russian Combat Methods in WW2. In: *Fighting in Hell: The German Ordeal on the Eastern Front*. Edited by Tsouras, Peter Greenhill, London.

Rastorguyev, S. (1999). *Informatsionnaya voina*. Moscow: Radio i sviaz.

Razumov, A. Kryukov, G. Kuznetsov A. (2022) Zhivu, srazhayus, pobezhdayu. Pravila zhizni na voynie. Published by Rossiyskiy Soyuz veteranov Afganistana I spetsialnykh operatsiy. Moskva.

Reznikov, O. (2023) Oleksiy Reznikov: rosya masovo krade ukrayinskih ditey z tymchasovo okupovanykh terytoriy. In: *Armyinform* online: https://armyinform.com.ua/2023/01/12/oleksij-reznikov-rosiya-masovo-krade-ukrayinskyh-ditej-z-tymchasovo-okupovanyh-teryt orij/?utm_source=mainnews&utm_medium=article&utm_campai gn=traficsource

Rid, T. (2020) *Active Measures. The Secret History of Disinformation and Political Warfare*. Profile Books: London.

RUSI report. (2023) Preliminary Lessons from Russia's Unconventional Operations during the Russo-Ukrainian War, February 2022-February 2023. https://rusi.org/explore-our-research/publications/speci al-resources/preliminary-lessons-russias-unconventional-operation s-during-russo-ukrainian-war-february-2022

RUSI. (2018) General Mark Carleton-Smith, Chief of the General Staff: RUSI Land Warfare Conference 2018, Video recording: https://www.you tube.com/watch?v=jurJ4hHpDAY

RUSI. (2022) Preliminary lessons in conventional Warfighting from Russia's Invasion of Ukraine: February-July 2022. RUSI Reports, November. Mykhailo Zabrodskyi, Jack Watling, Oleksandr Danylyuk and Nick Reynolds.

RUSI. (2023) Preliminary Lessons from Russia's Unconventional Operations During the Russo-Ukrainian War, February 2022-February 2023. https://rusi.org/explore-our-research/publications/special-r esources/preliminary-lessons-russias-unconventional-operations-d uring-russo-ukrainian-war-february-2022

Russia's Military Posture in the Arctic. (2019) *Chatham House Research Paper*, 28 June. https://reader.chathamhouse.org/russia-s-military-postur e-arctic-managing-hard-power-low-tension-environment

Russian Strategic Intentions (A Strategic Multilayer Assessment). (2019) *DOD White paper*. May.

Linda Robinson, Todd C. Helmus, Raphael S. Cohen, Alireza Nader, Andrew Radin, Madeline Magnuson, Katya Migacheva (2019) The Growing Need to Focus on Modern Political Warfare. In: RAND Reports online. https://www.rand.org/pubs/research_briefs/RB100 71.html

Satter, D. (2007) "Boris Yeltsin", Hudson Institute, 24 April 2007,

Savchenko, E. (2017) Current trends in the development of the British Armed Forces. In: *Voyennaya Mysl*. No. 6, June.

Scott, H. and W.Scott, eds. (1982). *The Soviet Art of War: Doctrine, Strategy, and Tactics*. Boulder, Co.: Westview.

Seely, B. (2018) If we are to counter Russian 'hybrid' war, we must understand it. In: *Politics Home*, online version: https://www.politicshome.com/thehouse/article/if-we-are-to-counter-russian-hybrid-war-we-must-understand-it

Security Service of Ukraine. (2022) Medvedchuk rozpoviv podrobytsi v spravakh vyvedennia z dezhavnoi vlasnosti naftoporovodu I zakuvivli vuhillia v LDNR. https://ssu.gov.ua/novyny/medvedchuk-rozpoviv-podrobytsi-u-spravakh-vyvedennia-z-derzhvlasnosti-naftoprovodu-i-zakupivli-vuhillia-v-ldnr

Sereda, O. (2019) Osmansko-ukrainska dyplomatiya v dokumentakh 17-17 stolitya [XVII.–XVIII. YüzyılbelgelerindeOsmanlı-Ukraynadiplomasisi], Kyiv—Stambul.

Sergeyev, L., Shemetov, M. (2019) Russia's first seaborne nuclear power plant sets sail across Arctic. In: Reuters. 23 August. online version https://www.reuters.com/article/us-russia-nuclear-floating-plant/russias-first-seaborne-nuclear-power-plant-sets-sail-across-arctic-idUSKCN1VD164

Shedd, D. (2021) The Curious Omission in Russia's New Security Strategy. In: *Defense One*, 25 August. https://www.defenseone.com/ideas/2021/08/curious-omission-russias-new-security-strategy/184854/

Shevtsov, L. (2022) Gibridnaya voina I spectsialnaya voyennaya operatsia v Ukraine. In: *Independent Military Review* https://nvo.ng.ru/concepts/2022-07-07/4_1196_ukraine.html

Shoigu, S. (2015) Shoigu: Rossiya gotova zaschishat svoi interesy v Arktike s pomoschyu oruzhiya. In: *RIA Novosti*, online version: https://ria.ru/20150225/1049600202.html

Shoigu, S. (2019) Interview in Moskovsky Komsomolets, 22 September.

Simonian, M. (2018) Pochemu my bolshe nie uvazhayem Zapad. In: *RIA Novosti*, 19 March. https://ria.ru/20180319/1516767644.html

Sipher, J. (2018) Russian "Active measures". In: *CHACR*, Issue 14. June. https://chacr.org.uk/docs/20180701-Issue14-Russian-Active-Measures.pdf

Slipchenko, V. (2005) For what kind of war Russia must be prepared? In: *Future War*. Moscow: Moskovskiy Obshchestvennyi Nauchnyi, pp.9-28.

Slipchenko, V. (2002) K kakoy voynie dolzhny gotovitsia vooruzhennyie sily. In: *Otechesvennyie Zapiski* 8 (9).

Skomorokhov, R. (2023) Mozhem povtorit? In: *Voyennoy Obozreniye* online topwar.ru

Snyder, T. (2018) Russia is winning the information war. Online version: https://lithub.com/russia-is-winning-the-information-war/

Snyder, T. (2022) Russia's genocide handbook. https://snyder.substack.com/p/russias-genocide-handbook

Snyder, T. (2022) To remember the Second World War is to remember Belarus. In: *Institute for Human Sciences* online https://www.iwm.at/blog/belarus-15-the-worst-war#:~:text=On%20the%20territory%20of%20today's,million%20were%20deported%20or%20displaced.

Snyder, T. (2023) Russia's Eugenic War. Four policies of racial cleansing. https://snyder.substack.com/p/russias-eugenic-war

Stalin, J. (1946) Answer to a letter of 30 January from Col.-Professor Rasin. Marxist Internet Archive. February 23. www.marxists.org/reference/archive/stalin/works/1946/02/23/htm.

Stoltenberg, J. (2023) Speech by NATO Secretary General Jens Stoltenberg at the Annual Conference of the Confederation of Norwegian Enterprises. https://www.nato.int/cps/en/natohq/opinions_210445.htm

Sukhankin, S. (2022) The 'Wagner Affair' in Belarus and Its Implications for Ukraine. https://jamestown.org/program/the-wagner-affair-in-belarus-and-its-implications-for-ukraine/

Sun Tzu. (2005) *The Art of War*. Harper Press.

Sonntagszeitung. (2023) Putins Patriarch war Spion in der Schweiz. 4 February. https://www.tagesanzeiger.ch/priester-spion-propagandist-das-geheime-leben-des-moskauer-kirchenfuersten-in-der-schweiz-566103963787

Surkov, V. (2018) Solitude of a half-blood. In: *GlobalAffair.ru* https://globalaffairs.ru/articles/odinochestvo-polukrovki-14/

Taylor, A. (2014) The Soviet War in Afghanistan, 1979-1989. In: *The Atlantic*, online: https://www.theatlantic.com/photo/2014/08/the-soviet-war-in-afghanistan-1979-1989/100786/

The Independent. (2019) Why a minor troop pullback in eastern Ukraine marks the end of President Zelensky's honeymoon. https://www.independent.co.uk/news/world/europe/east-ukraine-zelensky-honeymoon-impeachment-trump-latest-a9176536.html

The Guardian. (1999) Russian Patriarch 'was KGB spy'. 12 February. https://www.theguardian.com/world/1999/feb/12/1

The Guardian. (2023) Zelenskiy assassination plot foiled by security service, says Ukraine. 7 August. https://www.theguardian.com/world/2023/aug/07/volodymyr-zelenskiy-assassination-plot-foiled-by-security-service-says-ukraine

BIBLIOGRAPHY 209

The Huffington Post. (2014) 'You Have to Understand, George. Ukraine Is Not Even a Country', 16 March.

The Economist. (2023) What Russia's new budget reveals about the war in Ukraine. 31 October. https://www.economist.com/graphic-detail/2023/10/31/what-russias-new-budget-reveals-about-the-war-in-ukraine

The Hill. (2017) https://thehill.com/policy/cybersecurity/320650-russia-claims-to-add-information-warfare-troops/

The New York Times. (2023) Troop Deaths and Injuries in Ukraine War Near 500,000, U.S. Officials Say. 18 August. https://www.nytimes.com/2023/08/18/us/politics/ukraine-russia-war-casualties.html

The Patton Philosophy. (1998) The Unknown Patton by Charles M. Province (1998) quoted from Ch.10 In: *Free Republic*, online: https://freerepublic.com/focus/f-news/1775305/posts

The Arctic Council of the Russian Parliament. (2019). Online Report: http://council.gov.ru/media/files/VAzBy5r749GuZRCQD6zKQ6N0UzKAICAg.pdf

The Times. (2021) Revealed: how Russia invaded the heart of British power. Online version: https://www.thetimes.co.uk/article/revealed-how-russia-invaded-the-heart-of-british-power-qtmnrb5fm

The Washington Post. (2022) Putin's attack on Ukraine echoes Hitler's takeover of Czechoslovakia. Online: https://www.washingtonpost.com/history/2022/02/24/hitler-czechoslovakia-sudeten-putin-ukraine/

Thom, F. (2021) What does the Russian ultimatum to the West mean? In: *Desk Russie* (desk-russie.eu). Online: https://en.desk-russie.eu/2021/12/30/what-does-the-russian-ultimatum.html

Thomas, T. (2004) "Russia's Reflexive Control Theory and the Military", In: *Journal of Slavic Military Studies* 17.

Tolstoy, L. (1867) *War and Peace*, Part Ten, XXV, online version: https://www.gutenberg.org/cache/epub/2600/pg2600-images.html#link2HCH0215

Tolstoy, L. (1895) Christianity and Patriotism. Quoted from Tolstoy.ru

Trotsky, L. (1922) Military Knowledge and Marxism: Speech at the Meeting of the Military Science Society Attached to the Military Academy of the Workers and Peasant's Red Army. In: *The Military Writings of Leon Trotsky*, May 8. Marxist Internet Archive. https://www.marxist.org/archive/trotsky/1922/military/ch40.htm

Turchynov, O. (2018) Russia planned full-scale offensive against Ukraine in March 2014. In: *UNIAN* online https://www.unian.info/politics/10041461-russia-planned-full-scale-offensive-against-ukraine-in-march-2014-turchynov.html

Tylor, Edward B. (1881) *Anthropology: An Introduction to the Study of Man and Civilization.* London: Macmillan and Co.

V Krym posle okupatsii pereselilis ne menee 200,000 rosiyan. In: *Crimeahrg.org* https://crimeahrg.org/ru/v-krym-za-period-okkupaczii-pereselilis-ne-menee-200-tysyach-rossiyan%e2%80%af/

Varadarajan, T. (2018) Will Putin Ever Leave? Could He if He Wanted? In Wall Street Journal. 9 March, online version: https://www.wsj.com/articles/will-putin-ever-leave-could-he-if-he-wanted-1520635050

Vatsetis Ioakim, I. (1923) O voyennoy doktrine buduszchego. In: Scott, H and Scott, W. *Soviet Art of War*, London: Routledge, pp. 32-34.

Vedomosti. (2022) VTSIOM: 70% rossiyan podderzhivayut spetsoperatsiyu na Ukrainie. 6 September https://www.vedomosti.ru/society/news/2022/09/06/939470-70-rossiyan-podderzhivat-spetsoperatsiyu

Vortman, D. (2014) Formiovaniye ukrainsko-rossiyskoy sovetskoy administrativnoy granitsy (1918-1928) In: likbez.org.ua https://likbez.org.ua/formirovanie-ukrainsko-rossiyskoy-sovetskoy-administrativnoy-granitsyi-1918-1928.html

Volkava, E. (2012) The Kazakh Famine of 1930-33 and the Politics of History in the Post-Soviet Space. In: *Wilson Centre*, online: https://www.wilsoncenter.org/publication/the-kazakh-famine-1930-33-and-the-politics-history-the-post-soviet-space

Volkogonov, D. (1996) *Trotsky. The Eternal Revolutionary.* London: Harper Collins.

Wagener, V. (2017) Germany's role in the Russian Revolution. In: *DW* online 11 July https://www.dw.com/en/how-germany-got-the-russian-revolution-off-the-ground/a-41195312

Wallace, B. (2022) In: gov.uk An Article by the Defence Secretary "On the situation in Ukraine".

Walzer, M. (2015) *Just and Unjust Wars. A Moral Argument with Historical Illustrations.* Basic Books. 5th Edition.

Wilson, A. (2021) Russia and Ukraine: 'One People' as Putin Claims? In: Royal United Services Institute (rusi.org) https://rusi.org/explore-our-research/publications/commentary/russia-and-ukraine-one-people-putin-claims

UN Ukraine reports. (2021) Crimean Tatars in detention in the Russian Federation: solitary confinement, arbitrary punishments and inadequate medical care. 20 August, https://ukraine.un.org/en/140968-crimean-tatars-detention-russian-federation-solitary-confinement-arbitrary-punishments-and

UK Parliament. (2022) Russia's Grand Strategy. Vol. 706, 6 January. https://hansard.parliament.uk/Commons/2022-01-06/debates/6B5F9A7C-32FA-4D68-A50D-AA18D6C03D6C/Russia%E2%80%99SGrandStrategy

UK Parliament. (2017) https://b1cba9b3-a-5e6631fd-s-sites.googlegroups.com/a/independent.gov.uk/isc/files/2016-2017_ISC_AR.pdf?attachauth=ANoY7cqxsoXHtVXs7T71po0Sl5Fb50NO48FVIxB5ojp9IREWQfTnkCYJ3zw6xP39jC6NKMf5DW1TcWR9djy8Kgk-vboALg6XRrzFVWX7qPuUkOKCVK17MEU_LO6MxPWyM8Ck2I48RqUBFqj8PCIUfn2-FMGi6ov_-dxHf8Iw3QwLEiUuwKUBPjmt31B4DoL3UNuzcfS0rgT1rX1XYCSWSLE9mj4IkXh4uKnZahEzc9D21jv1PmUtQDQ%3D&attredirects=1

UK Parliament. (2018) "Moscow's Gold: Russian Corruption in the UK", House of Commons Foreign Affairs Committee, 8th Report. https://publications.parliament.uk/pa/cm201719/cmselect/cmfaff/932/932.pdf

UK Integrated Operating Concept 2025. (2021) https://assets.publishing.service.gov.uk/government/uploads/system/uploads/attachment_data/file/1014659/Integrated_Operating_Concept_2025.pdf

Ukraine's parliament declares 'Rashism' national ideology of Russia. (2023) In: *Novaya Gazeta*, online: https://novayagazeta.eu/articles/2023/05/02/ukraine-s-parliament-declares-rashism-national-ideology-of-russia-en-news

Ukrinform. (2023) Leopard tanks for Ukraine: Warsaw explains Berlin's reluctance. 20 January. https://www.ukrinform.net/rubric-ato/3655984-leopard-tanks-for-ukraine-warsaw-explains-berlins-reluctance.html

US House of representatives. (2018) "Social Media Advertisements,", Permanent Select Committee on Intelligence, May 10, 2018; the "Satan v Jesus" ad online at https//archive.org/details/2016-satan-v-jesus

US National Intelligence Council. (2021) Foreign Threats to the 2020 US Federal Elections, Intelligence Community assessment, 15 March. https://www.dni.gov/files/ODNI/documents/assessments/ICA-declass-16MAR21.pdf

Yampolsky, M. (2022) Regime of imperial paranoia: war in the age of empty rhetoric. In: *Re-Russia.net* https://re-russia.net/en/expertise/043/

Yegorov, I. (2014) Vtoraya "Kholodnaya". In: *Rossiyskaya Gazeta*, October 15. https://rg.ru/2014/10/15/Patrushev.html

Yefymenko, H. (2014) V 1917–1918 gg granitsy Ukrainy sformirovala Sovetskaya Ukraina, toyest bolsheviki? In: likbez.org.ua http://likbez.org.ua/in-1917-1918-border-of-ukraine-formed-the-soviet-ukraine-ie-the-bolsheviks.html

Zabuzhko, O. (2022) No guilty people in the world? Reading Russian literature after the Bucha massacre. In: *The Times Literary Supplement*, online: https://www.the-tls.co.uk/articles/russian-literature-buch a-massacre-essay-oksana-zabuzhko/

Zavadski, I. (1996). Informatsionnaya voiyna — chto eto takoye. In: *Zaschita informatsii*. Konfident. № 4. Moscow.

Zaxid.net (2011) Newsweek Polska: Yanukovychvykorystovuye"Svobodu" https://zaxid.net/newzweek_polzka_yanukovich_vikoristo vuye_svobodu_n1123010

Zinoviev, A. (1995) Russkiy experiment. (Russian experiment). Moskva: L'age d'Homme.

UKRAINIAN VOICES

Collected by Andreas Umland

1 *Mychailo Wynnyckyj*
   Ukraine's Maidan, Russia's War
   A Chronicle and Analysis of the Revolution of Dignity
   With a foreword by Serhii Plokhy
   ISBN 978-3-8382-1327-9

2 *Olexander Hryb*
   Understanding Contemporary Ukrainian and Russian Nationalism
   The Post-Soviet Cossack Revival and Ukraine's National Security
   With a foreword by Vitali Vitaliev
   ISBN 978-3-8382-1377-4

3 *Marko Bojcun*
   Towards a Political Economy of Ukraine
   Selected Essays 1990–2015
   With a foreword by John-Paul Himka
   ISBN 978-3-8382-1368-2

4 *Volodymyr Yermolenko (Ed.)*
   Ukraine in Histories and Stories
   Essays by Ukrainian Intellectuals
   With a preface by Peter Pomerantsev
   ISBN 978-3-8382-1456-6

5 *Mykola Riabchuk*
   At the Fence of Metternich's Garden
   Essays on Europe, Ukraine, and Europeanization
   ISBN 978-3-8382-1484-9

6 *Marta Dyczok*
   Ukraine Calling
   A Kaleidoscope from Hromadske Radio 2016–2019
   With a foreword by Andriy Kulykov
   ISBN 978-3-8382-1472-6

7 *Olexander Scherba*
   Ukraine vs. Darkness
   Undiplomatic Thoughts
   With a foreword by Adrian Karatnycky
   ISBN 978-3-8382-1501-3

8 *Olesya Yaremchuk*
   Our Others
   Stories of Ukrainian Diversity
   With a foreword by Ostap Slyvynsky
   Translated from the Ukrainian by Zenia Tompkins and Hanna Leliv
   ISBN 978-3-8382-1475-7

9 *Nataliya Gumenyuk*
   Die verlorene Insel
   Geschichten von der besetzten Krim
   Mit einem Vorwort von Alice Bota
   Aus dem Ukrainischen übersetzt von Johann Zajaczkowski
   ISBN 978-3-8382-1499-3

10 *Olena Stiazhkina*
   Zero Point Ukraine
   Four Essays on World War II
   Translated from the Ukrainian by Svitlana Kulinska
   ISBN 978-3-8382-1550-1

11 *Oleksii Sinchenko, Dmytro Stus, Leonid Finberg (compilers)*
Ukrainian Dissidents
An Anthology of Texts
ISBN 978-3-8382-1551-8

12 *John-Paul Himka*
Ukrainian Nationalists and the Holocaust
OUN and UPA's Participation in the Destruction of Ukrainian Jewry, 1941–1944
ISBN 978-3-8382-1548-8

13 *Andrey Demartino*
False Mirrors
The Weaponization of Social Media in Russia's Operation to Annex Crimea
With a foreword by Oleksiy Danilov
ISBN 978-3-8382-1533-4

14 *Svitlana Biedarieva (ed.)*
Contemporary Ukrainian and Baltic Art
Political and Social Perspectives, 1991–2021
ISBN 978-3-8382-1526-6

15 *Olesya Khromeychuk*
A Loss
The Story of a Dead Soldier Told by His Sister
With a foreword by Andrey Kurkov
ISBN 978-3-8382-1570-9

16 *Marieluise Beck (Hg.)*
Ukraine verstehen
Auf den Spuren von Terror und Gewalt
Mit einem Vorwort von Dmytro Kuleba
ISBN 978-3-8382-1653-9

17 *Stanislav Aseyev*
Heller Weg
Geschichte eines Konzentrationslagers im Donbass 2017–2019
Aus dem Russischen übersetzt von Martina Steis und Charis Haska
ISBN 978-3-8382-1620-1

18 *Mykola Davydiuk*
Wie funktioniert Putins Propaganda?
Anmerkungen zum Informationskrieg des Kremls
Aus dem Ukrainischen übersetzt von Christian Weise
ISBN 978-3-8382-1628-7

19 *Olesya Yaremchuk*
Unsere Anderen
Geschichten ukrainischer Vielfalt
Aus dem Ukrainischen übersetzt von Christian Weise
ISBN 978-3-8382-1635-5

20 *Oleksandr Mykhed*
„Dein Blut wird die Kohle tränken"
Über die Ostukraine
Aus dem Ukrainischen übersetzt von Simon Muschick und Dario Planert
ISBN 978-3-8382-1648-5

21 *Vakhtang Kipiani (Hg.)*
Der Zweite Weltkrieg in der Ukraine
Geschichte und Lebensgeschichten
Aus dem Ukrainischen übersetzt von Margarita Grinko
ISBN 978-3-8382-1622-5

22 *Vakhtang Kipiani (ed.)*
World War II, Uncontrived and Unredacted
Testimonies from Ukraine
Translated from the Ukrainian by Zenia Tompkins and Daisy Gibbons
ISBN 978-3-8382-1621-8

23 *Dmytro Stus*
   Vasyl Stus
   Life in Creativity
   Translated from the Ukrainian by
   Ludmila Bachurina
   ISBN 978-3-8382-1631-7

24 *Vitalii Ogiienko (ed.)*
   The Holodomor and the
   Origins of the Soviet Man
   Reading the Testimony of
   Anastasia Lysyvets
   With forewords by Natalka
   Bilotserkivets and Serhy
   Yekelchyk
   Translated from the Ukrainian by
   Alla Parkhomenko and
   Alexander J. Motyl
   ISBN 978-3-8382-1616-4

25 *Vladislav Davidzon*
   Jewish-Ukrainian Relations
   and the Birth of a Political
   Nation
   Selected Writings 2013-2021
   With a foreword by Bernard-
   Henri Lévy
   ISBN 978-3-8382-1509-9

26 *Serhy Yekelchyk*
   Writing the Nation
   The Ukrainian Historical
   Profession in Independent
   Ukraine and the Diaspora
   ISBN 978-3-8382-1695-9

27 *Ildi Eperjesi, Oleksandr
   Kachura*
   Shreds of War
   Fates from the Donbas Frontline
   2014-2019
   With a foreword by Olexiy
   Haran
   ISBN 978-3-8382-1680-5

28 *Oleksandr Melnyk*
   World War II as an Identity
   Project
   Historicism, Legitimacy
   Contests, and the (Re-)Con-
   struction of Political Commu-
   nities in Ukraine, 1939–1946
   With a foreword by David R.
   Marples
   ISBN 978-3-8382-1704-8

29 *Olesya Khromeychuk*
   Ein Verlust
   Die Geschichte eines gefallenen
   ukrainischen Soldaten, erzählt
   von seiner Schwester
   Mit einem Vorwort von Andrej
   Kurkow
   Aus dem Englischen übersetzt
   von Lily Sophie
   ISBN 978-3-8382-1770-3

30 *Tamara Martsenyuk,
   Tetiana Kostiuchenko (eds.)*
   Russia's War in Ukraine
   During 2022
   Personal Experiences of
   Ukrainian Scholars
   ISBN 978-3-8382-1757-4

31 *Ildikó Eperjesi, Oleksandr
   Kachura*
   Shreds of War. Vol. 2
   Fates from Crimea 2015–2022
   With an interview of Oleh
   Sentsov
   ISBN 978-3-8382-1780-2

32 *Yuriy Lukanov*
   The Press
   How Russia Destroyed Media
   Freedom in Crimea
   With a foreword by Taras Kuzio
   ISBN 978-3-8382-1784-0

33 *Megan Buskey*
   Ukraine Is Not Dead Yet
   A Family Story of Exile and
   Return
   ISBN 978-3-8382-1691-1

34 Vira Ageyeva
 Behind the Scenes of the
 Empire
 Essays on Cultural
 Relationships between Ukraine
 and Russia
 With a foreword by Oksana
 Zabuzhko
 ISBN 978-3-8382-1748-2

35 Marieluise Beck (ed.)
 Understanding Ukraine
 Tracing the Roots of Terror and
 Violence
 With a foreword by Dmytro
 Kuleba
 ISBN 978-3-8382-1773-4

36 Olesya Khromeychuk
 A Loss
 The Story of a Dead Soldier Told
 by His Sister, 2nd edn.
 With a foreword by Philippe
 Sands
 With a preface by Andrii Kurkov
 ISBN 978-3-8382-1870-0

37 Taras Kuzio, Stefan
 Jajecznyk-Kelman
 Fascism and Genocide
 Russia's War Against
 Ukrainians
 ISBN 978-3-8382-1791-8

38 Alina Nychyk
 Ukraine Vis-à-Vis Russia
 and the EU
 Misperceptions of Foreign
 Challenges in Times of War,
 2014–2015
 With a foreword by Paul
 D'Anieri
 ISBN 978-3-8382-1767-3

39 Sasha Dovzhyk (ed.)
 Ukraine Lab
 Global Security, Environment,
 and Disinformation Through the
 Prism of Ukraine
 With a foreword by Rory Finnin
 ISBN 978-3-8382-1805-2

40 Serhiy Kvit
 Media, History, and
 Education
 Three Ways to Ukrainian
 Independence
 With a preface by Diane Francis
 ISBN 978-3-8382-1807-6

41 Anna Romandash
 Women of Ukraine
 Reportages from the War and
 Beyond
 ISBN 978-3-8382-1819-9

42 Dominika Rank
 Matzewe in meinem Garten
 Abenteuer eines jüdischen
 Heritage-Touristen in der
 Ukraine
 ISBN 978-3-8382-1810-6

43 Myroslaw Marynowytsch
 Das Universum hinter dem
 Stacheldraht
 Memoiren eines sowjet-
 ukrainischen Dissidenten
 Mit einem Vorwort von Timothy
 Snyder und einem Nachwort
 von Max Hartmann
 ISBN 978-3-8382-1806-9

44 Konstantin Sigow
 Für Deine und meine
 Freiheit
 Europäische Revolutions- und
 Kriegserfahrungen im heutigen
 Kyjiw
 Mit einem Vorwort von Karl
 Schlögel
 Herausgegeben von Regula M.
 Zwahlen
 ISBN 978-3-8382-1755-0

45 Kateryna Pylypchuk
 The War that Changed Us
 Ukrainian Novellas, Poems, and
 Essays from 2022
 With a foreword by Victor
 Yushchenko
 Paperback
 ISBN 978-3-8382-1859-5
 Hardcover
 ISBN 978-3-8382-1860-1

46 Kyrylo Tkachenko
Rechte Tür Links
Radikale Linke in Deutschland, die Revolution und der Krieg in der Ukraine, 2013-2018
ISBN 978-3-8382-1711-6

47 Alexander Strashny
The Ukrainian Mentality
An Ethno-Psychological, Historical and Comparative Exploration
With a foreword by Antonina Lovochkina
Translated from the Ukrainian by Michael M. Naydan and Olha Tytarenko
ISBN 978-3-8382-1886-1

48 Alona Shestopalova
From Screens to Battlefields
Tracing the Construction of Enemies on Russian Television
With a foreword by Nina Jankowicz
ISBN 978-3-8382-1884-7

49 Iaroslav Petik
Politics and Society in the Ukrainian People's Republic (1917–1921) and Contemporary Ukraine (2013–2022)
A Comparative Analysis
With a foreword by Mykola Doroshko
ISBN 978-3-8382-1817-5

50 Serhii Plokhy
Der Mann mit der Giftpistole
Eine Spionagegeschichte aus dem Kalten Krieg
ISBN 978-3-8382-1789-5

51 Vakhtang Kipiani
Ukrainische Dissidenten unter der Sowjetmacht
Im Kampf um Wahrheit und Freiheit
Aus dem Ukrainischen übersetzt von Christian Weise
ISBN 978-3-8382-1890-8

52 Dmytro Shestakov
When Businesses Test Hypotheses
A Four-Step Approach to Risk Management for Innovative Startups
With a foreword by Anthony J. Tether
ISBN 978-3-8382-1883-0

53 Larissa Babij
A Kind of Refugee
The Story of an American Who Refused to Leave Ukraine
With a foreword by Vladislav Davidzon
ISBN 978-3-8382-1898-4

54 Julia Davis
In Their Own Words
How Russian Propagandists Reveal Putin's Intentions
With a foreword by Timothy Snyder
ISBN 978-3-8382-1909-7

55 Sonya Atlantova, Oleksandr Klymenko
Icons on Ammo Boxes
Painting Life on the Remnants of Russia's War in Donbas, 2014-21
Translated from the Ukrainian by Anastasya Knyazhytska
ISBN 978-3-8382-1892-2

56 Leonid Ushkalov
Catching an Elusive Bird
The Life of Hryhorii Skovoroda
Translated from the Ukrainian by Natalia Komarova
ISBN 978-3-8382-1894-6

57 Vakhtang Kipiani
Ein Land weiblichen Geschlechts
Ukrainische Frauenschicksale im 20. und 21. Jahrhundert
Aus dem Ukrainischen übersetzt von Christian Weise
ISBN 978-3-8382-1891-5

58 Petro Rychlo
„Zerrissne Saiten einer
überlauten Harfe ..."
Deutschjüdische Dichter der
Bukowina
ISBN 978-3-8382-1893-9

59 Volodymyr Paniotto
Sociology in Jokes
An Entertaining Introduction
ISBN 978-3-8382-1857-1

60 Josef Wallmannsberger
(ed.)
Executing Renaissances
The Poetological Nation of
Ukraine
ISBN 978-3-8382-1741-3

61 Pavlo Kazarin
The Wild West of Eastern
Europe
A Ukrainian Guide on Breaking
Free from Empire
Translated from the Ukrainian
by Dominique Hoffman
ISBN 978-3-8382-1842-7

62 Ernest Gyidel
Ukrainian Public
Nationalism in the General
Government
The Case of Krakivski Visti,
1940–1944
With a foreword by David R.
Marples
ISBN 978-3-8382-1865-6

63 Olexander Hryb
Understanding
Contemporary Russian
Militarism
From Revolutionary to New
Generation Warfare
With a foreword by Mark Laity
ISBN 978-3-8382-1927-1

64 Orysia Hrudka, Bohdan Ben
Dark Days, Determined
People
Stories from Ukraine under Siege
With a foreword by Myroslav
Marynovych
ISBN 978-3-8382-1958-5

65 Oleksandr Pankieiev (ed.)
Narratives of the Russo-
Ukrainian War
A Look Within and Without
With a foreword by Natalia
Khanenko-Friesen
ISBN 978-3-8382-1964-6

66 Roman Sohn, Ariana Gic
(eds.)
Unrecognized War
The Fight for Truth about
Russia's War on Ukraine
With a foreword by Viktor
Yushchenko
ISBN 978-3-8382-1947-9

67 Paul Robert Magocsi
Ukraina Redux
Schon wieder die Ukraine ...
ISBN 978-3-8382-1942-4

68 Paul Robert Magocsi
L'Ucraina Ritrovata
Sullo Stato e l'Identità Nazionale
ISBN 978-3-8382-1982-0

69 Max Hartmann
Ein Schrei der Verzweiflung
Aquarelle von Danylo Movchan
zu Russlands Krieg in der
Ukraine
Mit einem Vorwort von Mateusz
Sora
Paperback
ISBN 978-3-8382-2011-6
Hardcover
ISBN 978-3-8382-2012-3

70 Vakhtang Kebuladze (Hg.)
Die Zukunft, die wir uns
wünschen
Essays aus der Ukraine
ISBN 978-3-8382-1531-0

71 Marieluise Beck, Jan Claas
    Behrends, Gelinada
    Grinchenko und Oksana
    Mikheieva (Hgg.)
    Deutsch-ukrainische
    Geschichten
    Bruchstücke aus einer
    gemeinsamen Vergangenheit
    ISBN 978-3-8382-2053-6

72 Pavlo Kazarin
    Der Wilde Westen Ost-
    Europas
    Der ukrainische Weg aus dem
    Imperium
    Aus dem Ukrainischen übersetzt
    von Christian Weise
    ISBN 978-3-8382-1843-4

73 Radomyr Mokryk
    Die ukrainischen »Sechziger«
    Chronologie einer Revolte
    ISBN 978-3-8382-1873-1

74 Leonid Finberg
    My Ukraine
    Rethinking the Past, Building
    the Present
    ISBN 978-3-8382-1974-5

75 Joseph Zissels
    Consider My Inmost
    Thoughts
    Essays, Lectures, and Interviews
    on Ukrainian Matters at the
    Turn of the Century
    ISBN 978-3-8382-1975-2

76 Margarita Yehorchenko,
    Iryna Berlyand, Ihor
    Vinokurov (eds.)
    Jewish Addresses in Ukraine
    A Guide-Book
    With a foreword by Leonid
    Finberg
    ISB 978-3-8382-1976-9

77 Viktoriia Grivina
    Kharkiv—A War City
    A Collection of Essays from
    2022–23
    ISBN 978-3-8382-1988-2

78 Hjørdis Clemmensen,
    Viktoriia Grivina, Vasylysa
    Shchogoleva
    Kharkiv Is a Dream
    Public Art and Activism 2013–
    2023
    With a foreword by Bohdan
    Volynskyi
    ISBN 978-3-8382-2005-5

79 Olga Khomenko
    The Faraway Sky of Kyiv
    Ukrainians in the War
    With a foreword by Hiroaki
    Kuromiya
    ISBN 978-3-8382-2006-2

80 Daria Mattingly, Jonathon
    Vsetecka (eds.)
    The Holodomor in Global
    Perspective
    How the Famine in Ukraine
    Shaped the World
    ISBN 978-3-8382-1953-0

81 Olga Khomenko
    Ukrainians beyond Borders
    Nine Life Journeys Through the
    History of Eastern Europe
    With a foreword by Zbigniew
    Wojnowski
    ISBN 978-3-8382-2007-9

82 Mykhailo Minakov
    From Servant to Leader
    Chronicles of Ukraine under the
    Zelensky Presidency, 2019–2024
    With a foreword by John Lloyd
    ISBN 978-3-8382-2002-4

83 Volodymyr Hromov (ed.)
    A Ruined Home
    Sketches of War, 2022–2023
    ISBN 978-3-8382-2008-6

84 Olha Tatokhina (ed.)
    Why Do They Kill Our People?
    Russia's War Against Ukraine as
    Told by Ukrainians
    With a foreword by Volodymyr
    Yermolenko
    ISBN 978-3-8382-2056-7

Book series "Ukrainian Voices"

Coordinator
Andreas Umland, National University of Kyiv-Mohyla Academy

Editorial Board
Lesia Bidochko, National University of Kyiv-Mohyla Academy
Svitlana Biedarieva, George Washington University, DC, USA
Ivan Gomza, Kyiv School of Economics, Ukraine
Natalie Jaresko, Aspen Institute, Kyiv/Washington
Olena Lennon, University of New Haven, West Haven, USA
Kateryna Yushchenko, First Lady of Ukraine 2005-2010, Kyiv
Oleksandr Zabirko, University of Regensburg, Germany

Advisory Board
Iuliia Bentia, National Academy of Arts of Ukraine, Kyiv
Natalya Belitser, Pylyp Orlyk Institute for Democracy, Kyiv
Oleksandra Bienert, Humboldt University of Berlin, Germany
Sergiy Bilenky, Canadian Institute of Ukrainian Studies, Toronto
Tymofii Brik, Kyiv School of Economics, Ukraine
Olga Brusylovska, Mechnikov National University, Odesa
Mariana Budjeryn, Harvard University, Cambridge, USA
Volodymyr Bugrov, Shevchenko National University, Kyiv
Olga Burlyuk, University of Amsterdam, The Netherlands
Yevhen Bystrytsky, NAS Institute of Philosophy, Kyiv
Andrii Danylenko, Pace University, New York, USA
Vladislav Davidzon, Atlantic Council, Washington/Paris
Mykola Davydiuk, Think Tank "Polityka," Kyiv
Andrii Demartino, National Security and Defense Council, Kyiv
Vadym Denisenko, Ukrainian Institute for the Future, Kyiv
Oleksandr Donii, Center for Political Values Studies, Kyiv
Volodymyr Dubovyk, Mechnikov National University, Odesa
Volodymyr Dubrovskiy, CASE Ukraine, Kyiv
Diana Dutsyk, National University of Kyiv-Mohyla Academy
Marta Dyczok, Western University, Ontario, Canada
Yevhen Fedchenko, National University of Kyiv-Mohyla Academy
Sofiya Filonenko, State Pedagogical University of Berdyansk
Oleksandr Fisun, Karazin National University, Kharkiv
Oksana Forostyna, Webjournal "Ukraina Moderna," Kyiv
Roman Goncharenko, Broadcaster "Deutsche Welle," Bonn
George Grabowicz, Harvard University, Cambridge, USA
Gelinada Grinchenko, Karazin National University, Kharkiv
Kateryna Härtel, Federal Union of European Nationalities, Brussels
Nataliia Hendel, University of Geneva, Switzerland
Anton Herashchenko, Kyiv School of Public Administration
John-Paul Himka, University of Alberta, Edmonton
Ola Hnatiuk, National University of Kyiv-Mohyla Academy
Oleksandr Holubov, Broadcaster "Deutsche Welle," Bonn
Yaroslav Hrytsak, Ukrainian Catholic University, Lviv
Oleksandra Humenna, National University of Kyiv-Mohyla Academy
Tamara Hundorova, NAS Institute of Literature, Kyiv
Oksana Huss, University of Bologna, Italy
Oleksandra Iwaniuk, University of Warsaw, Poland
Mykola Kapitonenko, Shevchenko National University, Kyiv
Georgiy Kasianov, Marie Curie-Skłodowska University, Lublin
Vakhtang Kebuladze, Shevchenko National University, Kyiv
Natalia Khanenko-Friesen, University of Alberta, Edmonton
Victoria Khiterer, Millersville University of Pennsylvania, USA
Oksana Kis, NAS Institute of Ethnology, Lviv
Pavlo Klimkin, Center for National Resilience and Development, Kyiv
Oleksandra Kolomiiets, Center for Economic Strategy, Kyiv

Sergiy Korsunsky, Kobe Gakuin University, Japan
Nadiia Koval, Kyiv School of Economics, Ukraine
Volodymyr Kravchenko, University of Alberta, Edmonton
Oleksiy Kresin, NAS Koretskiy Institute of State and Law, Kyiv
Anatoliy Kruglashov, Fedkovych National University, Chernivtsi
Andrey Kurkov, PEN Ukraine, Kyiv
Ostap Kushnir, Lazarski University, Warsaw
Taras Kuzio, National University of Kyiv-Mohyla Academy
Serhii Kvit, National University of Kyiv-Mohyla Academy
Yuliya Ladygina, The Pennsylvania State University, USA
Yevhen Mahda, Institute of World Policy, Kyiv
Victoria Malko, California State University, Fresno, USA
Yulia Marushevska, Security and Defense Center (SAND), Kyiv
Myroslav Marynovych, Ukrainian Catholic University, Lviv
Oleksandra Matviichuk, Center for Civil Liberties, Kyiv
Mykhailo Minakov, Kennan Institute, Washington, USA
Anton Moiseienko, The Australian National University, Canberra
Alexander Motyl, Rutgers University-Newark, USA
Vlad Mykhnenko, University of Oxford, United Kingdom
Vitalii Ogiienko, Ukrainian Institute of National Remembrance, Kyiv
Olga Onuch, University of Manchester, United Kingdom
Olesya Ostrovska, Museum "Mystetskyi Arsenal," Kyiv
Anna Osypchuk, National University of Kyiv-Mohyla Academy
Oleksandr Pankieiev, University of Alberta, Edmonton
Oleksiy Panych, Publishing House "Dukh i Litera," Kyiv
Valerii Pekar, Kyiv-Mohyla Business School, Ukraine
Yohanan Petrovsky-Shtern, Northwestern University, Chicago
Serhii Plokhy, Harvard University, Cambridge, USA
Andrii Portnov, Viadrina University, Frankfurt-Oder, Germany
Maryna Rabinovych, Kyiv School of Economics, Ukraine
Valentyna Romanova, Institute of Developing Economies, Tokyo
Natalya Ryabinska, Collegium Civitas, Warsaw, Poland
Darya Tsymbalyk, University of Oxford, United Kingdom
Vsevolod Samokhvalov, University of Liege, Belgium
Orest Semotiuk, Franko National University, Lviv
Viktoriya Sereda, NAS Institute of Ethnology, Lviv
Anton Shekhovtsov, University of Vienna, Austria
Andriy Shevchenko, Media Center Ukraine, Kyiv
Oxana Shevel, Tufts University, Medford, USA
Pavlo Shopin, National Pedagogical Dragomanov University, Kyiv
Karina Shyrokykh, Stockholm University, Sweden
Nadja Simon, freelance interpreter, Cologne, Germany
Olena Snigova, NAS Institute for Economics and Forecasting, Kyiv
Ilona Solohub, Analytical Platform "VoxUkraine," Kyiv
Iryna Solonenko, LibMod - Center for Liberal Modernity, Berlin
Galyna Solovei, National University of Kyiv-Mohyla Academy
Sergiy Stelmakh, NAS Institute of World History, Kyiv
Olena Stiazhkina, NAS Institute of the History of Ukraine, Kyiv
Dmitri Stratievski, Osteuropa Zentrum (OEZB), Berlin
Dmytro Stus, National Taras Shevchenko Museum, Kyiv
Frank Sysyn, University of Toronto, Canada
Olha Tokariuk, Center for European Policy Analysis, Washington
Olena Tregub, Independent Anti-Corruption Commission, Kyiv
Hlib Vyshlinsky, Centre for Economic Strategy, Kyiv
Mychailo Wynnyckyj, National University of Kyiv-Mohyla Academy
Yelyzaveta Yasko, NGO "Yellow Blue Strategy," Kyiv
Serhy Yekelchyk, University of Victoria, Canada
Victor Yushchenko, President of Ukraine 2005-2010, Kyiv
Oleksandr Zaitsev, Ukrainian Catholic University, Lviv
Kateryna Zarembo, National University of Kyiv-Mohyla Academy
Yaroslav Zhalilo, National Institute for Strategic Studies, Kyiv
Sergei Zhuk, Ball State University at Muncie, USA
Alina Zubkovych, Nordic Ukraine Forum, Stockholm
Liudmyla Zubrytska, National University of Kyiv-Mohyla Academy

Friends of the Series

Ana Maria Abulescu, University of Bucharest, Romania
Łukasz Adamski, Centrum Mieroszewskiego, Warsaw
Marieluise Beck, LibMod—Center for Liberal Modernity, Berlin
Marc Berensen, King's College London, United Kingdom
Johannes Bohnen, BOHNEN Public Affairs, Berlin
Karsten Brüggemann, University of Tallinn, Estonia
Ulf Brunnbauer, Leibniz Institute (IOS), Regensburg
Martin Dietze, German-Ukrainian Culture Society, Hamburg
Gergana Dimova, Florida State University, Tallahassee/London
Caroline von Gall, Goethe University, Frankfurt-Main
Zaur Gasimov, Rhenish Friedrich Wilhelm University, Bonn
Armand Gosu, University of Bucharest, Romania
Thomas Grant, University of Cambridge, United Kingdom
Gustav Gressel, European Council on Foreign Relations, Berlin
Rebecca Harms, European Centre for Press & Media Freedom, Leipzig
André Härtel, Stiftung Wissenschaft und Politik, Berlin/Brussels
Marcel Van Herpen, The Cicero Foundation, Maastricht
Richard Herzinger, freelance analyst, Berlin
Mieste Hotopp-Riecke, ICATAT, Magdeburg
Nico Lange, Munich Security Conference, Berlin
Martin Malek, freelance analyst, Vienna
Ingo Mannteufel, Broadcaster "Deutsche Welle," Bonn
Carlo Masala, Bundeswehr University, Munich
Wolfgang Mueller, University of Vienna, Austria
Dietmar Neutatz, Albert Ludwigs University, Freiburg
Torsten Oppelland, Friedrich Schiller University, Jena
Niccolò Pianciola, University of Padua, Italy
Gerald Praschl, German-Ukrainian Forum (DUF), Berlin
Felix Riefer, Think Tank Ideenagentur-Ost, Düsseldorf
Stefan Rohdewald, University of Leipzig, Germany
Sebastian Schäffer, Institute for the Danube Region (IDM), Vienna
Felix Schimansky-Geier, Friedrich Schiller University, Jena
Ulrich Schneckener, University of Osnabrück, Germany
Winfried Schneider-Deters, freelance analyst, Heidelberg/Kyiv
Gerhard Simon, University of Cologne, Germany
Kai Struve, Martin Luther University, Halle/Wittenberg
David Stulik, European Values Center for Security Policy, Prague
Andrzej Szeptycki, University of Warsaw, Poland
Philipp Ther, University of Vienna, Austria
Stefan Troebst, University of Leipzig, Germany

[Please send requests for changes in, corrections of, and additions to, this list to andreas.umland@stanforalumni.org.]

ibidem.eu